THE QUICK &EASY HOME DIY MANUAL

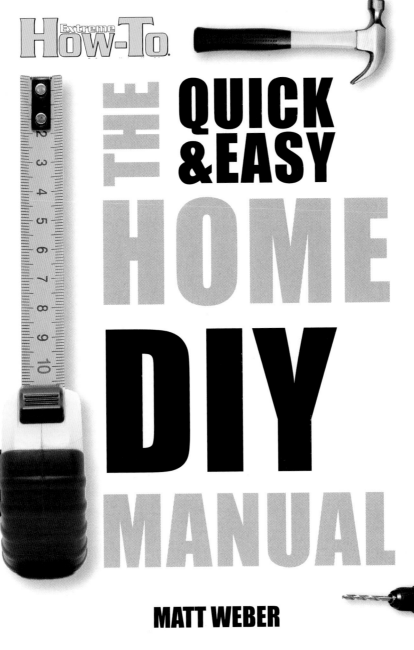

Extreme How-To

THE QUICK & EASY HOME DIY MANUAL

MATT WEBER

weldon**owen**

CONTENTS

INTRODUCTION

TOOLS AND SKILLS

DIY NATION

For a certain type of person, the sound of surrender is the ring of a phone as they call a repairman. That's me. I will invariably attempt a home repair or improvement before I pay good money to someone else for a job I can do myself.

Does that make me arrogant? Maybe. Stubborn? Absolutely. Am I a cheapskate, too? I prefer the word "frugal."

And I'm not alone.

From long-running television programs like *This Old House* to cable channels such as HGTV and the DIY Network, it should be obvious that do-it-yourself home improvement isn't a passing trend so much as a lifestyle that's been embraced for years by hard-working individuals from coast to coast. I mean, heck, the first settlers built their own homes long before building developers were throwing up high-rise condos, and we're simply carrying the torch of that rich tradition of self-reliance.

For someone to follow this path requires an independent spirit, a willingness to break a little sweat and—maybe most important—an eagerness to learn new things.

I came aboard as editor of *Extreme How-To* in 2003 with a college degree and a raft of work experience from time spent laboring in a steel fabricating plant, an aluminum warehouse, a shipping hub, a framing shop—I could go on and on; I even once had a gig selling knives (and hated it). Although I was no home improvement expert at the time, I was young and ambitious and eager to learn. I was unafraid to try new things, and no matter what challenges I faced, I'd figure them out on the job.

I then spent many years studying all the things I realized I didn't know about home improvement.

That's where this book comes in. A collection of hundreds of tried-and-true techniques and pro tips for success, we cover the most common DIY projects inside and outside the home. For years the aim of *Extreme How-To* has been to demystify professional-grade projects for the do-it-yourselfer, to equip our readers with the know-how to "build it yourself, and build it better."

If you're willing to learn new things and you don't worry about getting your hands dirty, this manual will help conquer your repairs and remodels without ever having to say "I surrender."

READ THIS FIRST

If you're new to home improvement, get ready for a wild ride. It's a fun and satisfying journey, but as your projects grow more ambitious than simple fixes and minor improvements, you'll find the big jobs can require a lot of work—much more than you'll see edited into split-second TV clips on your favorite home show. Any job can be rife with unforeseen pitfalls, but trial-and-error can be a powerful teacher.

The best way to minimize errors is to gather as much information as you can prior to beginning your project. The Internet is a goldmine of home-improvement information, from *Extreme How-To*'s website to many others. You'll find all sorts of helpful videos on Youtube—it's amazing how detailed some of instructional clips are. For large projects like deck-building or shed construction, buy a book dedicated to the subject that details the various design options and techniques for construction. Another great way to soak up knowledge is to observe a jobsite. For example, if you spend a few minutes watching a

roofing crew tear off and replace a home's shingles, you might quickly decide that since you can't be in that many places at once, maybe roofing is a project best left to the professionals.

GET A PERMIT

Some projects will require a permit from your local building department. In general, building codes are developed by industry associations "to provide minimum safety standards for a home's occupants, the environment and the public at large." The codes are adopted and enforced by local governments and vary based on local political issues, environmental regulations, and so forth. Check with your local building inspector to determine all local requirements.

Although codes vary from state to state, a permit is generally required for remodeling projects that involve changes to the building's existing footprint, electrical system or plumbing. Adding new windows to existing walls usually requires a permit. You're likely to need a permit for projects that go beyond a simple repair or cosmetic improvement, such as:

- adding supporting walls or removing load-bearing walls,
- in-ground concrete pool or a porch/deck,
- replacing the roof,
- backyard shed,
- concrete sidewalks, driveways and slabs

When a permit is filed, city officials will usually inspect the work completed at different stages to ensure it complies with current safety and health building codes.

When work is done to refresh the home, however, a permit is not usually required. Updating kitchen cabinets and countertops, for example, does not require a permit. Other remodeling updates such as flooring/ceiling coverings, painting/papering, tiling or carpeting can usually be done without a permit. Even if a permit isn't required, certain projects may require licensed professionals for structural, electrical and plumbing work. If you're not sure, check with your local city or county government office.

TOOLS
AND
SKILLS

THE RIGHT TOOLS FOR THE JOB

Some things you learn the hard way. For example, I once drilled into my hand. On a separate occasion I nearly electrocuted myself. While tools for home improvement can certainly prove handy, their associated work can often be hazardous, especially if you don't know what you're doing.

It's smart to always use the right tool for the job and to use it the way it was intended. And those little instruction manuals that are included by the manufacturer—read those, too, because it's more fun to learn the easy way.

My first toolbox was a gift from my dad and contained your basic hammer, screwdriver, pliers and a wrench. It grew over the years. These days I have a backyard garage to store all my stuff. You might never require quite that much room for your equipment, but the more projects you take on, the more your tool collection will expand. Start with the basic essentials and add items as you need them. Before you know it, tool collecting will get in your blood, and you'll start picking up gadgets that you might not need today, but you might need someday.

This chapter will overview common toolbox essentials as well as highlighting some slightly more obscure devices that might just help your next project go smoothly. We'll offer some basic instruction on how to use them, and provide professional insight that you won't find in the product literature. We'll show when to grab the right glue, and when to use the right clamp. You'll get some good advice on how to gear up for a safe work area, as well as how to keep the house as clean as possible while you repair and remodel. So, get ready to review some cool tools and learn how to get the most out of them.

001 BUILD A BASIC TOOLBOX

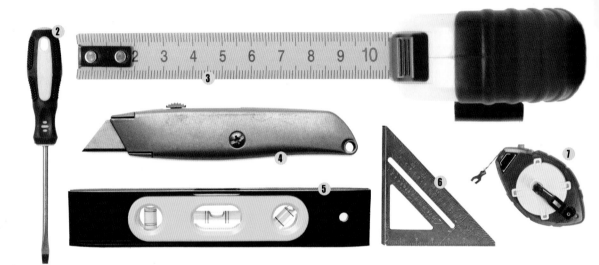

From simple fix-ups to major home improvements, the right tools make all the difference. Novice DIYers should assemble a toolbox with a handful of essential tools that are most widely applicable to any job. Additional materials can be purchased as required, expanding your arsenal as your experience and skill set improve. Choose a toolbox with ample storage space for large, irregular items such as a hammer and square, but one that's light and compact enough for easy portability.

1 HAMMER From hanging a picture frame to building a wall, the right hammer is an essential household tool. You'll find specialized models for heavy-duty framing and for fine woodwork, but a good basic model should be medium weight (16 to 20 ounces) with a smooth-faced head, rip claw, and non-wood handle.

2 SCREWDRIVERS Whether you're putting something together or taking it apart, the right screwdriver makes all the difference. You'll find various types of screws in everything from woodworking to automotive work, and each type requires a matching screwdriver, so you'll need a variety. Common screw types include flat-head, Phillips, square-drive, Torx™, and Pozidriv.

3 TAPE MEASURE The tape measure will likely get the most mileage of all your tools. A 25- to 30-foot tape will suffice for most jobs, big and small.

4 UTILITY KNIFE You can use a razor-sharp utility knife to open up packages, cut roof shingles, trim insulation, and so much more. Choose a model that offers convenient in-handle storage for extra blades.

5 TORPEDO LEVEL This handy tool utilizes a bubble vial to check for level and plumb on anything from picture frames and shelves to fence posts. Although longer levels are more accurate, a torpedo level comes close and fits in a toolbox.

6 SPEED SQUARE This is a very handy tool used for simple measuring, drawing straight lines, and marking angles. It also makes a grade-cutting guide for a circular saw.

7 CHALK LINE Another member of the marking and measuring family of tools, a chalk line can be very useful when working with drywall, roofing, floor installation, or any other unusually large piece of construction material.

8 SAFETY GOGGLES Arguably the most important item to keep in a toolbox is a pair of safety goggles. These will obviously help keep dangerous particles out of your eyes while cutting or performing demo work, but they can also be worn while painting to protect from flying specks.

9 **WOOD CHISEL** A ½-inch wood chisel is useful for many different applications, not just carving and shaping wood, as it's actually intended to do. Much to the manufacturer's chagrin, chisels can be used as everything from a miniature pry bar to a paint scraper. Keep two chisels handy: One for cutting wood and another for general usage.

10 **WRENCHES** Available with adjustable jaws or with fixed box-end designs, wrenches provide a firm grip for loosening and tightening bolts, nuts, and other faceted fasteners.

11 **PLIERS** Available in many sizes and designs, pliers tightly grasp and hold items that can't be held by your fingers alone.

12 **TONGUE-AND-GROOVE PLIERS** The adjustable mouth of tongue-and-groove pliers makes this tool handy for grabbing large items as well as small. Its primary use is for grabbing plumbing fixtures too big for standard wrenches, and the long handles provide plenty of leverage.

13 **LOCKING PLIERS** Known by the brand name Vise-Grip, this tool works like adjustable pliers but locks into place with incredible grip, freeing your hands for other work.

14 **ALLEN WRENCHES** Appliances, machinery, and power equipment often have screws with a hexagonal recess set in their heads. These screws require Allen wrenches, which are small L-shaped tools in sets of both metric and imperial measurements.

15 **SOCKET WRENCH SET** These modular systems include a wrench handle and individual sockets of different sizes, as well as extenders and adapters. The steel sleeve of the socket slips over a hexagonal nut or bolt head, and the wrench's ratcheting action turns the fastener in only one direction while "freewheeling" in the other for fast tightening and loosening.

16 **TOOL BELT** A good tool belt will keep your tape measure, pencil, fasteners, and other small items right at your side, saving you repeat trips back and forth to the toolbox to search for and retrieve supplies.

002 MASTER LAYOUT AND MEASURING

You've probably heard the phrase, "measure twice, cut once." The following tools help make that a reality.

FRAMING SQUARE The metal L-shaped framing square has a 24-inch leg (the blade) and a shorter 16-inch leg (the tongue). The  rigid 90-degree heel can easily verify the accuracy of right angles found inside and outside corners. Most framing squares also come with reference tables to assist in determining roof pitch and calculating rafter heights, along with other general applications.

T-SQUARE For large areas, drywall, and sheet goods, a T-square can be used to measure and mark straight, accurate lines up to 48 inches. It can also be edge-clamped in place and used as a guide for making straight cuts.

COMBINATION SQUARE The combination square consists of the blade (a metal ruler) and a stock, which slides along the blade and may be completely removed. A thumb-screw tightens the stock in place. The combo square can be used to check inside and outside corners for 90 and 45 degrees. It can be used as a marking gauge to draw a parallel line against an edge, and the blade can be used to measure the depth of a hole or mortise (notch). The stock features a bubble vial for checking level and plumb.

LEVELS Both a 2-foot and a 4-foot level are handy for determining if an object is indeed level. When the bubble rests evenly between the marks on the vial, the tool is level (or plumb). The longer a level's length, the greater its accuracy. However, in many cases a 4-foot level is too long and cumbersome for a small job, making the 2-foot version a better option.

003 SCREW IT BETTER

As your projects get more complex, you'll want to consider adding to your screwdriver collection.

MULTIPURPOSE This option can reduce the number of tools you need to carry with you. A variety of bits, usually stored in the handle, insert into a hexagonal drive shaft. Compare models to find the best bit selection for you.

MINI Eyeglasses, mobile phones, computers, and personal electronics often have very small screws, which in turn will require very small screwdrivers. Minis are available in flat-head, Phillips, Torx™, Pozidriv, and more.

004 SMOOTH THINGS OUT

Whether you're removing paint or prepping a new piece of furniture to stain and finish, sanding will be a necessary step in the process. The abrasive particles in the sandpaper are graded and numbered as "grit," indicating how coarse or fine these particles are. A good approach for a DIYer is to select three grits to have on hand. Start with the sandpaper that's just coarse enough to get rid of the worst surface defects. An 80-grit sandpaper is usually a good place to start. However, coarse grits will leave fine scratches on the wood, so the next step will be to turn these large scratches into smaller scratches with a finer paper of around 120-grit. For the final sanding phase, sandpaper at 220-grit will work for most types of wood. Wood with dense grain may require finer grits, such as 320-grit, to remove the last of the scratches, thus resulting in a smooth, ready-to-finish surface.

RATCHETING As with a socket wrench, the quick-drive ratcheting action drives screws fast while "freewheeling" in the opposite direction. This eliminates the need for the user to release and re-grip the screwdriver, saving time and labor.

CORDLESS A rechargeable battery-powered screwdriver can be fitted with any number bits in a wide range of sizes and drive-styles. When you're dealing with a lot of screws, you'll appreciate the high-productive efficiency this basic power tool brings to your projects. Keep one on the charger for grab-and-go convenience.

Power sanders do the work for you. Small palm sanders can smooth a wood surface in preparation for staining and sealing. Aggressive belt sanders can tear away an old wood surface with ferocious efficiency. And oscillating disc sanders strike a balance between aggressive material removal and finish-sanding.

005 SPLURGE ON THESE TOOLS

Many people find themselves buying expensive tools they almost never use. Be smart about purchases, but sometimes it does make sense to spend the money, as in the following cases.

STUD FINDER If you plan to hang anything heavy on a wall, you'll need to mount it into a solid stud in the wall's framing. To do so, you must first locate the stud. When passed over a wall, an electronic stud finder uses internal sensors to find the stud and signal its location for you to mark.

WORK LIGHTS Task-specific lighting in the form of tripod flashlights or LED headlamps are great for DIY. These low-wattage, low-heat lights come in handy beneath sinks, inside closets, and in any work circumstance when the power has been shut off.

NAIL-PULLING PLIERS Remodeling work will usually involve demolition, which often necessitates removing all those nails and fasteners installed by the original builder. A hammer claw won't grab onto a headless brad nail, and standard pliers don't offer adequate leverage for pulling them out. To remove pesky old nails, invest in specialty pliers constructed with an angled head to grip and pry them loose.

LASER MEASURING DEVICE A relative newcomer to the hardware store shelves, this tool is also called a distance meter, range finder, or laser "tape" measure, depending upon the manufacturer, and is great for taking precise measurements. Once you have the laser aimed, just press a button and the device calculates the distance and then displays it on the screen. This measurement is taken with precision laser optics that accurately measure the distance of the beam that hits a target object.

You'll find a wide range of electric drills in corded and cordless versions. With a corded drill you will always have 120 volts of power, more than enough juice to power the biggest drill that you're apt to use. A battery-powered cordless drill offers freedom of movement without being tethered to an outlet, but it requires time to recharge the battery and, depending on the size of the drill, the battery can add significant size and weight to the tool. Specifically designed and geared to bore holes in a variety of materials, drills come in a range of power classes and tool sizes, but most DIYers prefer a cordless drill/driver combo. Here are some other options as well.

1 DRILL/DRIVER A combination drill/driver offers variable speed adjustment to function as a versatile drill as well as a powered screwdriver. The ability to reduce speed and torque increases user control for screwdriving applications.

2 IMPACT DRIVER Specifically made for fastening applications, an impact driver employs an internal anvil to deliver much higher rotational torque than conventional drill/drivers. When the power needed to drive the fastener exceeds the torque of the tool's rotational force, a drive gear with two matching lugs strikes the anvil to nudge the bit along.

3 HAMMER DRILL Fastening items to concrete or masonry often requires boring a hole, inserting an anchor of some sort, then bolting or screwing the item in place. Drilling pilot holes into these harder materials is most easily accomplished with a masonry bit attached to a hammer drill, which uses an electro-mechanical hammering system. This consists of a gear assembly that delivers an impact to the chuck ranging from 20,000 to more than 50,000 blows per minute. A good choice for a DIYer is an 18-volt drill/driver that offers a hammer-drill function.

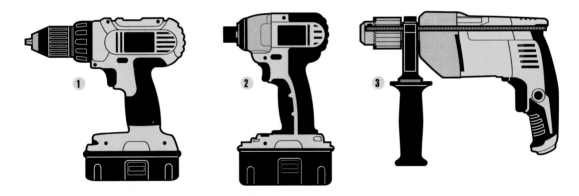

007 AVOID TEAROUT

To drill perfect holes in fine woodwork with no tearout, there are two possible methods.

METHOD 1 Use a backer board that's clamped to the workpiece. Select a good-quality bit with a starting point and side cutters, such as a Forstner or brad point. The bit treats the two clamped pieces of wood as a single piece.

METHOD 2 For applications in which a precise hole is not required, use a spade bit to drill out the hole. When you've just about pierced the back side, stop and flip the workpiece over. Use the hole pierced through the back side of the workpiece as a centering guide, and finish off the hole from the back side.

008 GET THE RIGHT DRILL BIT

Drill bits are indispensable tools, and new technologies are giving all these toolbox staples more cutting power than ever before. The standard twist-type drill bit is the most commonly produced drill bit available, and it's suited for a wide range of general-purpose tasks. However, the world is made up of a lot of different materials, and the right bit makes a big difference in drilling performance.

Bit Type: Twist

Description: Point angle is between 90 and 150 degrees; 118 degrees is the most common point

Uses: Sharper points work for aggressive cutting into softer materials; the shallower tip is designed for drilling harder materials such as drilling steel (but requires a starter hole)

Bit Type: Brad point

Description: Has a spur with a sharp point in the tip

Uses: The brad point's tip penetrates the work surface to hold the bit in position, while the sharp corners drill a clean hole in wood or plastic

Bit Type: Spade

Description: Has a flat, paddle-like shape with two cutting edges flanking a spur, which guides the trajectory of the drilling

Uses: For quick drilling of large holes intended for rough-in work such as framing, plumbing and electrical work; the aggressive cutting and high-speed action can leave a splintery hole

Bit Type: Forstner

Description: Forstner bits have a center spur as a guide and radial cutting edges that shear wood fibers at the edge and bottom of the hole, creating a smooth bore with an exact diameter

Uses: Forstner bits are the best choice for drilling precise, flat-bottomed holes in wood. They can cut on the edge of a block of wood to create channels and can also be used to create overlapping holes

Bit Type: Hole saw

Description: A cup-shaped bit set with a repeating pattern of teeth

Uses: Made to cut out large circles or cores of wood for tasks ranging from plumbing to installing doorknobs

Bit Type: Countersink

Description: Has an adjustable twist bit that locks into the countersink body with a set screw

Uses: Allows you to simultaneously pre-drill screw holes in wood and countersink the holes for recessed screw heads

Bit Type: Concrete/masonry

Description: Has a chisel-like tungsten carbide tip to break up stone, brick, or concrete, while the flutes pull back the chipped material

Uses: Excellent for installing wiring and plumbing into existing concrete, blocks, or bricks, as well as drilling pilot holes to set fasteners into concrete

Bit Type: Glass and tile

Description: Some feature spear-pointed carbide tips; some feature hole saw–type cylinders with diamond-grit cutting edges

Uses: Accurate drilling for fastener holes in ceramic tile, marble, china, mirrors, and glass. The bits are ideal for drilling in bathroom tile or wall mirrors. (Use water spray to cool down the cutting)

From metal and masonry to plastics and wood, you'll use a saw on virtually every major home project. There's a wide range of options out there for both general and specific uses. Here are all the basics you're likely to run into as you plan basic home DIY projects.

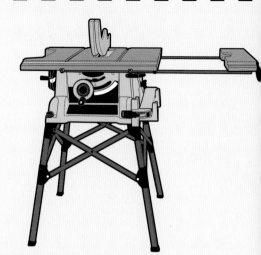

HANDHELD CIRCULAR SAW No other power saw can perform as many cutting tasks in such an affordable, storage-friendly package. Ripping, crosscutting, plunge cutting and more; circular saws do it all and can even make partial kerfs, beveled edges, and compound angles.

TABLE SAW Although table saws can crosscut short boards, their primary purpose is to rip long boards into thinner workpieces. A circular blade protrudes through a smooth table surface to cut the material as you feed it into the blade. Since the user guides the material along a rip fence, table saws offer superior control and accuracy for long rips and bevels.

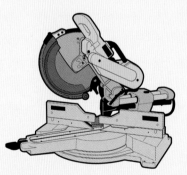

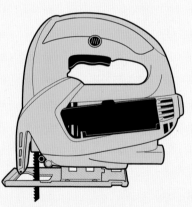

MITER SAW From deck building to intricate finish carpentry, a miter saw utilizes a circular blade to crosscut boards at the critical angles to build inside and outside corners. If you have a compound miter saw, not only can you turn the saw for a miter, you can tilt the blade to cut a bevel as well.

JIGSAW Also called saber saws, jigsaws are exceptionally useful tools for making tight, intricate cuts. The traditional "jigsaw" puzzle's tightly curved and complex network of cutout pieces demonstrates the saw's maneuverability. The straight, narrow blade can make curves, small holes, and detailed cuts that larger blades can't accomplish.

RECIPROCATING SAW Similar in design to a jigsaw, a reciprocating saw is larger and more aggressive. These versatile straight-bladed tools are designed to make cutouts and cutoffs, disassemble wood framing, trim branches, make tough cuts in tight quarters, and much more.

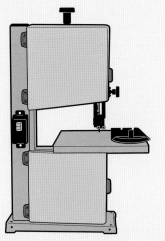

BAND SAW Commonly used to cut curves, a band saw consists of a pair of wheels that hold a narrow band of toothed metal. This band rides on the wheels in the same vertical plane, and a steel table is used to guide the workpiece into the cutting edge. A band saw can rip thick lumber into thinner slabs as well as cut metal and other materials. Portable versions are also available.

010 DO IT BY HAND

HANDSAWS The basic handsaw is good for large, rough cuts, plus it works when no power is available. When used with a miter box for improved accuracy, handsaws can also make angled cuts.

COPING SAWS Handsaws with a thin, flexible blade, they are used to make very small, detailed cuts for joining trim carpentry such as crown molding.

011 USE THE RIGHT TERMS

Different saws are made to make different cuts, so you should know all the terms.

RIP CUT To rip a board is to cut it into thin boards of equal length, sawing parallel to the wood grain.

CROSSCUT This means to cut a board down into shorter lengths of equal width, sawing perpendicular to the wood grain.

MITER This refers to an angled crosscut for joining two boards at an angled joint.

BEVEL A bevel is a cut that is made when the saw's blade is tilted at any angle other than 90 degrees.

012 GET INTO A SPIRAL (SAW)

From drywall and carpentry to flooring and HVAC, very few tools offer the versatility of a spiral saw. ❶ Originally designed to make drywall cutouts an easy chore, the RotoZip is a construction-grade spiral saw that uses thin cylindrical bits, similar to drill bits, but with the ability to make lateral cuts along the shank. Equipped with the right bit, the tool can cut through virtually any building material up to 1 inch thick. A RotoZip can also be equipped with a circular saw attachment. ❷

Smaller rotary tools, such as a Dremel, function in the same manner, but they operate with variable speed and can be outfitted as detail sanders for working around odd shapes and small nooks in woodwork. When equipped with small sanding drums, Dremels are frequently used for craft projects and millwork, such as window and door casings.

Both the heavy-duty RotoZip and the DIY-friendly Dremel are available in corded and cordless models and usually come with multiple attachments. Spiral saws are generally used with a depth-gauge attachment that rests flush against the cutting surface, and the bit is raised or lowered via an adjustable sleeve around the head of the saw. The right bits can cut through a wide range of material from wood and metal to tile or cement board.

For grout removal, you can select an angled depth gauge for your spiral saw to slide smoothly along the tile surface. These attachments are used in conjunction with specialized heavy-duty, grout-removal cutting bits. ❸

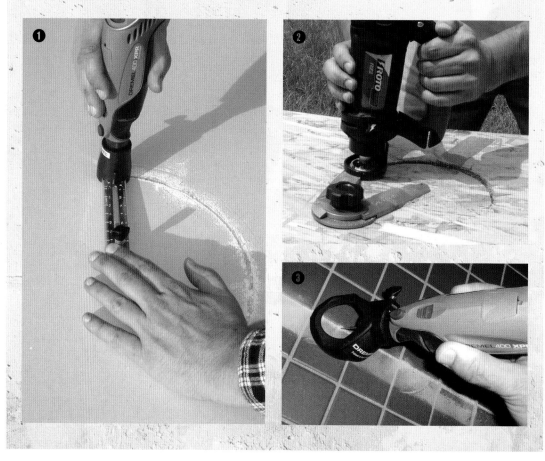

013   MEET THE MULTI-TOOL

The oscillating multi-tool is quickly becoming a must-have item, as it can equip a variety of different blades for notching wood, cutting metal, removing grout, sanding, making electrical cutouts, and much more. By utilizing high-speed oscillation, these versatile instruments can scrape, sand, make cuts flush with adjacent materials, and more, using a broad assortment of accessory blades. This allows the user to perform either fine detail work or to tackle more aggressive applications.

014   SCOUT OUT ROUTERS

Routers are used to hollow out or "rout" an area in the face of a workpiece. The router has a broad base and a bit projecting beyond its base plate. Depending on the router, the bit can be guided into the edge of a workpiece or plunged into the surface, where it cuts any number of straight, curved, or decorative profiles.

FIXED BASE The tool's base plate is attached in a fixed position to the motor, which is a great setup for cutting a profile in the edge of a board. Smaller trim routers take advantage of the fixed-base design to cut down on tool weight, which makes them easier to maneuver.

PLUNGE ROUTER Both the motor and cutter head slide along guide bars that are attached to the base. Plunge routers can begin cutting the center of a piece of wood, where the router bit is lowered or "plunged" into the workpiece. However, plunge routers often cost more and are heavier than fixed-base models.

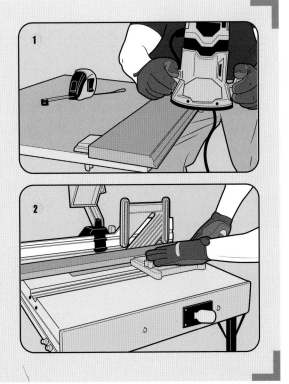

015 GET A GOOD COMPRESSOR

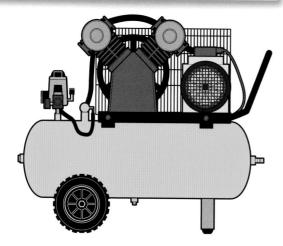

The most popular air compressors among DIYers and pros are midsize portable units that can be carried to a job site while still providing ample power. Here are factors to consider when making a choice.

OUTPUT The most important rating for any size air compressor is the standard cubic feet per minute (SCFM) output. To determine the size of compressor you need, first consider the tools you will use. The tool that has the highest SCFM rating will be your guideline for choosing a compressor. For the best results, purchase a compressor with an output of 1.5 times that rating. For example, if you want to use an impact wrench that requires 5.0 SCFM, you would purchase a compressor that puts out 7.5 SCFM. If you anticipate using multiple tools simultaneously, add the SCFM requirements for all tools that will be used at one time, and multiply the sum by 1.5.

TANK SIZE If you'll be using tools that require a high volume of air for continuous use, such as a pneumatic sander, then you need a larger tank. If you only intend to use the tool for intermittent use, your compressor can have a smaller tank size. For intermittent use, you can save money by choosing a unit with a smaller pump/motor (the most costly part of the unit) and a larger tank. A large enough tank with a pump that exceeds the SCFM requirement of your tools will allow the compressor time to cool between cycles. Tools requiring only quick bursts of air, such as brad and finish nailers, will deplete the tank much more slowly, so a 2- to 6-gallon tank should suffice.

016 GET SOME AIR

Air power is great way to take your home shop to the next level. Whether you need to run anything a framing nailer or a sandblaster, the right air compressor can handle the job. These versatile, economical machines, provide a single power source for a wide range of tools. Small inflators can air up basketballs and leaky car tires. Larger, compressors can be used in construction; there are also professional-grade stationary models for carpentry shops and automotive garages.

An air compressor is only as useful as the set of pneumatic tools that do the work. They require connection to a compressor hose, but air tools offer significant advantages over their electric cousins. They don't need their own motors, so air tools are more compact, lighter, and easier to handle—with less moving parts to malfunction.

Versatility is another advantage. You can easily switch tools at a single compressor, including a ratchet wrench, paint sprayer, angle nailer, finish nailer, or impact wrench.

017 RENT THE BIG STUFF

018 POWER UP

You may want to look into a generator that can be used if the power goes down for an extended time. You will need an adequate electrical to run large appliances or multiple tools simultaneously. High-power generators, however, cost more to purchase and require more room for storage.

To calculate wattage requirements, first make a list of all electrical devices you will be powering at one time with the generator. Next to each device, list the greater of the running or starting wattage. (If only the running wattage for a device with an electric motor is known, estimate the starting wattage to be at least three times the running wattage.)

If wattage is not given on the nameplate, the wattage may be calculated by multiplying the nameplate voltage by nameplate amperage. For example, 120 volts × 5 amps = 600 watts.

Add the wattages for all devices on your list. Choose a generator with a higher continuous output rating than the sum total wattage.

You can increase the number of devices your generator can power by staggering the load on the generator. For example, you could alternately power your refrigerator and air conditioner for limited periods of time.

A heavy, bulky item like a plate compactor can be not only cost prohibitive, but require storage space and maintenance as well. However, your local equipment rental outlet can provide you a well-maintained tool at a reasonable price, and then take it back off your hands. Some public libraries even maintain a tool library with equipment that locals can check out for little or no cost.

Common rental items include generators for remote power supply, plate compactors for tamping down foundations and patios, jackhammers for concrete demolition, and blowers for installing cellulose insulation. If you're working in the dark you can rent lighting equipment. If you're working in the cold, you can rent a kerosene heater. Check out your local supplier to explore the many rental options.

019 GET STUCK ON GLUES

The glue aisle of a hardware store is cluttered with countless tubes and bottles, and it can be pretty tough to determine the right product for the job. The table below should help determine the best adhesive for the application at hand. For any home project, it's helpful to know the glue's setting time (how long until it's initially bonded), drying time (when the adhesive is dry), and curing time (when it's fully bonded). Err on the side of caution: Keep the project clamped longer than needed to avoid messy and annoying failures.

TYPE OF GLUE	USED FOR	SETTING TIME	DRYING TIME	CURING TIME
Wood glue	As the name would suggest, it's for joining wood.	20 to 30 minutes	1 hour	24 hours
Superglue	Also sold as Krazy Glue, cyanoacrylates are good choices for metal, glass, ceramics, plastic, and rubber.	5 to 15 minutes	1 hour	24 hours
Silicone adhesive	Often used in plumbing projects or for glass repair; crates a flexible, waterproof bond for metal, glass, rubber, wood, and ceramics.	5 minutes	1 hour	24 hours
Epoxy	Epoxy consists of two parts—an adhesive resin and an activator/hardener—that mix to form an extremely durable, waterproof bond that works best on rigid surfaces like metal, ceramics, and plastics.	5 minutes to 2 hours	12 hours	24 to 48 hours
Hot glue	This comes in stick form and must be used with heated glue guns. It creates fast-setting, moderately strong bonds, ideal for lightweight materials and temporary adhesion.	15 to 30 seconds	5 to 10 minutes	24 hours
Spray adhesive	This glue disperses in fine droplets to provide a thin, uniform bonding surface that works best on lightweight materials such as paper, fabric, and small or thin pieces of plastic, wood, and metal.	Low-tack formulas will give you a few minutes before it sets; high-tack will set instantly	30 minutes	24 hours
Expandable glue	Known under brand names such as Gorilla Glue, these polyurethane-based products have foaming properties that expand and fill cracks in the material to create an extremely durable bond once cured, ideal for heavy-duty materials including wood, metal, ceramics, glass, plastic, and stone.	Varies depending on type	1 to 2 hours, or 30 minutes for fast-dry type	24 hours
Construction adhesive	This industrial-grade adhesive is sold in caulking tubes used in conjunction with fasteners for adhering plywood, cement board, treated lumber, and other building materials. Polyurethane-based versions are available for bonding plastics, vinyl, ceramics, mirrors, granite, and marble.	15 minutes to 1 hour	24 hours	24 hours to 7 days, depending on product

020 CLAMP DOWN

Here are the clamps you should consider adding to your burgeoning toolbox.

C-CLAMP The most basic and versatile member of this family can be used to hold together items you're gluing. Typically made of steel or cast iron, they tighten using a large, threaded screw.

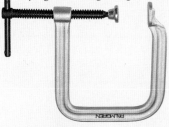

PIPE CLAMPS Clamp hardware that you add to your own pipe. Cut the ½-inch- or ¾-inch-diameter pipe as long or short as you want it.

BENCH CLAMPS They look like only half a clamp because bench clamps are bolted to a workbench, and the single upper jaw holds work securely down onto the tabletop.

STRAP CLAMP Utilizing a flexible band, strap clamps are designed for clamping rectangular, round, or any irregularly shaped projects.

SPRING CLAMPS They resemble giant clothespins and make a handy third hand to hold items for small repairs, painting, or gluing.

ANGLE CLAMPS Apply multidirectional pressure to 90-degree mitered corners.

BAR CLAMPS An adjustable lower jaw slides on a bar to bracket the work, and a threaded screw tightens the clamp with impressive force. Consider investing in a variety of sizes.

BENCH VISE Often used for metalwork, this heavy-duty metal clamp is typically bolted to a workbench and used to hold an object securely while work is performed on it.

021 GLUE IT RIGHT THE FIRST TIME

When gluing wood pieces together, make sure all surfaces are smooth and clean. The adhesive can be applied with a glue-bottle applicator tip, but it's important to evenly coat the wood surface. Thin strips of wood can be used as "paddles" to smooth out beads of glue to more thoroughly coat the surface of narrow joint pieces. If coating larger surfaces, such as when gluing down veneers, a roller is the best choice for a smooth and thorough application.

022 STICK TO IT

The right tape can work wonders for quick repairs, and some are made for specific purposes around the house. Here are the most widely used tapes for the do-it-yourself crowd..

TYPE	USES	GOOD TO KNOW
Duct tape	This is an excellent general-purpose tape for quick fixes, temporary bonds, and emergency repairs. Use it to bundle wires, seam together floor underlayment, or patch a vacuum hose.	Newer versions have twice the adhesive as standard duct tape. Not meant for use on ducts!
Foil tape	This tape is the best choice for use on home air ducts.	High-quality adhesive foil tape is more tolerant of temperature changes and creates a tighter seal than duct tape.
Painter's tape	Use it to mask off areas for crisp color lines and to protect areas you don't want painted.	Some new versions are treated with an absorbent polymer that reacts with latex paint and instantly gels to form a seal against paint bleed.
Electrical tape	Use this to bundle and splice electrical wires.	Most commonly made of vinyl, it's thin and stretchable to provide long-lasting insulation of electrical wires.
Self-fusing tape	This is a non-tacky, silicone-rubber tape that, when stretched and wrapped around hoses, cables, and pipes, fuses to itself to form a seamless rubbery bond that is waterproof and insulates electrical connections.	This handy multipurpose repair tape is sold under brand names such as Rescue Tape and Mighty Fixit tape.
Thread seal tape	This tape is a thin polytetrafluoroethylene film used for sealing pipe threads.	It lubricates the connection for a deeper seating of the threads, and it also fills minor deformities to create a better seal.
Drywall tape	Combine it with joint compound to seam drywall to prepare a new wall or ceiling for primer and paint.	It's available in paper and fiberglass versions.

023 SEAL UP WINDOWS

Window insulation kits sold at hardware stores and home centers come with double-sided adhesive tape and a large sheet of plastic film. Apply the tape around the window frame on all four sides, and then apply the film onto the tape so it completely covers the window, creating a sealed air space. Cut away the excess film and use a hair dryer to heat-shrink the film so it tightens the seal and shows no wrinkles.

025 **WRAP THREAD SEAL TAPE**

Employ thread seal tape on any threaded plumbing connections (not gas) that don't already have a rubber seal. After cleaning the male threads of a pipe with a rag, place the end of the tape on the second thread (not first), hold it in place with one hand, and wrap the tape 3 to 6 times in the same direction that the fitting will be tightened, which is usually clockwise. Wrapping against the thread direction might cause the mating threads to unwrap the tape when the connection is screwed together.

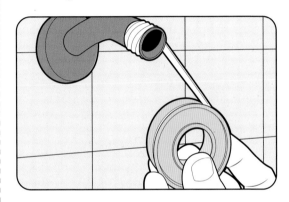

026 **PRESS IT DOWN**

Paint rollers and brushes leave a slightly uneven, stippled surface on the wall. When you're masking a room to repaint it, the flat underside of the painter's tape can bridge these irregularities and cause paint to bleed past the tape edge. To help improve surface contact with the wall and ensure the best adhesion, use a small rubber roller to press down the tape.

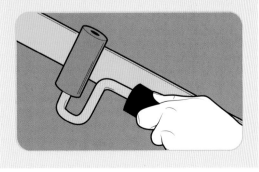

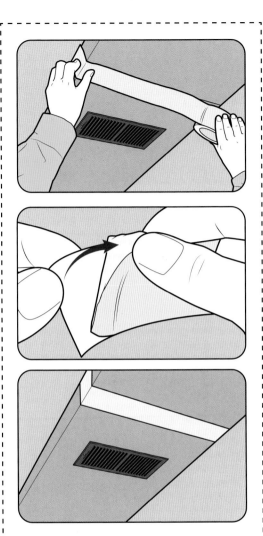

024 **USE FOIL TAPE GENTLY**

Measure and cut the length of tape you need by pulling it off the roll and holding it against the duct seam. Foil tape has a paper backing that's removed prior to application. Peel about 2 inches of backing, apply the adhesive end to the seam with one hand while holding the backing with the other, and slowly peel it away as you wrap the seam. Foil tape is very tacky; if the adhesive side folds on itself, it'll tear before releasing. Press down the tape evenly with a straight edge such as a credit card.

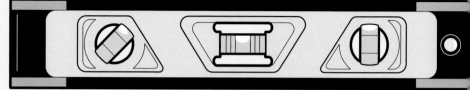

Just about everyone has used a basic carpenter's level or a small torpedo level. They are still incredibly useful tools, but widening your (level) horizons may be helpful for a wider range of DIY projects. Here are some options to consider.

1 6-FOOT LEVEL This option is even more accurate than a 4-footer for critical installations such as door installation, where the hinges need to be perfectly plumb for the door to swing properly.

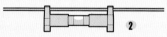

2 STRING LEVEL The longer a level is, the greater its accuracy. Sometimes the hardware store doesn't carry a version that's long enough, in which case a string level can help save the day. Pull a string tight between two points then hook the string level (a short cartridge with a bubble vial) onto it. Keep adjusting the string until the bubble reads level.

3 MAGNETIC LEVEL This option can attach to pipes and other metal objects to determine level or plumb, and it frees your hands while you work.

4 POST LEVEL A bifold level with multiple vials, this can be strapped around a fence post or support column to check for plumb in several directions at once.

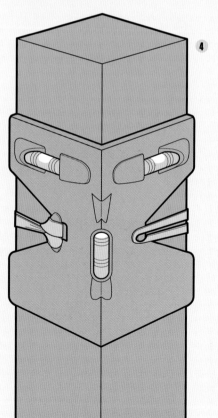

028 ENJOY THE LASER SHOW

If you're an ambitious DIYer with a house where you'll be painting, installing trimwork, hanging pictures, mounting shelves or cabinetry, then a laser layout tool may be well worth the investment. To project perfectly plumb and level guidelines onto walls and ceilings. We recommend buying a model that easily mounts to a common camera tripod so you can position it at any location with adjustable height.

029 USE A MULTIPURPOSE SPEED SQUARE

The Speed square is a five-in-one layout tool that offers a handy balance of simplicity and versatility. A Speed square is a very useful 90-degree shape that makes a quick marking gauge for simple crosscuts.

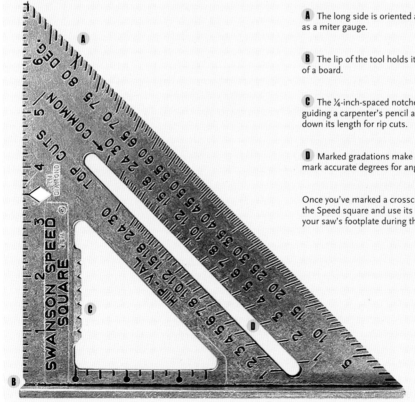

A The long side is oriented at 45 degrees for use as a miter gauge.

B The lip of the tool holds it square to the edge of a board.

C The ¼-inch-spaced notches are excellent for guiding a carpenter's pencil as you slide the square down its length for rip cuts.

D Marked gradations make it easy to read and mark accurate degrees for angled cuts.

Once you've marked a crosscut, simply slide over the Speed square and use its straight edge to guide your saw's footplate during the cut.

Painting a home's interior is hands down the most popular DIY project. New colors can dramatically change a room's décor and completely alter the look and feel of the living space. Here are the essential tools you'll need for your basic painting tool kit.

1 PAINTER'S TAPE Essential for masking off anything you don't want to paint.

2 PAINTBRUSH Your go-to application tools for trimwork, details, and tight spots.

3 PAINT ROLLER Applies paint to large, flat surfaces quickly and efficiently.

4 PAINT TRAY Holds a modest amount of paint or primer while you paint.

5 DROP CLOTH Protects flooring and furniture from accidental messes while painting.

6 SANDPAPER AND ABRASIVES Smooth down surfaces in preparation for painting.

7 PAINT SCRAPER Removes old, loose paint and preps surfaces for new paint.

031 APPLY YOUR PAINT

Paint jobs need brushes for fine detail and trim, and rollers for main surfaces. Here's what to use.

BRUSHES For latex paint you'll need synthetic bristles; for oil-based paint or varnish, choose a good-quality natural-bristle brush. The better the quality of natural bristles, the smoother the paint finish will be. You'll regret buying a super cheap brush when the bristles fall out of the brush and stick to your new paint surface. Brush handles are made of a variety of wood or plastics and come in several shapes and sizes. Choose a handle that feels comfortable in your hand for the type of work you're doing. Smaller trim brushes are intended for tight spaces, and some have tapered bristles to get into grooves and corners. Larger brushes are less accurate but apply paint more quickly. Keep a variety of brushes on hand for remodeling and maintenance.

ROLLERS These essential tools are available in small 3- and 4-inch models for tight or small spaces, as well as standard 12-inch sizes for painting walls. Paint rollers consist of a cage (the skeletal frame that spins on a handle) and a cover (the fabric cylinder that applies paint to the wall). The cover consists of the roller nap, which is made from natural or synthetic fibers. The nap is available in various lengths to apply different finishes. In general, ⅜- or ½-inch nap makes a good general-purpose roller cover.

NAP	USES
¼ inch	Smooth surfaces on new walls, ceilings, doors, and trim
⅜ inch	Smooth to lightly stippled walls
½ inch	Most walls and medium-rough surfaces, including textured plaster and concrete
¾ inch	Rough surfaces such as textured walls, concrete, and masonry

032 CLEAN UP

There's nothing worse than crusty brushes and other tools, so be sure to clean up promptly and correctly. Roller cages and paint trays can be cleaned with either clean water or mineral spirits, depending on the type of paint. Disposable roller covers should be discarded after use. Brushes can be a little trickier. When using water-based latex paint, it's smart to clean your brushes every 2 hours. Here's how.

STEP 1 Remove excess paint from the bristles with the edge of a paint scraper and then rinse the bristles with water.

STEP 2 Mix 1 gallon of warm water and ½ cup of fabric softener in a bucket.

STEP 3 Whisk the brush through the mixture for 15 seconds and allow the fabric softener to release the paint.

STEP 4 Remove the brush and spin it thoroughly to dispel the water, then wipe it dry on a towel.

If you've been using oil paint, you'll need more specialized cleaning supplies. As with latex paint, start by removing excess paint with a scraper. Next, clean the brush with mineral spirits for about 10 seconds to break down the binders in the paint. Spin the excess out of the brush, then clean it for 10 to 20 seconds in denatured alcohol to strip out the oils. Finish by whisking the brush for 10 seconds in the fabric softener mixture to recondition the bristles.

The workbench is usually the hub of all your shop operations. A common height for workbenches is just a couple of inches below the user's waistline. The surface should be clear and flat, and its size can be built to fit your needs—before you build or purchase a bench, be sure it makes sense for the size of your miter and/or table saw.

Many people often add an extension panel to their workbench that can fold up level with the tabletop for work with large pieces, and then can unlock and fold out of the way when not needed. Lockable wheels will also allow you to easily move the bench around and then secure it in a stationary position. And don't forget to outfit the area with a comfortable stool.

034 GET OUT OF THE SHOP

What if you don't have a whole garage or a spare room to make into a workshop? Although you can optimize interior spaces with shelves and other wall storage, you're ultimately limited by the size of your house. But overlooked areas of the home can be modified to provide extra storage space. Convert the space beneath a staircase into a closet, build a plywood bin under your deck, add a garden shed for lawn tools, or install a subfloor in the attic to create storage space above the joists. With a little creative thinking, you can find a number of storage options outside the typical work space.

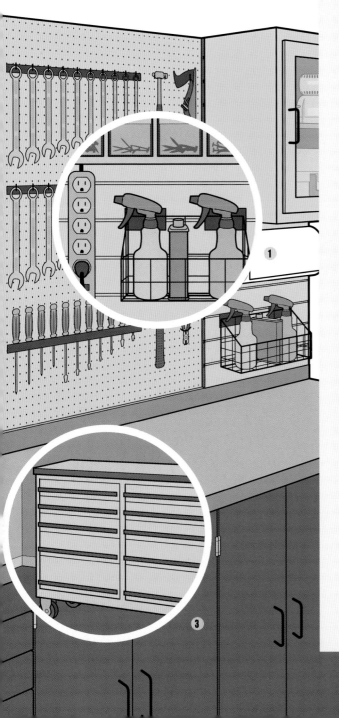

035 STORE SMARTER

You can add significant square footage of elevated storage space by building shelves. Wall-mounted shelves can be hung with store-bought brackets screwed into the framing studs. Two-tiered shelves can be built with simple legs and rails made of 2x4s and shelving made of 2x6s or 2x8s. Screw or nail the shelves together and then use diagonal bracing to keep the structure square. Some workshop shelves utilize 2x2 ladder brackets with three-tiered plywood shelving. Styles vary, but most shop shelves are built with simple construction from inexpensive materials.

1 WALL-STORAGE SYSTEMS Popular because they make use of otherwise unused wall space to organize tools and supplies, many of these systems consist of slat-wall panels fastened to the wall, which hold various hooks, shelves, and straps to keep items off the floor.

2 PEGBOARD PANELS These panels, which are mounted to the wall, have long been popular for storing small items including wrenches and screwdrivers. A wide range of hooks and holders can be mounted to the pegboard holes with almost limitless versatility to keep your hand tools handy.

3 TOOL CABINETS Bigger cabinets are an excellent option for serious DIYers who have a lot of equipment that needs to be sorted by type and application. The number of drawers varies, and many versions include caster wheels to easily roll the cabinet around the shop.

036 DEAL WITH RUST

To avoid rust, always store metal tools away from moisture, and dry them thoroughly if they get wet. Routinely wipe off grease and grime, which can accumulate grit that wears down moving parts and interferes with their function. Keep construction tools rust free with an occasional light coating of lubricating oil. Available in liquid and spray versions, it delivers a colorless oil coating that eases sticking parts, and the thin, wet film can also protect the tools against wear and corrosion.

RENEW RUSTY TOOLS First, clean off the tool using hot water and detergent. For light rust, use steel wool or fine-grit sandpaper; scrub the rust off in thorough circular motions. For heavy corrosion, use a wire brush. Rinse with water, dry the tool and then apply a sufficient amount of solvent or WD-40 to any leftover rust and scrub it away. Repeat until the tool is clean,

and apply a protective coat of lubricant before storing it.

HANDLE TOUGH JOBS Renew multiple tools or machinery with small components by using a liquid rust remover, which makes even deep rust disappear without scrubbing. Some removers rely on harsh chemicals, but Evapo-Rust is an environmentally friendly, water-based product that comes in a 3.5-gallon bucket with a dip basket so small parts don't get lost.

GO NATURAL Combine salt and lemon juice in a container, then apply the solution with steel wool. The salt works as an abrasive, and the acid in the lemon juice cuts through corrosion. Leave the solution on the tool's surface for a while before scrubbing to agitate the rust. Once the corrosion has been removed, clean and dry the tool with a rag.

037 RECYCLE WHAT YOU CAN

What building material can be recycled and how varies from city to city; check with your local authorities to be sure you're doing it right. One good thing is that recycling services for hazardous materials are becoming common, at least for some of the more common items such as motor oil, electronics, and batteries.

In fact, 96 percent of all lead-acid batteries are recycled. This includes automobile and lawnmower batteries. Almost any retailer that sells lead-acid batteries collects used batteries for recycling, as required by most state laws. Not only is recycling your battery a responsible environmental decision, but the recycler will typically offer you a battery-core "credit" that reduces the cost of your replacement battery.

038 GREASE IT UP

Lubricants have a wide range of uses—they can loosen tight parts, protect against rust or other damage, and make things run more smoothly. Here are the common types you'll see.

MULTIPURPOSE SPRAY Popular general-use product that protects metal from rust and corrosion, penetrates stuck parts, displaces moisture, and lubricates almost anything.

PENETRATING OIL Quickly loosens any corroded bolts, nuts, and parts on hinges, clamps, or frozen shafts/pulleys.

SILICONE SPRAY Provides super-slippery protection in a clear, non-staining film to prevent rust and corrosion; protects rubber gaskets and prevents sticking in cold temperatures.

WHITE LITHIUM GREASE Ideal all-weather application because it will not freeze or melt. Provides long-lasting, heavy-duty grease coat for joints, hinges, and connections.

LUBRICATING OIL Protects objects against moisture, stops squeaks, and loosens any sticking parts on locks, hinges, and garage door rollers. Prevents rust and corrosion on spark plugs, coils, wiring, hand/electric tools, and outdoor power equipment.

DRY LUBRICANT A long-lasting dry film that cuts friction and protects against water and corrosion without staining. Lubricates and silences slides and glides, window tracks, extension ladders, control cables on snow blowers, and more.

CHAIN LUBRICANT Stays in place to help lubricate and prevent corrosion on fast-moving chains or wire cables such as a garage door opener, chain-drive equipment, throttle, and brake.

039 WINTERIZE TOOLS

After the lawn and garden season, you're going to want to repair and winterize your yard tools so everything's in great shape when the time rolls around to get outdoors again. Even if you live in a climate where you'll be using some of those tools most of the year, the turn of the seasons is a good time to take a look at your toolshed and see what needs loving care.

MAINTAIN THE LAWNMOWER If you have major small-engine or lawnmower problems, have them taken care of in fall rather than waiting for spring when all repair shops are busy. Sharpen or replace lawnmower blades. Drain the oil and replace it along with the filter. Drain the gas or add a fuel stabilizer to engines in lawnmowers, pressure washers, generators, or similar items. Do any minor repairs while it's easier to get parts during the off-season.

STRING IT ALONG Get ready for spring by replacing the line in string trimmers. In cold winter climates, make sure the snowblower is working properly.

DON'T IGNORE HAND TOOLS Clean and sharpen all gardening equipment such as rakes, hoes, shovels, and shears, and give all wooden handles a coating of linseed oil.

040 FIRE IT UP

Don't wait for a wintertime power outage to discover your generator doesn't function. Exercise your generator every 4 weeks. Start the engine and let it run for 10 to 15 minutes with a small load plugged in, such as a lamp or fan. Exercising the generator monthly will dry out any moisture that has accumulated in the windings, which could otherwise cause corrosion.

041 RAISE AN EXTENSION LADDER PROPERLY

The easiest way to raise a long extension ladder is to do it with two people. One person "foots" the first rung, holding the bottom of the ladder securely to the ground, as the second person walks toward the house with the other end of the ladder, raising it with the first person's help, as needed.

STEP 1 If you need to raise the ladder alone, it needs to be collapsed to its shortest height. First, brace the foot of the ladder against the wall and walk it slowly toward the base, rung by rung and hand by hand, until the ladder is upright. Rest the top of the ladder against the wall, roof, or other solid surface. Then lift the base out to a slight angle where it can temporarily rest without your support.

STEP 2 Extension ladders are equipped with a lanyard and pulley to help extend the ladder. To use a lanyard, first foot the bottom rung, then carefully tilt the ladder backward with one hand, and pull the rope with the other to extend the ladder as necessary. Be careful of hazards to nearby power lines or other people.

STEP 3 An extension ladder should be set with the base 1 foot away from the wall for every 4 feet the ladder reaches, or roughly a 75-degree angle.

STEP 4 Once you've got it positioned right, you need to secure the feet. The base of the ladder should rest on level ground with the feet flipped into position. On a wooden deck, you can nail a board down behind the feet to act as a cleat and prevent slippage. When setting up on uneven ground, it helps to dig a small trench beneath the high foot of the ladder to level the base.

STEP 5 Make sure all locks are engaged and that the ladder is supported securely at all contact points. If it seems the least bit unstable, tie ropes to the ladder stiles beneath the lowest rung and anchor them to something solid. You can also secure the top of the ladder using rope or wire fastened to a couple of eye screws mounted into the house's fascia.

042 CHOOSE THE RIGHT LADDER

Your work environment, including the physical size restrictions, is probably the most important factor in determining the type of ladder to use for a given job. Plenty of purpose-built ladders are available for specific jobs. A long extension ladder ❶ is required for accessing the roof of multilevel homes, while smaller A-frame ladders ❷ and fold-out stepladders ❸ make sense for interior jobs like installing crown molding. Multipurpose ladders offer a versatile solution that combines ladder types into a single unit. By articulating like an A-frame ❺ and also extending and collapsing just like an extension ladder, a multipurpose ladder can serve as a stepladder, an extension ladder ❹, even a 90-degree ladder (for getting close to walls). By adjusting the length of each side of the ladder independently when in the A-frame mode, a multipurpose ladder can also give access over uneven ground and staircases. Plus, you only have one ladder to store.

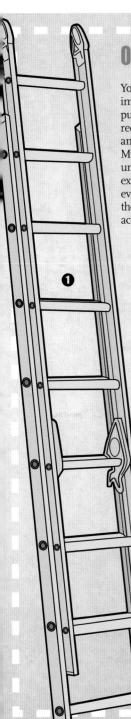

043 KNOW YOUR LADDER(S)

Ladders are essential. They can also be awkward, bulky, and hard to store. Here's what to consider when selecting one.

MATERIALS Ladders are constructed from one of three basic materials: wood, fiberglass, and metal (aluminum). If you're working near electricity, a metal ladder should be rejected since aluminum conducts electricity. However, if there aren't any electrical sources in your work area, aluminum is easier to transport.

HEIGHT A ladder must be long enough that the climber does not have to stand on the top rung or step. On the other hand, a straight ladder is too long, for example, if ceiling height prohibits the ladder from being set up at the proper angle (roughly 75 degrees). Likewise, an extension ladder is too long if the ladder extends farther than 3 feet beyond the upper support point. In this case, the portion of the ladder extending above the upper support point can act like a lever and cause its base to move or slide out. Safety standards require a label on the ladder to indicate the highest standing level.

FIT The ladder that you select also must be the right size for both your body and the job at hand. Check the ladder's duty rating—the maximum safe weight capacity for the task at hand. In other words, the duty rating of a given ladder has to be greater than the total weight of not just the person climbing but also their tools, supplies, and any other objects placed upon the ladder. If the total load outweighs the ladder's maximum capacity, the ladder could feasibly collapse.

DUTY RATING	LADDER USES
Type III 200-pound capacity	An economical design for light use
Type II 225-pound capacity	A basic design for those who don't use a ladder much
Type I 250-pound capacity	A good all-around ladder for most standard uses
Type IA 300-pound capacity	A more rugged ladder for the serious DIYer
Type IAA 375-pound capacity	An extra-tough ladder for professional uses

044 BE STABLE

For work on extension ladders, consider adding a stabilizer accessory to the top ladder. Stabilizers generally consist of extension braces with rubber pads that grip the work surface to help keep the top from slipping sideways. These accessories distribute the load to prevent damage to materials like metal siding. Ladder stabilizers are also made wide enough to span window openings, and they hold the ladder away from the building for easy, unobstructed access to gutters and overhangs.

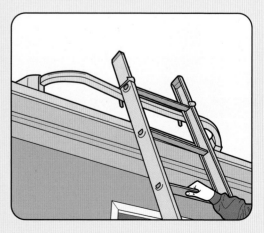

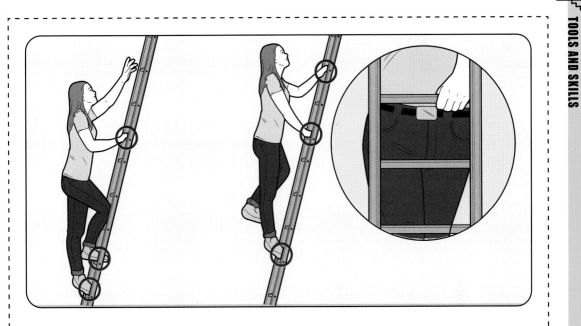

045 REACH NEW HEIGHTS

When climbing a ladder, you'll want to emulate rock climbers by using the "three points of contact" rule to reduce the chances of slipping and falling. At all times during ascent or descent, the climber should face the ladder and have two hands and one foot, or two feet and one hand, in contact with the ladder cleats and/or side rails. When working atop a ladder, keep the center of your belt buckle between the ladder side rails (or within the width of the cleats) rather than reaching or leaning too far to one side. It's also smart to use towlines or a tool belt to keep your hands free when climbing, or recruit an assistant to hand you the items you need. Wear only slip-resistant shoes, preferably with heels and heavy soles, to prevent foot fatigue.

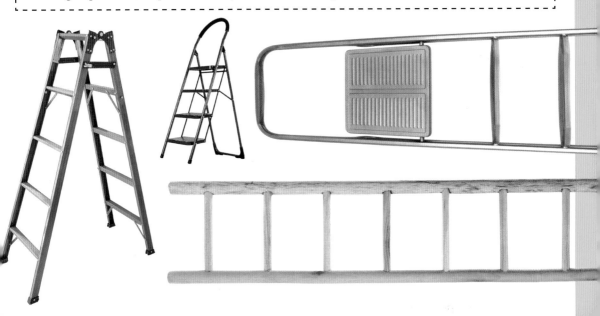

Remodeling a home comes with some safety hazards, so to avoid injuries you'll need to wear the right protective equipment.

1 SAFETY GLASSES Crucial for shielding your eyes from flying debris during demolition, sawing, drilling, and more. They're available in many styles and tints, from stylish eyeglass versions to goggles that seal around the perimeter of the eye area.

2 WORK GLOVES Protect from blisters, cuts, and repetitive stress abrasion to the hands. Work gloves vary greatly in style, and some include padded palms and fingers to absorb the shock and vibration of power tools.

3 RUBBER GLOVES When working with paint or chemicals, rubber gloves can protect your skin from burns and irritation as well as sticky messes that are tough to clean up. You'll also appreciate them when

working on dirty plumbing projects. Thin nitrile gloves allow dexterity when painting and staining, but heavier rubber gloves with extended cuffs work best for messy plumbing chores.

4 KNEE PADS Often overlooked by inexperienced DIYers, knee pads don't just reduce the wear and tear of working on your knees. You should view them as a comfort item that takes the pain out of installing new floors and baseboards—or any jobs where you work in a kneeling position.

5 RESPIRATOR Fresh air is a popular concept for a lot of good reasons. Use a simple dust mask to prevent inhaling sawdust during basic carpentry work, or use a filtered respirator for work around harsh chemicals, when cutting cement board, and so on.

6 WORK BOOTS Your feet are susceptible to three primary injuries during construction work: twisting

047 PUSH IT REAL GOOD

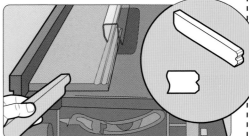

When ripping boards on a table saw or routing boards on a router table, the workpiece should be pushed forward and firmly against the rip fence, guiding it into the blade or bit. Use a "push stick" to push the workpiece completely past the blade to complete the rip or rout. A push stick is a tool made from a 15-inch piece of wood with beveled and notched ends to nudge the end of the workpiece clear of the blade and off the table. This simple tool keeps your hands away from the blade while cutting and is also useful for clearing the table of any wood scraps.

the ankle, a wound from puncturing the sole of the shoe, or an object falling on your foot from above. A quality work boot can firmly support the ankle joint, protect from nails and sharp objects with its thick, solid sole, and steel-toed versions can even protect your toes from falling boards or concrete blocks.

7 HARD HATS Not just for construction workers, you should use a hard hat any time you're present beneath a falling hazard, whether a crew of workers is replacing the roof or you're cutting a dead branch out of a tree.

8 SAFETY HARNESS Fall-protection equipment saves lives. Attached to a secure area of the roof's framing by a lanyard, these vest-like harnesses are required for working on roofs or any elevated surface where, if you fall, it would be better not to hit the ground. Many different options are available to suit individual size, comfort needs, and working habits.

048 SAVE YOUR EARS

Ask an old-time carpenter about hearing protection, and the response is likely to be: "What'd you say?" Exposure to noise is common in construction, and hearing loss is prevalent. DIYers should use earmuffs or earplugs to protect against noise from power tools such as air compressors, impact drivers, circular saws, and the like.

049 CHARGE AHEAD WISELY

You can perform most electrical work inside the home safely, but it's still important to shut off the power supply before getting on the job. Shut off the circuit you're working on at the circuit breaker box by flipping a breaker switch or unscrewing a fuse. This box should be labeled to help identify the appropriate circuits, but you should always verify that the power is off by testing the line with a voltage meter, which should read zero if there is no electrical current. Test all the wires in the outlet box (not just the ones you're working on), because more than one circuit might be running into the box.

While the power is off, post a sign on the breaker box warning other people not to reconnect power while you're working on the electricity. Use tools with rubber-insulated handles, and avoid touching metal while working around electricity. Wear non-conductive rubber-soled shoes, and never do this type of work in a wet environment. Most importantly, don't attempt an electrical repair or installation unless you know what you're doing.

Repairs to the outdoor service drop and the wires that feed the main shutoff to the breaker box should be left to your utility company.

050 STORE IT SAFELY

When it comes to DIY home improvement, "safety" should be your middle name. The improper storage of household chemicals can be hazardous to your family's health and the environment.

CONTAIN CORRECTLY Store all chemicals in their original labeled containers that list directions, ingredients, and first-aid steps in case of accidental poisoning. Use child-resistant packaging correctly, and close the container tightly for storage.

KEEP AWAY FROM FLAME Store flammable liquids outside your living area and far away from any ignition source such as a furnace, car, outdoor grill, or lawnmower.

BE PESTICIDE SMART Don't stockpile any pesticides; buy only the amount that you'll need in the near future or during the season when the pests are active. Follow all storage instructions on the pesticide label, and keep them out of reach of children and pets. If at all possible, store all pesticides in a locked cabinet in a well-ventilated area and never in cabinets near food, animal feed, or medical supplies. Avoid storing them where flooding is possible or where the chemicals might spill or leak into wells, drains, groundwater, or surface water.

051 GET THE LEAD OUT

Homes built as recently as 1978 may have paint that contains lead. Dust and chips from disrupted or degraded lead paint can cause serious health problems for the occupants of the house. Test sticks, which are available at home centers and paint stores, can easily detect the presence of lead in paint. Follow the manufacturer's instructions when testing the paint; the tip of the stick should turn red if it contains lead. For guidance on how to have lead paint safely removed from your home, contact the local authorities or the Environmental Protection Agency at www.epa.gov.

052 AVOID ASBESTOS

Asbestos can be found in building materials manufactured before 1978, such as vinyl and linoleum flooring and textured ceiling spray. It has long, thin fibers that can damage the lungs when breathed, which can cause scarring that can lead to cancer. Undisturbed asbestos usually poses no danger, and in some cases the material can be covered with new flooring to contain it.

Do not attempt to remove asbestos yourself. Standard respirators will be inadequate, and any damaged asbestos can send airborne fibers throughout your house. Check with state and local guidelines about professional asbestos-removal services located in your area.

053 TEST FOR RADON GAS

Radon gas sounds like something out of a scary 1950s sci-fi movie, but it's an actual danger you should take seriously. Radon is a radioactive gas that occurs naturally in soil from the breakdown of uranium. It can rise up from cracks in a home's foundation, or through other cracks or holes. It's a cancer risk that's associated with as many as 20,000 deaths a year in the United States alone.

The good news is that you can test for radon simply and cost-effectively, and if you find high levels, there are simple steps that you can take to mitigate the danger. Newer homes have likely been built to be radon-safe, but you should still test for the gas, just to be sure.

You can't see, smell, or taste radon, but it can be detected with a simple home test, which you can purchase at home-improvement stores or online through a number of other sources. Follow the instructions carefully; if you have a questionable result, test again in a week.

If you should discover that your home is contaminated by radon gas, don't panic. There are several proven methods you can employ to reduce radon in your home; the most common is a "soil-suction system," a pipe-and-fan system that pulls radon from beneath the house and vents it to the outside. Sealing any foundation cracks or other openings will make this system more effective and cost-efficient. Research what is the best for your home's structure and then act accordingly.

054 GET WIRED

Typical electrical supply wire for home use comes in an insulated sleeve that contains three wires. The black wire carries electrical current and is usually called the "hot" wire. The white wire is "neutral," and, finally, a bare copper wire is the ground wire. When electrical wires are joined each of them must be hooked to its mate: black to black, white to white, ground to ground. Otherwise, the circuit will not work.

USE THE RIGHT SIZE Electrical wiring can come in different gauges, or sizes. The smaller the number, the heavier the gauge. Heavier-gauge wire is thicker and can carry more electrical current without overheating. So, for example, 12-gauge wire is heavier and will carry more of a load than 14-gauge wire.

MATCH THE BREAKERS Electrical wire and circuit breakers are designed to work in tandem and must correspond correctly in size. For example, 14/2-gauge electrical wire is rated to a maximum of 15 amps and should not be used with any circuit breaker larger than 15 amps; 12/2-gauge wiring is rated to a maximum of 20 amps. These two sizes are the standard used in most homes today for lighting and wall outlets.

BE SAFE It is imperative to know the proper gauge wire and circuit breaker required for any given application. If the wrong gauge wire is used with the wrong size breaker, it can result in a fire or a malfunctioning electrical circuit. If too small a wire is used with a high-amp breaker, the wire can overheat and catch fire before the breaker ever trips. On the other hand, if a wire is too large then the breaker may continuously trip, disrupting the circuit before the wire ever reaches maximum load.

055 CONNECT IT RIGHT

Replacing light switches and wall outlets are great DIY projects. Building codes limit how many outlets and/or lights a particular circuit can have and even where they can be placed. Consult your local and state building codes before beginning any electrical work.

Switch and outlets are similar in that they have screws on both sides for connecting wires. The green screws are for the ground wires, the silver/stainless screws are for the white neutral wires, and the brass-colored screws are for the black "hot" wires. Wires are attached by bending the end into a hook shape that fits around the screws on each side of the outlet or switch to make a secure connection when tightened.

LIGHT SWITCHES To connect a switch, route the ends of the two wires into the switch box, strip the ends, and then connect the white wires together with a wire nut. Connect the ground wires

056 GO NUTS

For applications such as wiring a light, the fixture's wires are joined to the electrical supply wires with wire nuts. Like the wire itself, wire nuts come in different sizes to accommodate the various gauges of wire. To connect, strip back the insulation from the ends of the wires, hold them between your fingers, and use pliers to twist the wire nut onto the ends in a clockwise direction.

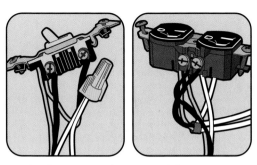

together by securing them around the green screw on the bottom of the switch. The black wires are each attached to the switch, one to each brass screw on the right-hand side.

PLUGS Receptacles (plugs or outlets) are all connected in a row, so to speak, by attaching the white wires to the silver/stainless metal screws on one side and connecting the black wires to the brass screws on the other side. The ground wire connects to the green screw at the bottom.

057 POWER UP

Every DIY homeowner should have a general understanding of the wiring that runs throughout the house. Electricity enters every home by traveling through a power meter supplied by the local utility company, then, in most cases, through a master 200-amp circuit breaker, and then to the home's breaker box. The flow of electricity is spread over numerous circuits to different parts of the home by first passing through individual circuit breakers that serve as a safety mechanism to prevent the system from overloading (and short-circuiting). A home's electrical system is designed to work off 120 volts with the exception of certain major appliances, such as an electric clothes dryer, which runs off 240 volts.

Before you do anything, always disconnect the electrical power supply before working with any part of the electrical system. Use a voltage meter on the circuit to verify it is off.

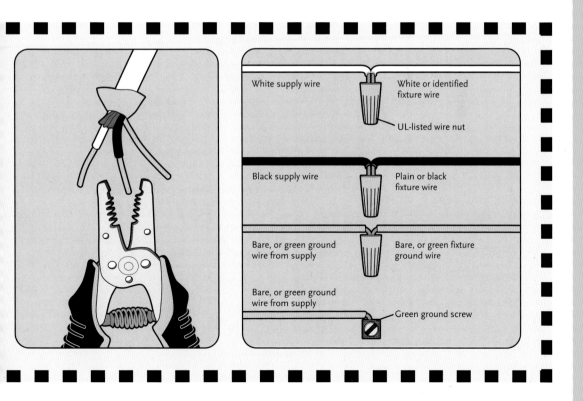

White supply wire

White or identified fixture wire

UL-listed wire nut

Black supply wire

Plain or black fixture wire

Bare, or green ground wire from supply

Bare, or green fixture ground wire

Bare, or green ground wire from supply

Green ground screw

058 KNOW YOUR PIPES

A range of pipes carry water to and through your home, and they may be made of a variety of materials. Here's what you may find.

1 PVC The most commonly used plastic piping material, PVC (polyvinyl chloride) was developed to replace cast iron and galvanized steel pipe because it's less expensive, easier to install, and will never corrode. It's made for both pressurized and non-pressure applications, including DWV applications, sewer hookups, water service, irrigation, and conduit.

2 CPVC PVC's "cousin," this similar material has an increased chlorine content that allows it to withstand a wider range of temperatures. Many building codes require the use of CPVC as opposed to PVC for hot-water applications; check those related codes before beginning any relevant project.

3 ABS A rigid plastic pipe developed for DWV systems, typically black or dark gray in color. It's inexpensive and easy to cut but is susceptible to cracking over time and is not allowed by some local plumbing codes.

4 COPPER Available as either rigid pipe or flexible tubing, copper has been the most popular supply line used in residential systems in the last several decades. It is durable, resistant to bacteria and corrosion, and unaffected by ultraviolet rays, so it can be exposed for outdoor applications—and it's also recyclable.

059 TRY SOMETHING NEW

Cross-linked polyethylene (also called PEX) is becoming a new standard for indoor pipes. This stuff is resistant to extreme temperatures and stress as well as to chemical damage from acids and alkalines. The material is flexible and suitable for use in temperatures below freezing and up to 200 degrees Fahrenheit, including potable water. PEX is easy to thread through stud holes without binding against the wood like a rigid copper pipe can do. When a pipe reaches a corner, simply bend the flexible pipe through the corner studs—no joint is necessary. With PEX supply line, fewer joints save time and reduce the likelihood of a leak. PEX is less expensive than copper, and PEX joints can be made with simple quick-connect couplers.

060 UNDERSTAND PLUMBING 101

Every DIYer should have a working knowledge of the home's plumbing system.

THE BASICS Water enters your house under pressure from your local utility's main supply line and then flows through pipes to various fixtures. Gravity then moves the water through a drain system into a septic tank or city sewer. You'll want to know where the water comes into your house and where the main shutoff valve is.

SUPPLY LINES As fresh water enters the property it passes through a water meter, and then a split in the line sends water either directly into the plumbing fixtures or to the water heater.

FIXTURES Plumbing fixtures are connected to the plumbing system to deliver and drain water (sinks, tubs, showers, washing machines, and so on). Before water reaches the fixtures, it usually passes through a shut-off valve protruding from the wall (or two valves, if hot water is also used). These valves can stop the flow of water to repair or replace the fixture. A separate valve inside the fixture delivers water to the user when opened.

DRAIN LINES Wastewater drains from the bottom of plumbing fixtures through a P-trap or S-trap just below the drain openings. The traps consist of bends in the pipe to hold water, forming a seal against sewer gases.

All these drain pipes lead to a drain-waste-vent (DWV) stack, the main vertical pipe leading to the sewer line. The DWV also vents outdoors, usually up through the roof, to release sewer gases. It helps equalize pressure in the system so water flows freely. Since water and sewage travel down drains by gravity, a downward slope must be maintained throughout the system.

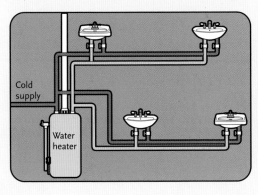

Cold supply

Water heater

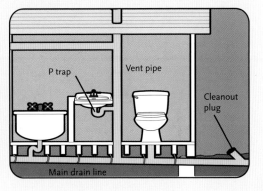

P trap

Vent pipe

Cleanout plug

Main drain line

061 KNOW YOUR LIMITS

Don't attempt a plumbing project if you don't know what you're doing. A flooded home can cost thousands in repairs and flooring replacement, which is a lot more money than a plumber would have charged to fix the problem that you bungled—and you'll still need that plumber in the end. Thoroughly research how to perform any repair or installation, and what materials and supplies you'll need. Seek expert advice for any questions, and expect to get wet. Plumbing projects are messy, time consuming, laborious, and often uncomfortable (ever spent much time working beneath a sink?). Proceed with caution and, when in doubt, hire a pro.

062 CHOOSE THE BEST CAULK GUN

②

Caulk guns are relatively inexpensive tools, so it makes sense to pay just a little extra for a gun with the right features.

① SPOUT CUTTER Every tube of caulk will need to have its spout clipped, and there's no reason to lug around an extra pair of snips. Look for a gun with an integrated spout cutter typically located in the handle.

② SEAL PUNCH This super simple feature should come on every gun, but it doesn't. It's a small metal rod that flips out from beneath the gun to puncture the caulk tube's interior seal, so you don't have to monkey around with a wire coat hanger or other makeshift implement.

③ PLUNGER TYPE Caulk guns use one of two drive mechanisms: ratchet rod or smooth rod. Ratchet rods have visible teeth that are ratcheted forward by a drive arm when you pull the trigger. Smooth rods are driven by a spring-loaded pressure bar and generally have twice the thrust for smoother bead control and less hand fatigue. The smooth-rod variety usually costs more, however, and some have a tendency to wear out and slip when the trigger is pulled.

063 SEAL IT UP

Caulk is available in a sometimes bewildering range of options—flexible, waterproof, mildew resistant, paintable, and more. Your best bet is to read the packaging carefully to ensure the uses and features listed match the job at hand.

TYPE	PROS
SILICONE SEALANTS	• Waterproof • Works well in kitchen and bathroom; available with additives that fight mold and mildew • Easy to remove and replace when the bead gets grimy
ACRYLIC CAULK	• Economical • Can be painted • Easy to apply and clean up
HYBRID CAULK/ SEALANT	• Combines attributes of silicone and acrylic • Comes in varieties for interior and exterior usage
FIRE-RESISTANT CAULK	• Fire resistant

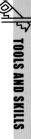

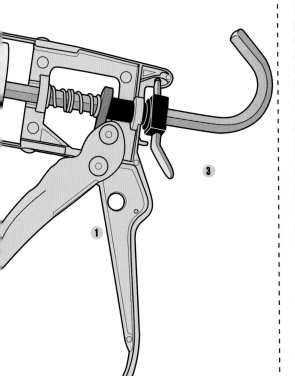

3	
1	

ONS	NOTES
Messy and sticky Many varieties cannot be painted	Read the package carefully to see if it can be painted and what additives it has
Not waterproof • Not very flexible • May crack over time	Only appropriate for interior projects
More expensive	These pro-grade sealants cost more but deliver excellent results
More expensive	Used around electrical wires and fixtures as an additional safety measure

064 CAULK LIKE A PRO

Caulking can be applied to door frames, moldings, and casings; exterior siding; and anywhere gaps need to be filled. Here are some common applications.

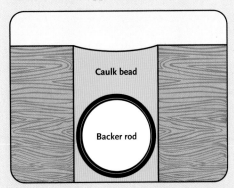

Caulk bead

Backer rod

SEAL BIG JOINTS To seal a joint larger than ¼-inch wide, use a foam backer rod as a filler before applying the caulk. The rods are a cheaper way to fill the empty space. Plus, when the caulk is applied over a backer rod, it will form an "hourglass" shape with large surface areas of adhesion at the sides of the joint. This caulk bead withstands joint movement better than any other.

CAULK A TUB When caulking a bathtub, first fill the tub with water. The weight will pull the tub downward and maximize the size of the joint. Apply a flexible, waterproof caulking along the edge of the tub in full contact with both vertical and horizontal surfaces. Once the bead is dry, then you can drain the water.

REMOVE OLD SEALANT To get rid of an old grungy bead of silicone for replacement, cut through each side of the bead using a utility knife and pull it away by hand. With any luck, most of the bead will stay intact as a strip. To remove any remaining sealant, scrape at it with a paint scraper held at a shallow angle. Finish up by scrubbing the surface with mineral spirits and an abrasive pad to get rid of any residue. Once clean and dry, apply a new bead of sealant.

Remodeling can be messy business, particularly if it involves any sort of demolition. Dust and debris have an uncanny knack for spreading throughout every crevice of the home if left unchecked. A clean job site keeps the house spick-and-span and even eliminates safety hazards.

You can take precautionary measures as you work to save lots of time during cleanup.

1 Protect carpet and hardwood by covering your floors with contractor's paper; tape sheets together and attach them to the baseboards of the room.

2 A canvas drop cloth can make a flexible and reusable protective cover for irregular shapes such as bathtubs and stairs.

3 Seal off the doorways leading to construction areas with plastic to inhibit dust from circulating throughout other rooms.

4 Place a box fan in an open window, pointing it to blow outside. Once all demolition is finished, sweep the floor in the direction of the fan to send the dust out the window. On outdoor projects, use tarps to cover the surrounding ground.

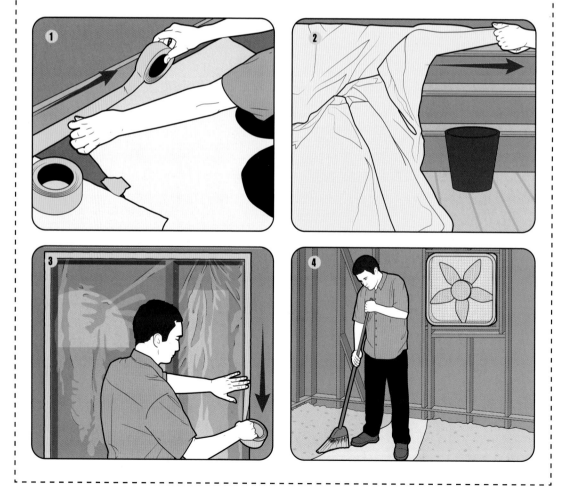

066 HANDLE HAZARDOUS WASTE

Certain types of household chemicals qualify as household hazardous waste (HHW), which contain corrosive, toxic, ignitable, or reactive ingredients. These can include paints, cleaners, oils, batteries, and pesticides that contain potentially hazardous ingredients. They will contaminate septic tanks or wastewater treatment systems if poured down drains or toilets, and they present hazards to children and pets if left around the house. Although federal law allows disposal in the trash, many communities have collection programs to reduce the potential harm posed by these chemicals. Call your local environmental, health, or solid-waste agency for the time and location of your HHW collection program.

067 STUDY CHEMISTRY

From cleaning up spills to repainting walls, chemical cleaners provide a powerful solution for certain household tasks. You should always wear eye protection and don heavy-duty rubber gloves when using these products. Follow the manufacturer's instructions, and remember to properly store and dispose of these or any materials that could be hazardous.

TSP Trisodium phosphate is an alkaline type cleaner that dissolves grease and can clean everything from laundry to concrete driveways.

MINERAL SPIRITS This is a petroleum-based solvent formulated to dissolve oil-based paints.

MURIATIC ACID Also known as hydrochloric acid, this highly corrosive chemical is used to clean masonry.

068 DISPOSE OF DEBRIS

Debris can be collected for disposal outside the home with a wheelbarrow. Inside the home, you can toss it all into 3-millimeter plastic contractor bags. For debris with nails or jagged edges that might tear the plastic, Demobags are woven, tougher, and more tear-resistant.

You can haul the bags of debris to your local dump, which will likely charge a disposal fee. Or, for larger projects (or lack of a truck), consider Waste Management's Bagster bags. This "dumpster in a bag" can be purchased at home centers and unfolds to offer a 3-cubic-yard capacity, with no container usage fees (unlike full-size dumpsters). Fill the Bagster with up to 3,300 pounds of waste, and then schedule your collection online or by phone.

Major remodeling jobs that require rental of a full-size dumpster will usually involve a contractor, who should be held responsible for job site cleanup. On jobs such as roof or siding tear-offs that involve lots of nails and fasteners, a responsible contractor will have a worker canvas the surrounding ground with a magnetic broom to collect all the debris, so that nails don't end up stuck in someone's heel or tire.

QUICK
FIXES

BE A HOME-IMPROVEMENT HERO

When a problem arises and the other members of your household are wailing and gnashing their teeth, it's always nice to be the hero. To stop a messy leak or to unclog a toilet—those are feats of great strength and brilliance, and your family will surely sing your praises as you come to the rescue.

This chapter will show you the typical systems and components of a house and how to make quick fixes that can save the day without delay. Every homeowner should have a firm grasp of how their home functions as a system, from the insulation to electrical wires to the moisture barriers that protect the living space from water intrusion. A basic understanding of these house components will help you locate problems and make simple repairs. Plus, you can identify areas in need of improvement.

We delve into basic plumbing techniques and electrical work. Learn to solder copper pipe and join PVC plumbing. Learn to replace a light fixture and how to wire an electrical outlet. Maintenance is another major focus, because it's smarter to make a small early repair than pay to fix major damage later. You'll even find advice on how to conduct your own home inspection, much like a pro does. Whether you need to patch a rotting window, silence a squeaking floor, or fight mold in the household, we show how to get it accomplished with minimal headache. Keep this book in safe, dry place to grab whenever you need to a fast answer.

069 INSPECT YOUR HOME

The purpose of a professional home inspection is to examine the grounds, structure, and mechanical systems for defects, broken or obsolete components, and any damage from weather, rot, or wear and tear. Making your own annual home inspection can help to determine any necessary repairs you can make to prevent bigger problems in the future.

A home inspection will have three major considerations: water, safety, and HVAC (heating, ventilation, and air conditioning). For example, the primary concern for a site's grounds is ensuring that water drains away from the house. Another area to inspect is the sidewalks, making certain that cracks won't be a trip hazard.

070 WATCH FOR WATER

❶ Water should always be diverted 10 feet from the house foundation. This can be accomplished by using a gutter system's downspout extensions, splash blocks, or downspout drains. The grading should be sloped away from the house, dropping 6 inches for every 6 feet. Poor drainage can lead to accumulated hydrostatic pressure against the home's walls, which can cause basement walls to buckle, or lead to water erosion, which can weaken the home's foundation.

071 CHECK THE EXTERIOR

A home's exterior reveals a lot about potential issues you may face. Here's what to check for.

❷ PLANT INVASION Inspect tree overgrowth that causes excessive shade, which can contribute to mildew and rot on the house. Overgrown trees and shrubs that contact the house can lead to pest infestation and should be trimmed back.

❸ WALL TROUBLE Any evidence of bulging or bowing exterior house walls could indicate a

072 GET UP ON THE ROOF

Check all these basic roofing components, too.

❻ SURFACE Use a ladder and binoculars to inspect the roof exterior. Missing or damaged shingles, or gutters full of granules, indicate a need for replacement. Check all roof penetrations for worn or missing roof flashings. Look out for bowing, expansion, or waviness in the roof deck, indicating a problem with the framing.

❼ CHIMNEY Look for cracks in the chimney or evidence of any smoke escaping through mortar joints. A distorted or discolored rain cap, creosote flakes on the roof and ground, or damaged roofing material could indicate a dangerous creosote buildup in the chimney.

❽ GUTTERS Inspect gutters and downspouts for leaks or cracks. Ensure that they're free of leaves or other debris that impede drainage. Gutter covers help keep them clog-free.

❾ EXTERIOR WALLS Check the exterior siding for structural integrity, secure attachment, and signs of rot or water penetration. Weep holes in brick and veneer should be open. Look for cracks in stucco—due to expansion of plywood sheathing beneath—that can allow moisture to penetrate. Inspect the exterior insulating finish system (EIFS) with a moisture meter to check unseen areas behind the wall surface.

problem with the studs. Studs can warp if water has penetrated the wall and contacted the wood.

❹ A TIGHT SEAL Use a pick or awl to prod at the wood casing and trim of your doors and windows. Look for peeling paint and soft, spongy wood. Make sure that the flashing is installed above and around the windows to divert water. At the doors, check the thresholds for normal wear and tear and any wood rot. All of a home's wood trim is susceptible to rot; check for warping, splitting,

peeling paint, and missing caulking. Cut away deteriorated caulking and replace with a new high-quality exterior sealant.

❺ DECK DAMAGE Check every single deck, porch, and balcony for structural integrity. For any decks attached to the house, pay close attention to the ledger board connection, which is prone to rot and water damage if improperly installed. If damaged, it can be a common cause of deck collapse.

After examining a home's exterior, it's time to look inside for the following things.

❶ **WATER DAMAGE** Examine all surfaces, doors, and windows for any water issues. Check the basement, fireplace, and attic. Stuck interior doors can be a sign that the foundation is moving due to water pressure. A wall or ceiling may sag if it's been exposed to water. Plaster walls exposed to water can lose all structural integrity. On walls that have wood paneling, ensure the panels aren't bowed or warped, which could indicate moisture behind the wall. The attic needs proper ventilation; humidity can originate from a bathroom vent that terminates in the attic, as well as from roof leaks. Find and repair the source immediately. In bathrooms, check out the ceiling beneath the shower pans for signs of moisture. Test behind tiling using a moisture meter.

❷ **STRUCTURAL ISSUES** Popping nails might be a sign of inadequate wall framing. Check for any floor framing problems in the basement. Look for twisted, damaged, or rotted joists that can cause a weakness in the floor area. Sagging floors may be caused by a sagging main bearing beam. Check ceilings for nail pops, cracks, or sags that could indicate underlying structural problems. If the ceiling joists are causing the ceiling to sag, this will put stress on the adjacent walls as well as the ceiling.

❸ **ELECTRICAL SAFETY** Check all smoke detectors, and use a three-prong circuit analyzer to ensure that outlets work in the proper 120-volt range. Wiring problems can cause shocks, sparks, fires, equipment failures or poor performance. Low voltage may be caused by wiring too small for the electrical load, overly long circuits, or conductors with a higher resistance when operating at high temperatures.

074 CHECK PIPES AND DUCTS

❹ Check the plumbing pipes room by room for leakage, corrosion, and adequate insulation. In older homes, the plumbing may be lead, which is a health hazard. Apply a magnet to metal pipes. If the magnet adheres, the pipe is made of galvanized steel; if not, it's likely a lead pipe. One way to verify that the house has adequate water pressure is to turn on all faucets.

075 GET A GOOD FOUNDATION

Inspect crawlspaces and basements for signs of water penetration or cracks in foundation walls. Water forced through below-grade walls indicates drainage problems outside the home. Check foundation and retaining walls with a 4-foot level. If they list or bow from external pressure, they may eventually collapse, and you should consult a structural engineer.

⑤ CRACKS Hairline cracks in a foundation may simply be cosmetic (occurring as the foundation cures), but they should still be monitored. V-shaped cracks (wide at top, narrow at bottom), or ones extending the wall's full height, are likely caused by uneven settlement of the footing and will usually worsen over time. A floor slab that cracks or heaves upward may indicate a high water table. Install footing drain tiles to counteract the issue.

⑥ DRAINAGE If a home has a sump pump, drainage is a possible issue. Check the outside foundation perimeter for ruts on the ground or bare spots from erosion, which indicates more water flow than the soil can absorb. Installation of drainage conduit can provide a solution.

⑦ WOOD ROT Use a screwdriver or awl to check areas for wood rot or decay inside the framing. Wood rot is caused by a fungus and is as damaging as termites. Inspect framing members near the ground for signs of termite infestation, such as mud tubes lined with dirt. Termites' wings fall off easily, so a pile of wings is another clue to their presence.

⑧ EXTERIOR WALLS Check exterior siding for structural integrity, secure attachment and signs of rot or water penetration. Look for functional weep-holes in brick and brick veneer. In stucco, check for cracks due to the expansion of the plywood sheathing beneath it. Cracks of any size in the stucco will allow moisture to penetrate. When inspecting the EIFS, use a moisture meter to inspect unseen areas that might contain moisture behind the wall surface.

A steady stream of water should come from each one. If not, the pipe diameter could be too narrow. A professional inspector often checks for gas leaks in plumbing and appliances with a battery-operated combustible gas detector; you can buy one at a home center. The HVAC system isn't inspected for safety or water, but for its performance. In older systems, an inspector would open the furnace to inspect the flames and other parts; newer furnaces cannot be inspected in that manner. HVAC systems can be powered by electricity, gas, or oil, and can be configured as forced air, boiler, steam, or radiant systems. If you aren't well versed in the technology of your system, then it's a good idea to have your home's HVAC system inspected annually by a certified technician.

Insulation helps keep a home warm in the winter and cool in summer. It saves energy, lowers your utility bills, and can makes for a more comfortable home. Any exterior walls that separate conditioned and unconditioned spaces should be insulated to create a thermal envelope. There are several insulation products designed for specific uses. For the best energy efficiency, you should combine several of them to make a total insulating system, including products for insulating the foundation walls, exterior walls, crawlspace (underfloor), floors, basement walls, HVAC ducts, and more. Here are some other things you should know.

MIND THE GAP Maintain a minimum 3-inch space between any electrical fixtures and their surrounding insulation. This is mandated by electrical code, and if necessary you can nail wood barriers between ceiling joists to keep the insulation away.

KNOW THE R-VALUE Insulation levels are determined by the R-value, a measure of the insulation's ability to resist any heat traveling through it. The higher the R-value, the better the thermal performance.

Your recommended insulation level will depend upon the geographic area where your home is located. According to the Department of Energy, the warm, southern regions of the country should have enough attic insulation to achieve a value of R-30 to R-60. The northern, colder areas of the United States, meanwhile, require attic insulation of at least R-49 to be properly cost effective.

DO THE MATH The amount of insulation that you need to achieve a certain R-value depends on the type of insulation that's being used. For example, 3½ inches of fiberglass will achieve R-13, while 2 inches of rigid foam polystyrene achieves R-10. The R-value will be printed on the package of the insulation product so that you can easily calculate how much is required. R-values of individual products can be added to achieve recommended levels. For example, an R-38 added to an R-11 results in R-49.

A home's exterior walls should include both a moisture barrier and insulation installed upon construction. Any other areas of your home that you determine to have inadequate insulation can usually be retrofitted to increase the R-value.

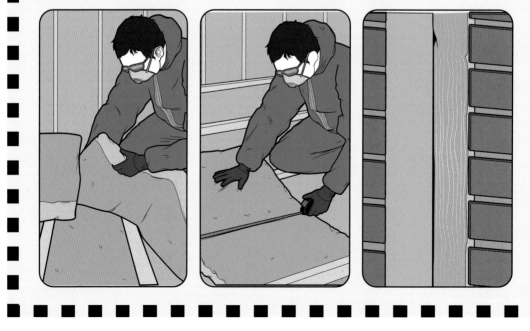

077 KNOW YOUR MATERIALS

A wide range of insulation products is available to totally envelope and insulate a building. The major types of insulation include fiberglass, blow-in, spray foam, rigid foam, and various types of loose fill. Here are the basics on each kind.

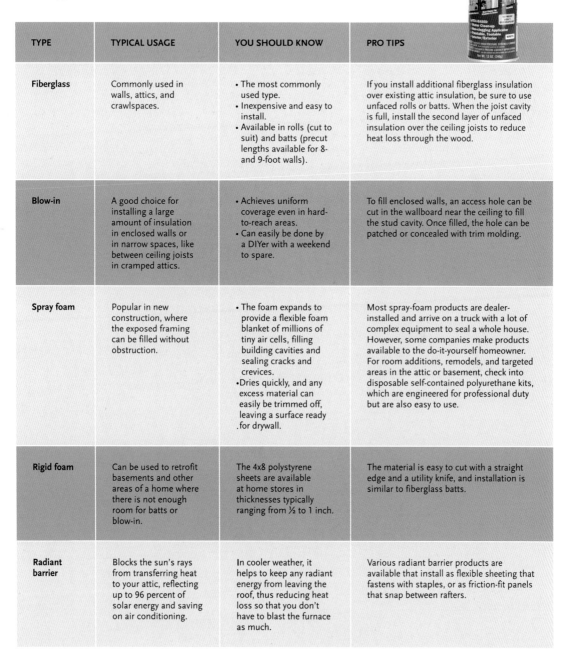

TYPE	TYPICAL USAGE	YOU SHOULD KNOW	PRO TIPS
Fiberglass	Commonly used in walls, attics, and crawlspaces.	• The most commonly used type. • Inexpensive and easy to install. • Available in rolls (cut to suit) and batts (precut lengths available for 8- and 9-foot walls).	If you install additional fiberglass insulation over existing attic insulation, be sure to use unfaced rolls or batts. When the joist cavity is full, install the second layer of unfaced insulation over the ceiling joists to reduce heat loss through the wood.
Blow-in	A good choice for installing a large amount of insulation in enclosed walls or in narrow spaces, like between ceiling joists in cramped attics.	• Achieves uniform coverage even in hard-to-reach areas. • Can easily be done by a DIYer with a weekend to spare.	To fill enclosed walls, an access hole can be cut in the wallboard near the ceiling to fill the stud cavity. Once filled, the hole can be patched or concealed with trim molding.
Spray foam	Popular in new construction, where the exposed framing can be filled without obstruction.	• The foam expands to provide a flexible foam blanket of millions of tiny air cells, filling building cavities and sealing cracks and crevices. • Dries quickly, and any excess material can easily be trimmed off, leaving a surface ready for drywall.	Most spray-foam products are dealer-installed and arrive on a truck with a lot of complex equipment to seal a whole house. However, some companies make products available to the do-it-yourself homeowner. For room additions, remodels, and targeted areas in the attic or basement, check into disposable self-contained polyurethane kits, which are engineered for professional duty but are also easy to use.
Rigid foam	Can be used to retrofit basements and other areas of a home where there is not enough room for batts or blow-in.	The 4x8 polystyrene sheets are available at home stores in thicknesses typically ranging from ½ to 1 inch.	The material is easy to cut with a straight edge and a utility knife, and installation is similar to fiberglass batts.
Radiant barrier	Blocks the sun's rays from transferring heat to your attic, reflecting up to 96 percent of solar energy and saving on air conditioning.	In cooler weather, it helps to keep any radiant energy from leaving the roof, thus reducing heat loss so that you don't have to blast the furnace as much.	Various radiant barrier products are available that install as flexible sheeting that fastens with staples, or as friction-fit panels that snap between rafters.

078 SEARCH FOR LEAKS

Whether from drywall, carpentry, flooring, or HVAC, air leaks represent money out the window. In cold weather, warm air rises into the attic of the home. As it enters the attic, it leaves the living space, which you're paying to heat. It also pulls in cold air from other cracks and crevices in the home, around doors and windows, and through the basement. In essence, these leaks create a vicious cycle that can drain away energy and money. Inspect your home carefully for any leaks, which can be difficult to find when hidden beneath insulation. Some common problem areas include the attic hatch, plumbing vents, wiring holes, recessed lights, and the soffit boxes that contain them.

LIGHT A CANDLE A simple way to check for air leaks is to use a burning candle. On a cool, windy day, close all doors and windows and turn off the furnace. Turn on all the vent fans in the house to encourage the leaks. Move the lit candle around the edges of doors and windows. Look for the smoke to flutter or the flame to flicker, which indicates a leak.

TEST THE TEMPS If temperatures differ more than 1 or 2 degrees in various areas of a room, it may be poorly sealed. Use weather-stripping and/or caulking, then retake the temperatures. (If the differences persist, you may have an HVAC airflow problem.)

KNOW YOUR WEAKNESS Certain spots in the home are particularly vulnerable. Check round the furnace flue or the duct chaseway (the box that hides the ducts) for leaks. Next, investigate indoor areas including heating and dryer vent penetrations, gaping baseboards and cracks along sill plates ,and floor-to-wall junctions. On the outside, look for leaks at the bottom of siding edges where they meet the foundation, along garage ceiling and wall joints, and all electric, gas, and A/C penetrations. Also examine the basement rim joists and all windows and doors.

DO AN AUDIT Consider investing in an infrared thermometer, for a DIY home energy audit. For as little as a hundred bucks, handheld laser-sighted tools can detect energy loss around doors and windows, insulation, ductwork, and other areas throughout the home.

PRO TIP

APPLY CAULK Sprayable release agents can prevent caulk from sticking to the surrounding areas, making shaping the joint that much easier. Similarly, masking the joint with painter's tape can also help to eliminate mess if you are not fully comfortable with your prowess with using caulk.

079 FILL THE GAPS

Seal leaks between moving parts with weather stripping. Use caulking between non-moving parts. You can use a wide variety of products, such as caulk and foam backer rods, silicone or water-based sealants, or rolls of foam. Another popular sealant is spray-in expandable foam, which comes in an aerosol can. It's important to select the right insulating foam for the job; too much expansion in the wrong place can put unwanted stress on the construction. Use "no warp" formula around windows and doors.

080 LAY A BETTER BEAD

Caulking is a necessary evil. Applying the stuff is a messy job, whether you're sealing the home or filling joints on trim to achieve the finished look that separates professional jobs from amateur attempts. Control and consistency are the keys to a better caulk bead.

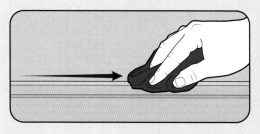

STEP 1 Clean the work area before application to promote adhesion, to prevent debris from disrupting application of the bead, and to keep any unsightly dirt from being embedded in your fresh caulk.

STEP 2 Cut off the tip of the tube at a straight 90-degree angle. Start at the tip to keep the hole small. If the hole is too big you'll sacrifice control of the bead. Puncture the seal inside the nozzle with a stiff wire or thin rod.

STEP 3 With the tube loaded in the caulk gun, pull the trigger several times to advance the caulk to the tip of the nozzle. Release pressure from the plunger any time you're not applying caulk to prevent excess from squirting out of the gun's tip.

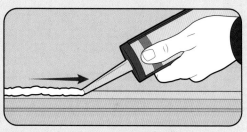

STEP 4 Begin at the horizontal joints. To ensure that a full bead adheres to both planes of the caulk joint, rest the tip of the nozzle equally on both surfaces. Depress the trigger with one hand to force caulk into the joint as you stabilize the gun and move the bead with the other.

STEP 5 Keep the gun at a 90-degree angle to the wall for consistent application and easy visibility. Move steadily to keep the bead as consistent as possible to avoid gaps. If you cross any vertical joints, caulk a few inches up or down the joints, which makes it easier to connect the caulk beads later.

STEP 6 Fill in all the vertical joints, tying them into your horizontal runs. Wet a short wooden dowel or shaping tool, and draw its tip over the bead to scrape away excess caulk and to press it into a concave shape. Keep plenty of paper towels for cleanup.

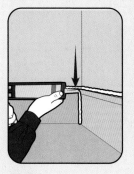

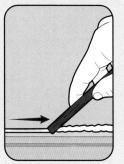

081 SEAL A LEAKY DOORWAY

Even the most energy-efficient HVAC systems can still cost plenty if warm or cool air is wasted through leaky doors. As a house settles over time, door frames often shift, creating a gap around the perimeter. A general rule of thumb: If you can see light between the closed door and the jamb, you have a problem. If this happens to a door leading outdoors or to an unconditioned living space, it equates to leaving a window cracked. The solution here is to install a simple weather-stripping kit.

WHAT YOU'LL NEED:
- Weather-stripping kit
- Drill or driver
- Measuring tape
- Hacksaw

Hardware stores sell several varieties of weather stripping, but the best type for doors has a rigid aluminum bar along with a soft rubber gasket, called a bulb. The bulb compresses against the closed door to prevent the passage of air and moisture. The kits are usually sold with three pieces—one for the top and two for the door sides (screws included). The pieces often come in standard door heights, but any of the three components can be trimmed to size.

STEP 1 Measure from the door sill to the upper jamb.

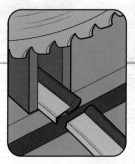

STEP 2 Cut the weather-stripping to length using a hacksaw.

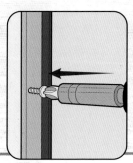

STEP 5 Close the door and position the strips so that the gasket is compressed.

STEP 6 Measure between the side strips for the top piece of stripping.

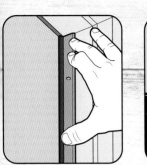

STEP 3 Close the door and press the weather-stripping firmly onto it.

STEP 4 Drive screws into the slots, but leave them all loose (predrill holes if fastening into a metal door frame). Repeat for the door's opposite side.

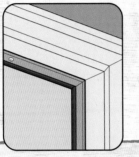

STEP 7 Cut the top strip to fit, and fasten tightly in place when compressed.

STEP 8 Close the door a few times to check the seal and make minor adjustments. Retighten until you've completely closed off the gap.

082 BE A HAPPY HACKER

A hacksaw is a frame-type saw that cuts metal. The blade is replaceable, thin ,and flexible, with fine hardened teeth that are held in tension by the frame. Plenty of people own a hacksaw but feel uncomfortable using it, since cutting metal can be tricky. Here are basic hints for happy hacking.

STAY SHARP Hacksaw blades are cheap; there's no excuse for using a dull one. Buy a box of at least two different teeth; change a blade when it begins to grab.

STIFFEN UP Flexibility is your enemy here. If your blade isn't screwed in as tight as possible, it's possible that it may twist or flex during sawing, making the process less efficient (and your arms more sore). Tighten the nut until the blade is totally rigid, then see if you can tighten it a little more.

TRY THE TEETH Blades range from 14 to 32 TPI (teeth per inch); coarser blades are suited for soft metals like brass or aluminum, and finer blades are best for thin, harder materials. Use the right blade to ensure a precision cut.

PRESS HERE, PLEASE Keep in mind that the blade's teeth face forward, so cutting will only occur on the forward stroke. You shouldn't be using any pressure at all on the backstroke.

STROKE SMOOTHLY Use long strokes that allow you to use as much of the blade as possible on each pass. Push firmly, but not so hard that you bend the blade or move more quickly than the saw's capabilities, and maintain a smooth, constant pace. Lubricate the teeth with a little oil or WD-40 to cut down on friction and help remove metal particles from the teeth.

083 STAY IN THE ZONE

Zone heating is an efficient method for optimizing the way you warm your home. Typical occupants spend 80 percent of the time in 20 percent of the house, so it makes sense to only heat or cool the area that's currently in use.

A basic technique with an existing forced-air heating system is to adjust the vents in the unoccupied rooms. Do not close the vents completely, however. Sealing the vents closed could decrease airflow through the air handler, cause pressure imbalances, and put stress on the duct connections. Closing vents by 75 percent can be effective. (The vent closest to the thermostat should always be open.)

SPACE HEATERS A simple and cost-effective way to supplement your central heating system is with a plug-in heater. The most common are ceramic space heaters with fan-forced air. Available in a wide range of designs, these are safe, compact, and ideal for heating spaces up to 150 square feet.

INTEGRATED SYSTEM ZONING This involves a set of multiple thermostats connected to a control panel that operates different dampers within the HVAC ductwork. Radiant floor heating is another option for controlling heat zones.

FORCED-AIR SYSTEMS These work best inside homes where the different zones can be isolated from each other by closing doors. Avoid shutting off the heat entirely in an unused part of your home, because condensation could form on cold interior wall surfaces and lead to mold. Also, keep all rooms at a minimum of 50 degrees Fahrenheit during the winter to keep water pipes from freezing.

084 SAVE ENERGY

Heating and cooling system costs account for approximately 45 percent of the average home's utility bill, or about 45 cents of every dollar. For lower bills, use less energy.

One good way is with modern energy-efficient windows. These include spacer systems, inert gas fillings, and special glass options that reduce energy usage by 34 percent compared to non-coated, single-pane windows. The space between the double panes may be filled with argon, an odorless, colorless, nontoxic gas six times denser than air. This design prevents air infiltration and acts as an added barrier to prevent harmful ultraviolet rays from entering the home. Low-E (emissivity) glass also has a transparent metallic oxide coating to reflect heat.

Aluminum storm windows are another alternative, installed over existing windows to insulate and block drafts. Some storm windows even come with Low-E glass.

085 JOIN THE PROGRAM

Programmable thermostats automatically adjust your home's temperature settings several times a day to fit your lifestyle. They can save money on energy costs and allow you to program when the system should scale back on heating or cooling. In winter, set the heat to kick on during your commute home so you step into a warm house. In summer, keep air conditioning low in the morning to avoid cooling an empty house while you're out.

PRO TIP

STAY DRY, KINDA Indoor humidifiers soothe irritation from dry air, but any excess humidity can breed mold or bacteria. Ideal humidity in your home should be kept between 30 and 50 percent.

086 CHANGE YOUR FILTER

Be diligent about regularly replacing the filters that remove dust from the air as it circulates through the HVAC system. Most systems use disposable filters. Some furnaces have an electrostatic filter, which is a sturdy metal filter that needs to be cleaned every few months. In either case, a clogged filter hinders airflow, and your system has to work harder to get the temperature set by your home's thermostat.

When the temperature drops and cold weather rolls in, it's time to prepare your home—inside and out—for the winter elements because, yes, winter is coming. Sealing off air leaks and installing adequate insulation are two of the most effective ways to save energy, but your efforts shouldn't end there. When giving your house its annual physical exam, don't overlook any of these crucial areas.

1 WINDOWS Ideally, your home should have double-pane and low-emissivity coated window glass. You can also insulate your windows using heat-shrink plastic insulation. One option for wooden-frame windows is to cover the outside with heavy plastic to reduce cold air infiltration. Staple the sheeting over the outside, leaving a 4-inch overhang at the perimeter. Secure the edges with wooden furring strips, fasten to the outside window frame, then trim off the excess plastic.

2 HVAC Have an HVAC technician do a full inspection of your furnace for proper performance. If the furnace is made of old-fashioned sheet metal ductwork, consider replacing it with insulated ducts, including the plenum. If you use propane or heating oil, ensure that the tank has been filled.

3 PLUMBING Insulate outdoor hose bibs and exposed plumbing, including those in unheated crawlspaces. If you go on a winter vacation, leave your heat set to at least 50 degrees Fahrenheit so pipes don't freeze.

4 GUTTER AND ROOF Replace worn or damaged shingles or flashing. An ice dam is a ridge of ice that forms at the edge of a roof, preventing melting snow from draining and causing backed-up water to leak into the home. To prevent ice dams, clean your gutters to ensure proper drainage, and install gutter covers to prevent debris accumulation. Proper attic ventilation removes heat and keeps the roof deck evenly cool to prevent melting of the ice.

5 FIREPLACE CHIMNEYS Have a pro chimney sweep inspect, clean, and repair any fireplaces, flues, or wood stoves. Add chimney or flue caps to keep out birds and pests. Tuck-point or repair any loose masonry, and make sure the dampers work on fireplaces and stoves. Store a winter's supply of firewood and kindling away from the house (for safety), and cover it for protection.

6 ATTIC Inspect the attic for evidence that the weather seal of the house has been broken. Check for any wet or damp insulation and moldy, rotted attic rafters or ceiling joists, any of which could indicate a leaky roof. Address any problems before they can worsen.

7 BASEMENT/FOUNDATION Install covers over the crawlspace ventilation openings. Cover basement windows with plastic shields. Rake leaves and debris away from the foundation. Seal foundation cracks and other openings to keep out mice and other pests.

088 KEEP WARM FOR LESS

Energy bills aren't getting any lower—even if you've done your inspection properly and fixed everything you can, you will still need to turn on the heat this winter. Here are a few ways to minimize your heating costs.

ADJUST YOUR FAN It may sound counterintuitive to turn on a ceiling fan in the winter, but most ceiling fans have a switch that has two settings. The counterclockwise setting cools a room during the summer. However, since heat rises, during winter the fan's clockwise setting forces warm air downward into the living space.

ADD MOISTURE Anyone who's spent a steamy summer in the South can attest that humid air feels warmer than dry. For a more comfortable rest, and to soothe sinuses irritated by cold, dry air. use a humidifier. Both cool- and warm-mist humidifiers are available, and either can help make a room feel warmer.

LET THE SUN SHINE The radiant heat of the sun can be harnessed to keep your home toasty warm by strategically adjusting the blinds and curtains. On sunny days, open up the curtains that face southward to let in the sunlight. You should remember to keep the curtains closed at night, however, in order to provide an extra insulating barrier between your home's interior and the cold outdoor air.

089 HIT THE DECKS

Sweep away leaves, needles, and branches from between the deck boards and off the surface. Debris can retain water and lead to mildew. Mildew should be removed from a deck as soon as it appears. Make a mildew-killing solution with 3 quarts of water, 1 quart of oxygen bleach, and ¼ cup of ammonia-free liquid dishwasher detergent. Apply with a garden sprayer, let set, then rinse clean. For tougher stains, use a soft bristle brush.

090 FLIP THE DECK BOARDS

In some cases of weathered deck boards, you can try prying them up and flipping them over. The underside of the boards are often in good condition because they have been hidden from water and sun exposure. If so, just turn them over, fasten them down, and then stain and seal them for an economical way to renew your worn deck's appearance.

PRO TIP

THINK AHEAD Take care of problem with small engines in your yardwork machinery, or similar issues, in winter, instead of spring when the repair shops are busy. Drain oil and replace it along with the filter. Drain the gas from lawnmowers and similar equipment, or add a fuel stabilizer to all engines.

091 CLEAR THE CLOGS

Plumbing can be a very messy, smelly, and altogether nasty job, but if your pipes are clogged, you can often solve the problem by simply following the guidelines detailed here.

Gravity carries water away from appliances and sinks, and out of the house via drainpipes ranging in size from 1¼ to 4 inches in diameter. The size of the pipe depends on the size of the fixture. Each fixture also has a trap that holds water to seal off sewage gases, and the traps are handy for catching wayward objects that go down sink drains, such as toothbrushes or hair clasps, which can be rescued by unscrewing the trap.

It will be easier to unclog a slow drain than it is to open one that is completely stopped, so look for signs of a sluggish drain. Pour scalding water down the pipe to loosen any grease buildup. If this doesn't solve the problem, check the other household drains. Multiple clogged drains mean a clog in the main pipe. Here are some declogging methods to try.

TYPE	WHAT IT IS	WHEN TO USE
Cup-style plunger	The most common clog-fighting tool, found in just about every bathroom	Best for sinks and shower drains
Flanged plunger	Variation on the classic style	Designed to be more efficient in a toilet; flange makes it less useful in sinks and showers
Cylinder plunger	New design allows for drawing water into a cylinder and then pushing it out with sudden force	Good for toilets and drain clogs with standing water
Plumbing snake	Flexible steel cable that works its way through the drainpipe	If clogs are farther down a drainpipe
Compressed air	Cartridge shoots air down the pipe, blasting the clog away	If you don't have a snake or would like to avoid removing your traps
Chemical products	Various chemicals that dissolve clogs	Use judiciously in sinks and tubs; not for use in a toilet or laundry outflow

092 TRY THIS SOLUTION

Chemical clog removers can be helpful in opening the occasional plugged pipe. But don't be suckered by thin liquid products. If you pour a watery cleaner down a sluggish drain, it'll go right by the clog and into the depths of your plumbing system, leaving the problem stuck in the pipe. Choose a thicker product that sticks to the inside of the pipe. Chemical cleaners use either an acid or a base to dissolve stubborn clogs and organic matter; the thicker products have improved coverage and better contact with blockage. Allow the cleaner to sit as directed; follow with running water to test the drain.

Chemical cleaners come with a few red flags. The first is that the active ingredient is often chlorine bleach, which is bad for septic tanks because bleach can kill off the beneficial bacteria in a septic system. Bleach-based products are best suited for systems linked to a city sewer. Also, laundry drain clogs are often due to accumulated clothing fibers. Liquid drainers don't dissolve those particles, so all of those clogs will have to be removed physically, not chemically. Furthermore, liquid drain cleaners are not intended for every household clog. They're not designed to remove the waste that may be clogging your toilet.

The general rule of chemical cleaners: Read the instructions on the label and only use it as intended. Always use in a well-ventilated area, and wear rubber gloves. Don't use a plunger if a liquid cleaner is in the drain, because you risk splashing caustic chemicals onto your skin. And don't pour in a liquid cleaner if the drain is completely blocked or you will be faced with a sink full of caustic water—another mess that you'll have to deal with afterward.

093 PLUNGE A SINK

Most people think of plungers in terms of clearing a stopped toilet, but they're also great for blocked drains. Use a simple plunger with a large enough suction cup to completely cover the drain, creating an airtight seal around it. Fill the sink with water to completely cover the suction cup (it may help to coat the rim of the cup with petroleum jelly). Seal off any other outlets, such as the overflow drain in sinks, to create a vacuum. Push out any trapped air beneath the cup and give the plunger about 15 vigorous up-and-down pumping strokes to jolt loose the clog. This might take 3 to 5 sets of strokes.

If a plunger doesn't work and you end up needing to open the P-trap underneath the drain, then use a wrench to disassemble and inspect the trap. Often the trap is congested, and a thorough cleanout and replacement is all that's needed.

094 USE A SNAKE (OR NOT)

To clear stubborn clogs farther down the drain than a plunger can go, a plumbing snake is a handy tool. It's basically a flexible steel cable that goes through the pipework, physically removing clogs. However, the snake doesn't work very well in tight turns, so remove the P-trap and the horizontal trap arm from the rear wall first.

Insert the snake directly into the drain pipe. If snaking a tub's drain, remove the overflow plate and run the cable down the tube. Push the snake into the pipe until you run into the obstruction. Try to hook the clog by twisting the plumbing snake's handle; once it's hooked, push the snake back and forth to help break up the obstruction, then flush with cold water.

If you don't have a plumbing snake, or if you want to avoid removing the traps, try out one of the new clog-removal products that shoot compressed air into the drain and force the clog to move. Some products are available in disposable cans. Another type is a reusable device that uses cartridges of compressed CO_2. Once the cartridge is loaded, press down firmly on the tool handle; a needle punctures the cartridge, sending a powerful burst of air into the drain, instantly unclogging it.

PRO TIP

FILL YOUR BLADDER
Another drain-clearing tool is the reusable rubber drain bladder. This attaches to a standard garden hose and is inserted into the pipe. When the water is turned on, the bladder expands into the pipe while sending a powerful jet of water down the drain to force out the clog.

095 CLEAN THE MAIN DRAIN

If multiple fixtures are clogged, you may need to clear the main drain line. Locate the clean-out plugs on the large drainpipes in your basement or crawlspace; they may be in a garage or outdoors, along the foundation of the house. Each plug has a cap with a square fitting at the top. Remove the cap with a wrench. (Be sure no one uses the facilities while the main drain line is open.) Use a plumbing snake to break up any clogs in the open main line, running it in both directions of the pipe.

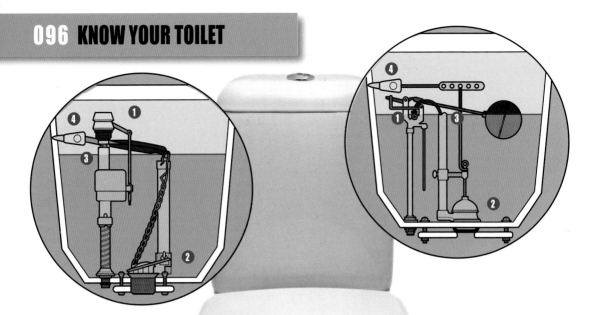

A toilet is something that everyone needs to have working. It must fill and flush, and if all is in proper working order, a toilet will do so with minimal noise and hassle. While fairly simple in design, over time any of these toilet components can wear out and corrode. This can lead to problems with flushing and refilling the tank.

❶ FILL VALVE Attached to a water-supply connector through the bottom of the tank, the fill valve controls the flow of fresh water into the toilet tank. The two main valve types used today are the traditional float ball (also called a ballcock) and the float cup type.

❷ FLUSH VALVE This valve consists of a flapper (or "stopper" or "tank ball") that aligns over the drain and is attached to the overflow pipe. It regulates the discharge of water from the tank to the bowl.

❸ OVERFLOW PIPE Often attached to the flush valve, this pipe supplies refill water to the bowl and prevents overflow of the tank.

❹ TANK LEVER Consisting of a lever arm and a flush handle, the tank lever allows water to flow into the bowl by lifting the flapper when the flush handle is pressed.

097 TROUBLESHOOT A TRICKLING TOILET

You might hear fresh water trickling into the tank when you haven't flushed the toilet. Here's how to figure out what's happening and fix it.

CHECK THE VALVES Look down inside the overflow pipe. If water is running through the refill tube into the overflow pipe, check the fill valve. For ballcock-type fill valves, the float ball rod will be at the top of the tank, with a hollow plastic or copper ball on the right-hand end. If it is bent in any direction, then carefully straighten it by hand. If the rod is straight and the float ball does not lightly rest on the tank's water surface, it probably has a leak and requires replacement.

LOWER THE LEVEL The tank's water level may also be set too high. Lower the water level by moving the adjustment clip located on the ballcock link. Simply squeeze the sides of the clip and then push down on the link to adjust the water. Float cup–type fill valves also feature a water-level adjustment clip located on the cup mechanism.

LOOK FOR CORROSION Look for any sticking or corrosion in the lever. If you do see rust, replace the entire mechanism.

CLEAN YOUR SEAL Remove any buildup beneath the fill valve seal. To do this, shut off the water and remove the top of the ballcock or the float cup valve.

Cover the opening with an upside-down glass. Turn the water on and off a few times, and any buildup should be flushed by the water stream. Turn the top over and rinse it under a faucet, then reattach.

FIX THE FLAPPER The trickling water may be due to a leaky flapper. If the flapper is dirty, you can simply clean it with a rag to remove any grime or buildup. If the stopper is damaged or worn, it can sit askew and not seal properly. Replace it along with the valve seat. If you've tried all of these aforementioned methods and the water is continuing to run through the refill tube, then the fill valve seal is probably defective and requires replacement.

GO BEYOND If you hear water trickling but you do not see water running from the refill tube into the overflow pipe, check the placement of the refill tube. The refill tube is the small vinyl tube that stretches from the fill valve on the left to the hollow pipe on the right. If the refill tube is stuck down inside the overflow pipe, raise the end until it is just above the top of the pipe. The adapter should hook to the top. If none of these troubleshooting tips work, the overflow pipe or flush valve may be corroded or leaking and need replacement.

098 GET A ROYAL FLUSH

A toilet that doesn't flush properly can be both gross and annoying. Inspect the shut-off valve at the wall; the water supply might be off or partly shut. Just turn the valve counterclockwise to open it. Then, tighten the top of the ballcock or float cup. Make sure it locks tightly into place. In some cases, the chain between the toilet lever and the flapper may have detached. If this is the case, the chain can easily be reattached or replaced.

If the toilet bowl doesn't totally flush or won't fill properly, the holes under the rim could be limiting the water flow. Use a coat hanger or stiff wire to clear them of any obstructions. Next, tighten the set screw attaching the flush handle; remember to allow a small amount of play up and down. If the handle or set screw is corroded, then replace the entire mechanism. Also, be sure that the flapper is closing only after the tank is emptied. Finally, adjust the chain, allowing ½ inch of slack. Test flush a few times, and you should be all set.

099 SOLDER COPPER PIPE

Most American homes have copper water lines. Soldering is the process of joining two copper or brass surfaces with metal by heating the solder to a little under 750 degrees Fahrenheit. When the joint cools, it will be as strong as the pipe. You need a few basic specialized tools to work with copper pipe, and they're worth putting in your toolbox. Here's what you'll need to get.

PIPE CUTTER This tool allows you to make a clean, square cut to ensure a good joint every time.

FOUR-IN-ONE TOOL This tool will quickly remove dirt and oxidization from the interior of fittings and the exterior of copper pipe in both ½- and ¾-inch sizes to increase your chances of a successful solder job.

PROPANE TORCH You can use a handheld, self-contained unit for basic soldering. Get one with an auto-ignite feature and locking ON/OFF switch or button.

100 PLAN THE INSTALLATION

For new plumbing installation, plan to have as few soldered joints as possible to reduce the chance of leaks. Determine the materials required for the task, and have them as well as extra parts on hand before beginning, including all flux, solder, pipe, valves, and elbows for male and female connectors. Note that building codes require leadless solder for domestic water lines, because lead-based solder can leach into the water standing in the pipe.

STEP 1 Measure, cut, and dry-fit all parts. This will ensure that the project works before soldering. Make certain there is no strain on the run of pipe or joints, because stress can result in failure over time.

STEP 2 Assemble and clean all parts to remove any surface oxidation. Clean both the exterior of copper pipe and the interior of all fittings. When this is done correctly, the pipe or fitting interior will shine like a new penny.

STEP 3 Apply a light coat of self-cleaning, non-acid flux to all mating surfaces. Use a small "flux brush" for this task. The purpose of the flux is to remove any unseen surface oxidation, to etch the copper to promote adhesion, and to help the solder bond well with the copper pipe and fitting. Reassemble the pieces. You're ready to solder!

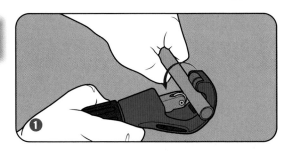

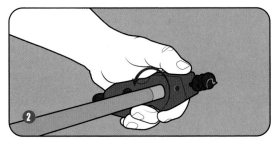

101 SOLDER SAFELY

Always wear safety glasses and gloves when soldering. If the project requires overhead soldering, never stand directly below the work. Next, follow the steps below to ensure a job well done.

STEP 1 Pull about 12 inches off the roll of solder and bend the top 3 inches to form a right angle. This will make it easier to deposit solder all around a joint.

STEP 2 Begin heating the fitting first, then apply heat to the pipe/fitting joint with a back and forth motion. When the pipe and fitting reach the proper temperature, the solder will melt when touched to the joint, and the heat will draw the solder into the joint. The flux will bubble and smoke slightly.

STEP 3 Make sure to fill the joint completely. Use a damp rag to quickly wipe off any excess solder from the joint. Continue soldering all joints in this manner. (While soldering around wooden framing members, be careful to avoid a fire.)

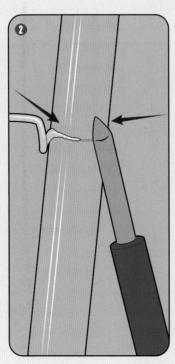

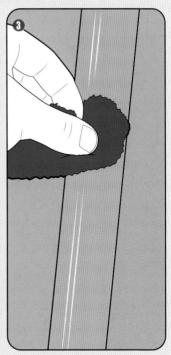

102 TACKLE TANK TROUBLE

A number of things could be causing issues with how the toilet tank functions. Here are some common issues.

FILL IT UP If your tank is refilling slowly, or not at all, you will need to clean the fill valve interior. Shut off the water at the wall connection, lift the float arm and twist the ballcock or float cup top until it unlocks. Use a coat hanger or other similar stiff wire to gently scrape out the inside of the fill valve. Hold an upside-down glass over the valve opening and turn the water on and off three or four times to flush deposits from the inside. Rinse the fill valve top under a faucet to clean the seal, and then replace the top, turning it clockwise until it locks. Turn on the water supply. If the tank still doesn't fill properly, replace the pipe that runs from the wall to the toilet. Braided stainless steel toilet connectors are preferred.

KEEP IT QUIET If the toilet is too loud when refilling, make sure the shut-off valve at the wall is completely open. Also, inspect the angle adapter, which is typically a rigid, plastic elbow on the end of the refill tube. Tweak the adapter slightly toward the inside wall of the overflow pipe to ensure that fresh water hits the pipe wall a couple of inches from the top before running to the bottom of the tank. If this didn't do the trick, replace the fill valve.

103 HANDLE BRASS VALVES

Brass valves require special treatment when soldering, and there are two commonly used approaches. The first is to remove the valve stem (along with its rubber washer) from the valve body and attach the pipe by soldering. Once the valve has cooled, reinstall the valve stem. Do not try to solder the valve with the stem in place because the heat from soldering will melt the rubber washer and thus render the valve ineffective.

The second method involves using a female threaded valve and attaching male threaded couplings to the ends of the copper pipe. After the pipe and couplings cool, thread them into both sides of the valve.

PRO TIP

SEAL WITH LIQUID SOLDER
For small, targeted repairs, liquid solders offer a strong, water-resistant alternative to conventional hot soldering. Once these molten metals are applied, the bond should be clamped together, then left undisturbed for up to 24 hours in order to achieve maximum strength.

104 JOIN PVC PIPING

PVC is the most commonly used plastic piping since it's corrosion-resistant, cost-effective, and promises a long service life. Pieces are joined with PVC cement. Each type of plastic pipe is made of different materials and requires its own blend of cement to ensure a proper bond. Here's how to put it all together. These same steps can be used to join CPVC pipe as long as you use CPVC cement.

MEASURE The ends of PVC piping will slide inside the fittings up to the shoulder. When measuring pipe length, always measure the distance between the shoulders of the fittings; transfer this measurement to the pipe.

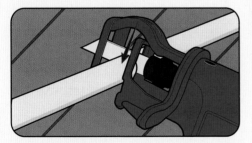

CUT Make the cut as straight and square as possible, using a standard hacksaw, miter saw, or reciprocating saw.

DEBURR Use a utility knife or file to remove burrs from inside the pipe joint.

CLEAN For good adhesion and a strong, leak-free joint, lightly scuff the ends of the PVC with fine-grit sandpaper to remove the sheen and any dirt. Clear off dust with a clean rag.

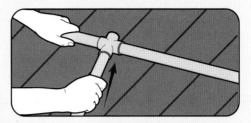

DRY-FIT Assemble everything to be sure it's the correct length. The orientation of certain fittings is critical to plumbing design. Make directional reference marks on the pieces for easy realignment during final assembly. Mark the depth of pipe concealed by the fitting to guide where to apply the primer and cement.

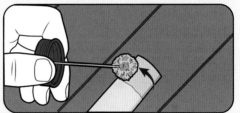

PRIME Apply PVC primer around the entire end of the pipe, as well as the inside of the fitting. The primer temporarily softens a thin layer of the PVC material, allowing the cement to create a strong, leak-free bond between the pipe and fitting.

CEMENT Brush PVC cement over the pipe end and inside the fitting, completely covering the contact surfaces of the joint.

CONNECT Slide the pipe into the fitting until it presses firmly against the shoulder. Give the pipe or fitting a ¼-inch turn to spread the adhesive and make sure it completely seals the joint. Make sure the reference marks on the fittings are properly aligned. Hold the joint for at least 30 seconds as the cement cures.

105 SHUT DOWN A LEAK

If you have a water leak, first shut off the water supply. If you have a leak at a toilet, sink, washing machine, or bathtub (with exposed plumbing), shut off the water at the valves located at the floor or wall, below or behind the fixture. But those aren't the only ones that you need to know about, so read on.

MAIN SHUTOFF VALVE To stop any leaks upstream of the fixture valves, you need to close the house's main shutoff valve, allowing you to open up any pipe within the house. Locate it prior to an emergency, check it periodically, and then keep it maintained—if you don't know where this crucial valve is, every minute spent searching for it during an emergency could result in gallons more water spilling into your home. The valve doesn't get used often, so don't let it rust and become nonfunctional. To locate the main water valve, look around the inside perimeter of your house at the ground level. Follow a straight path from the outdoor water meter to the home for the most likely location. Look for access panels in the walls, which often conceal the valve, or check your home inspection report.

OUTDOOR SHUTOFF VALVE If the previous options fail, or you have an outdoor leak in the yard, then shut off the water main outside. Look for a round or rectangular steel or iron lid. (Note: In cold climates the lid may be covered with sand or dirt to prevent pipes from freezing). Remove the lid to access the water meter and valve. Storm runoff may have covered outdoor valves with dirt or mud, requiring you to clear it with a hand spade. Connected to the water meter is the water company's shutoff valve, which usually needs a special wrench and can be very difficult to turn. Check for an additional residential valve on the house side of the meter that uses a nut or handle to close it, which is the simplest option. If there's no residential valve, use locking pliers and elbow grease to turn off the company valve until the leak can be fixed. (Special wrenches for outdoor valves are also sold in hardware stores.)

PRO TIP

USE PLUMBER'S EPOXY

You can quickly fix a leaky pipe with plumber's epoxy. Follow the manufacturer's instructions, and use the claylike epoxy ribbon to form a seal around the leak. Turn on the water and check for any leaks. This will only be a temporary solution, however, until permanent repairs can be performed.

106 THAW FROZEN PIPES

If pipes have frozen, shut off the water and inspect them for damage due to expansion from freezing water. If the pipe is undamaged, drain it by opening a downstream faucet. Use a hair dryer or heat gun to warm the pipe and melt the blockage. You can also wrap the pipe in a towel and pour hot water into the towel. After the pipe has thawed, turn on the water supply and check again for any leaks.

107 TRY PUSH-FIT CONNECTIONS

It's sometimes necessary to completely repair a pipe and/or joint to make a repair. Push-fit connections provide the fastest and easiest method to connect PEX, copper, or CPVC pipe. Push-fit connections utilize a compression fitting to join the pipes, requiring no soldering, clamps, or glue, and they're certified up to 200 PSI and 200 degrees Fahrenheit. Here's how to make a push-fit connection.

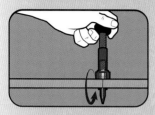

STEP 1 Make a square cut on the end of the pipe.

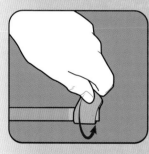

STEP 2 Sand down the rough edges.

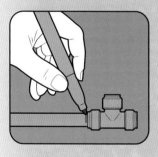

STEP 3 Some push-fit connections use a ring fitted in the end of PEX pipe to keep its round shape while the connector crimps over it. Mark the depth of the pipe that goes in the push-fit connection.

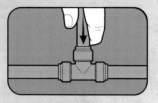

STEP 4 Push the fitting together to the depth mark so that it "clicks," then the permanent connection will be complete.

STEP 5 When a pipe goes in the fitting, stainless steel teeth grip it tightly, and the O-ring compresses to create a perfect seal. A disconnect tool releases the O-ring to easily change and reuse valves and fittings.

Push-fit plumbing connections range in size from 3/8 to 1 inch, available as couplings, elbows, tees, connectors, reducers, and end stops. More than just a quick fix, these connections can be used for all sorts of new plumbing installations.

108 USE SELF-FUSING TAPE

Since the water found in drainpipes is not under pressure, leaks can often be fixed using self-fusing silicone tape. Stretch a length of the tape and wrap it around the problem area, overlapping the tape and making sure to cover the surface on both sides of the leak. The tape will fuse to itself to form a waterproof seal.

People spend a great deal of time looking into the mirror, and they naturally want to see themselves in a complimentary light. Start your design for the bathroom lighting scheme with the vanity mirror, which typically has the brightest light, then decide what ambient or accent sources will work the best to complement the vanity station. Layer the light sources to fill in gaps and reduce glare.

Remember: Recessed or canned lighting is not ideal for a bathroom's only light source because it tends to cast a shadow across the face. The room decor is better when the design and finish of the light fixtures work together with all the plumbing accessories. A wide range of fixture styles, shapes, sizes, and finishes are available. Here are more hints to brighten the smallest room in the house.

❶ **WATCH THE WATER** Showers need light fixtures designed for use in wet areas. If you have room, table lamps can add a soft, human touch to bathrooms—but place them away from water sources.

❷ **TAKE RECESS** Tubs need good general light, which can be provided by a recessed fixture. To avoid glare, aim the light beam at the outside edge of the tub.

❸ **SHINE ON** Windows provide opportunity to add natural lighting or replace the electrical options.

❹ **LIGHT UP THE NIGHT** The toe space below vanities and cabinets can be lined with rope lighting for a nice night-light.

❺ **GET YOUR GLOW** Indirect (or cove) lighting, with its hidden light source, adds a soft, warm glow to the bathroom, but is purely aesthetic.

❻ **LOOK YOUR BEST** For the mirror, lighting from warm fluorescent vertical wall sconces can provide the kind of even facial illumination that eliminates dark circles and shadows. Halogen lighting above the vanity provides cross-illumination when used in conjunction with wall sconces.

❼ **GO HIGH** Ceiling fixtures suspended overhead can provide an elegant touch while adding extra light.

❽ **GET READY TO READ** Focused flood lights or halogen fixtures over the commode can provide good light for reading (you know you do it).

110 COOK UP A KITCHEN SCHEME

Today's kitchens are often the hub of family living. The lighting should be suitable for reading, paying the bills, feeding the kids, and more. A single kitchen light source means that work around the perimeter of this central light is relegated to the dimmer areas of the room. The proper lighting scheme depends on the size and complexity of the kitchen. Smaller kitchens may require only a central overhead fixture coupled with under-cabinet task lighting placed near your sink and stove. Larger kitchens may require a combination of general, task, and accent lighting.

1 PREPARE BEFORE SHOPPING When visiting a lighting showroom, bring photos of your kitchen and take note of the room's dimensions. How tall is the ceiling? Where are the doors? How much space is there between the cabinets and the countertop? This information will help determine your options.

2 START WITH THE BIG FEATURES Kitchen tables and islands are focal points; light them up first, then design your scheme outward. Try pendant lighting or a fixture with three lights over an island.

3 CREATE A BALANCED MIX The biggest mistake is overlooking subtleties in your lighting scheme. Recessed lighting can create a blanket of light, but it doesn't illuminate exactly where you need it. Don't just add more recessed fixtures, which will just over-saturate the room with light. Combine lighting types, and remember that dimmer switches add flexibility.

4 CHOOSE A NICE FINISH The topmost trends in decorative finishes for kitchen fixtures include: wrought iron, often used in rust and earth tones; pewter and satin nickel finishes, where brass used to be popular; painted finishes; and colored glass, as opposed to plain white. Of course, fashions change, and you may not want to remodel often, so go with what you love over what's in style.

5 DON'T OVERLOOK DETAILS Under-cabinet lighting can reduce shadows on the counter and add critical light to work space. Mini-pendants mounted over a kitchen island can make countertop activities easier for everyone. And step lights around an island prevent stubbed toes during midnight snack runs.

In modern wiring, individual wires are bundled together inside a sheathed cable. In older houses, knob and tube wiring is used in place of cables. Whatever your wiring system, the white wire is usually the neutral wire, and the black is the live or "hot" wire. Any red wires are hot, too. The unsheathed, exposed copper wires are ground wires. (Note: In some cases, a wiring installation may have required a white wire to be hot, in which case it should have been marked with black tape. However, just because it should be marked doesn't mean that it was marked.) Many light fixtures don't have black and white

wire, in which case, look for a rib on the wire sheathing to determine the neutral wire.

If only a single cable, or one set of black and white supply wires, enters the box, then the fixture is at the end of the circuit. This is common—but is not guaranteed—with ceiling fixtures and allows for the simplest method of installation. If two cables (or two sets of black and white wires) enter the box, then your fixture is in the middle of a circuit. If a light is in the middle of a circuit, you will have to twist multiple wires together.

TYPE	WHAT IT IS	DESCRIPTION
Two-wire with ground	Hot / Neutral / Ground	A black wire, a white wire, and an uninsulated ground wire
Three-wire with ground	Hot / Neutral / Ground	Used with three-way and four-way switches, and has a black wire, white wire, red wire, and an uninsulated ground
Knob and tube		A two-wire system in which individual wires are insulated with white or black treated fabric

112 USE THE RIGHT BULB

When purchasing a lighting fixture, check its maximum wattage. A bulb with more wattage than necessary can present a fire hazard from the excess heat. Wattage indicates the power a bulb consumes—not the light that it generates, measured in lumens. If you're getting excess light, use lower-lumen bulbs.

PRO TIP

GET HUNG UP Many ceiling fixtures are often positioned above focal points, such as a dining room table. A good rule of thumb is to install the fixture about 30 inches above the table. To shorten a chain, cut it to length with metal snips, and then cut the wiring 6 inches longer than the chain.

113 UPDATE FIXTURES

Your primary concern when you are selecting a replacement fixture is to ensure that the box and ceiling will support the fixture's weight. If a new fixture weighs about the same as the old one, the existing electrical box will likely suffice. If its new replacement is heavier, the ceiling box may need to be replaced. Have all of the work professionally inspected when you're done.

STEP 1 Turn off the power at the breaker box by flipping a circuit breaker or unscrewing a fuse. Use a voltage tester to make sure the power is off.

STEP 2 Use a work platform fastened to a ladder to support the weight of the old fixture while you remove the mounting screws from the electrical box. With the screws out, pull off the box cover and disconnect the wiring by unscrewing the wire nut and untwisting the wire pairs.

STEP 3 Organize the fixture's components, such as the canopy and hanging hardware. Ceiling fixtures vary greatly in style and construction, as do the related components and the assembly process. Any quality lighting manufacturer will include assembly instructions for the model; usually you need to use only a screwdriver.

STEP 4 Thread the box cover, mounting strap (which screws into the junction box), and any other necessary parts over the wire and chain before installing.

STEP 5 Strip about ¾-inch of insulation from the end of each wire. Match the fixture wires to the supply wires by color (see item III). Twist exposed ends together clockwise, securing them with a UL-listed wire nut. Ground wires can be connected to a ground screw on the junction box or joined to the supply ground using a wire nut.

STEP 6 Install a light bulb to test the connection before installing the fixture. If it won't light up, you probably have a loose connection. Once the light functions, protect connections by wrapping electrician's tape around the wire nuts.

STEP 7 If you haven't yet installed the mounting strap, screw it to the junction box.

Then screw the threaded mounting stem on the chain solidly into the mounting strap. Cover up the junction box with the cover or "canopy," and secure it in place with the locknut included with your light fixture.

STEP 8 Install the glass and light bulbs. Balance light output by using several sockets; use higher-wattage bulbs for fixtures with fewer sockets.

114 GET GROUNDED

A ground fault circuit interrupter (GFCI) is a type of electrical outlet that helps protect people from shocks due to hazardous ground faults. Ground faults occur when an electrical current "leaks" or follows an unsafe direction instead of following its intended path. When a ground fault occurs and electricity from an appliance passes through the person's body, the resulting shock can cause serious injury or even death. GFCIs detect when current is leaking from an electrical circuit to ground and automatically shut off the power at the receptacle in a fraction of a second.

GFCIs not only protect what's plugged into them but also provide feed-through protection to ordinary outlets wired downstream (other outlets on the same circuit). The UL standard has been recently updated to require that GFCIs be self-testing, which incorporates an auto-monitoring feature into the GFCIs, beginning in mid-2015.

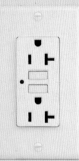

INDOORS Bathrooms, kitchens, laundry rooms, or any other place around the house with a water source within 6 feet of the receptacle needs GFCI protection. Remember: Electricity and water can be a deadly combination, so keep appliances such as radios or hair dryers away from sinks, tubs, or pools.

OUTDOORS Protect outdoor receptacles, including any around pools, decks, and patios, using GFCIs with weatherproof covers. Plug pool pumps, hot tubs, and any outdoor appliances into GFCI outlets.

115 KEEP UP WITH TECHNOLOGY

Technology is moving fast; electrical advancements are no exception. Here are a couple of cool options for your home.

USB ENABLED Offering a simple solution to charge a wide range of electronic devices, the newer duplex electrical receptacles now often come equipped with a USB interface. Increasingly popular in homes and businesses, these replace the standard AC duplex receptacle and eliminate the need for bulky adapters by including a set of integrated USB charging ports. These new receptacles make it easy to quickly charge virtually any applicable electronic device, including smartphones, tablets, e-readers, MP3 players, cameras, and more.

WIRELESS SWITCHES Another new home electrical trend is the growing popularity of wireless switches. These battery-powered switches control home lighting options by radio frequency. The advantage here is that you can place the light switch anywhere in the home without the need to wire it into the electrical system, which saves a lot of time and work. Mount it to any wall surface or even hold the device in your hand. A few of the new switches can wirelessly control up to five light sources simultaneously from anywhere in the home. Once the switch is installed, it searches for installable devices and ultimately synchronizes itself with them, granting remote-control capability. Using Z-wave wireless technology, the switch operates on a dedicated radio frequency so it does not interfere with Wi-Fi or other wireless communications in the house.

116 TEST YOUR GFCI

GFCIs sold today offer improved protection by automatically blocking the outlet's reset button (ensuring that no power is available) if they're improperly wired. With both newer and older models, it's important to periodically test your installed GFCIs (following the manufacturer's instructions as you do so) to ensure they're working properly.

STEP 1 Plug a night light or lamp into the GFCI.

STEP 3 Press the RESET button to reset the GFCI; the light should come back on.

STEP 2 Turn the light on and push the TEST button on the GFCI. The GFCI should trip and the light should go off.

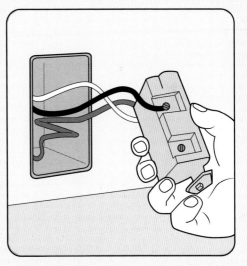

STEP 4 If the light either does not go off when the TEST button is pressed or does not come back on when the RESET button is pressed, the device is malfunctioning and should be replaced at once.

The basic outlet in the United States has a pair of vertical slots, the left slightly bigger than the right. The left slot is neutral, the right slot is "hot"; the hole centered below them is the ground. Outlets and plugs vary around the world, but these basic components are found everywhere in some configuration.

We probably don't have to tell you why grounding is so important, but it bears repeating since a good ground can literally mean the difference between life and death. Most of the things you plug in are made of metal, or at least have significant metal components, making for a potential shock risk. If a wire comes loose inside an appliance, contacting metal inside the case, the entire object is now "hot," and anyone who touches it can get a nasty shock. If it's plugged into a grounded outlet, as it should be, that charge will flow straight to ground instead of trying to go through you in a potentially deadly way.

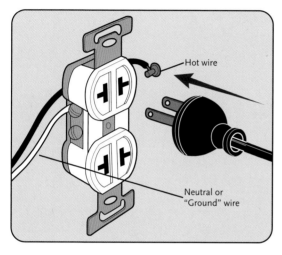

Hot wire

Neutral or "Ground" wire

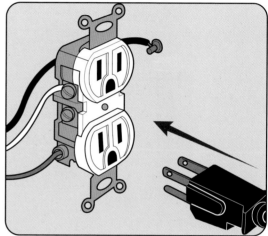

118 ASSESS YOUR OPTIONS

If you live in a home that was built before the 1970s, it likely has at least some two-pronged outlets. The now-familiar standard grounded, three-pronged model first appeared back in the 1960s and became mandatory for homes built after 1974 in the United States. Older houses were grandfathered in under most building codes, so you may not be required to replace the outlets—but you should consider it. If money and time is no object, the best thing would be to replace all the old outlets with grounded, three-prong outlets. But if time and money are tight, here are some options.

INSTALL A GFCI A two-pronged slot that's safe by your bed is a real risk in a kitchen or bathroom (or anywhere else it might get wet). A GFCI is a safer solution (see item 114). You need to put a warning label on any ungrounded GFCI (the labels come in the box when you buy one) and it's not as safe as a fully grounded outlet, but it will provide protection against electrical shocks.

REPLACE IT ENTIRELY Sensitive appliances (such as a computer or plasma TV) should be plugged into an outlet that has a properly grounded circuit all the way back to the circuit breakers. A DIYer who is comfortable with electrical work can easily take care of this.

119 REPLACE A TWO-PRONGED OUTLET

The first step below is absolutely crucial—do not continue if the metal box that's holding your current two-pronged outlet is not grounded. Even when the outlet isn't grounded, the box usually is, so it's unlikely to be an issue. The boxes in older homes are generally wired with armored (or BX) cable, which has a flexible metal jacket that essentially serves as a grounding wire for the box.

STEP 1 Check for ground. Insert one prong of a circuit tester into the shorter slot (the hot one), and touch the other to one of the screws securing the plastic cover plate. The tester should light up to indicate a proper ground. If it turns out not to be grounded, you can still install a GFCI safely, but installing a three-pronged receptacle will be a job for an electrician.

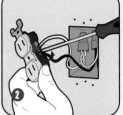

STEP 2 If the box is grounded, turn off the power at the breaker panel or fuse box, then unscrew the cover plate from the wall, remove the receptacle, and disconnect it from all wires.

STEP 3 To connect the new receptacle, attach the "hot" black wire to the brass terminal in the box and the white neutral wire to the silver one.

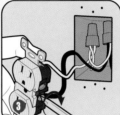

STEP 4 Twist one end of an 8-inch grounding wire (or pigtail) around the green ground screw in the outlet box, and tighten. If a ground screw isn't present, you can buy one in a hardware store.

STEP 5 Secure the other end of the grounding wire to the green grounding terminal on the new three-pronged receptacle. Screw the new receptacle into the box.

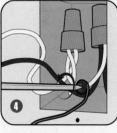

STEP 6 Turn on the power. Use a circuit tester to make sure the circuit is working.

PRO TIP

USE A USB PORT Are you annoyed by your phone trying to sync while you're busy working, or just have too may devices plugged into your phone and not enough of the charging-cord adapter plugs that are always underfoot until you really need one? Several manufacturers make a relatively easy-to-install three-pronged outlet that also incorporates a USB port, so you can charge devices without an adapter. Be aware that they're almost twice as thick as a standard receptacle, which may be more than an older junction box is engineered to handle. Check first to avoid wasting time.

120 REPLACE A STANDARD SINGLE-POLE BREAKER

When replacing a circuit breaker, stand on a rubber mat or a piece of plywood to insulate yourself against an electrical shock. Use an insulated screwdriver and insulated wire strippers. Most houses will have a combination panel, with a main breaker, and then all the branch circuit breakers below.

STEP 1 Remove the cover to the breaker panel and test the breaker to verify that it is faulty.

STEP 2 Before shutting off the main breaker, first shut off all branch circuit breakers. Double-check with a voltage meter that the faulty breaker and adjacent breakers are shut off. Most homes will have "push in" or "stab in" types of breakers.

STEP 3 Use a screwdriver to disconnect the wire from the load terminal of the breaker. Bend the wire out of the way.

STEP 4 Carefully pry the defective breaker out of its position. Take note as to how the breaker locks into position in the panel.

STEP 5 Connect the load wire to the new breaker. With the new switch off, push it firmly into place. Reattach the wire to the load terminal.

STEP 6 After the cover is back on, turn on the main breaker and then, one by one, all individual breakers. Test all systems to see if everything is normal. Replace the panel cover.

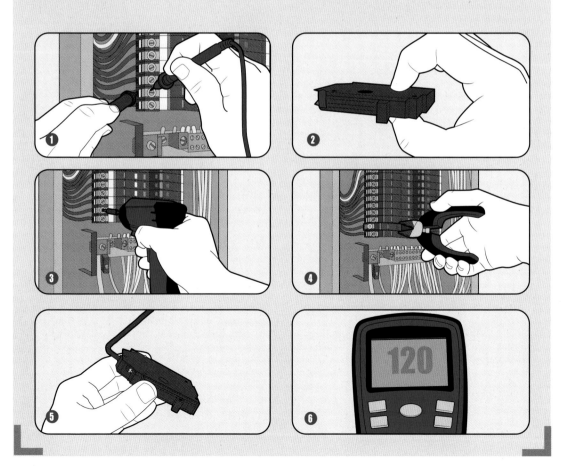

121 CHOOSE THE RIGHT REPLACEMENT

Circuit breakers are designed to protect your wires from carrying too much current by tripping off an overload or a short circuit. Whenever you need to add a new circuit, you'll need to install a new circuit breaker. Occasionally an existing circuit breaker fails and needs to be replaced. You can safely replace a circuit breaker in your electrical panel if you take the proper precautions.

Before you do anything, gather all the information that you can (the brand name, part number, breaker size, breaker type, and so on) to determine the proper replacement. Although some breakers are interchangeable, many are not, even if they look similar. Replacing with the wrong breaker can be dangerous and may void your breaker or panel warranty. Check the breaker panel door for information about which breakers are compatible with your panel. Here are some common types you may find yourself dealing with.

CIRCUIT BREAKER TYPE	WHAT IT DOES
Standard circuit breaker	Monitors the flow of electricity as it enters the home.
Single-pole breaker	Protects one energized wire and supplies 120V to a circuit. They're generally rated 15 or 20 amps, occupy one slot on a breaker panel, and are the most common breakers in a home.
Double-pole breaker	Typically occupies two slots on a breaker panel and consists of two single-pole breakers and a shared trip mechanism. They supply 120V/240V or 240V to a circuit, protect two energized wires, and range in capacity from 15 to 200 amps. Double-pole breakers are required for large appliances like dryers and water heaters.
GFCI circuit breaker	Cuts power to the circuit when they're tripped by an overload of current, a short circuit, or a line-to-ground fault. All GFCI breakers have test buttons on the front and coiled wires. They function in the same way as GFCI receptacles but protect an entire circuit, eliminating the need for GFCI receptacles on that circuit.
AFCI (arc-fault circuit-interrupter) breaker	Protects against an unintentional electrical discharge in wiring that could cause a fire. Once the breaker senses the abnormal electrical path, it instantly disconnects the damaged circuit before the arc builds enough heat to catch fire. AFCI breakers look like GFCI breakers with test buttons and coiled wires. The only way to tell them apart is to read the fine print on the breaker.

122 TEST A BAD BREAKER

Before you replace a circuit breaker, make sure that you've correctly diagnosed the issue.

STEP 1 Unplug any devices along the problem circuit, turn off all lights, and flip the switch on the breaker. If it resets, you can then reconnect the electronic devices one at time and turn on the lights to determine where the problem is.

STEP 2 Turn off the breaker before plugging each item back in, and then reset the breaker. This prevents a dangerous surge of current should you have a short circuit in a device, which can send a very high amount of electrical current before the breaker trips.

STEP 3 If the breaker won't reset, test it with a voltage meter. If the meter doesn't read voltage on the load terminal, even when all known loads are disconnected, then the breaker is probably faulty and needs replacement.

Thermostat installation is a fairly simple job. All that's typically required is a slotted screwdriver, a small Phillips screwdriver, a hammer, an electric drill/driver, a 3/16-inch bit, and two AA batteries.

STEP 1 Cut power to the thermostat and furnace. Remove the thermostat's cover, which is usually fastened with plastic push tabs.

STEP 2 Unscrew the old unit. The wires might be mounted to the thermostat or wall plate by screws. Each wire will be wrapped in color-coded insulation that corresponds to the terminals on the rear of the new thermostat (or wall plate). When connected to the existing thermostat, all of these wires are usually marked with a code letter. It may help to label them to avoid confusion. The number of wires in a system can vary from two (for heat only) to as many as eight.

STEP 3 Disconnect the wires and then unscrew the wall plate from the wall.

STEP 4 Pull out the wires and clip them so they don't slide back through the hole. Then screw them to the color-coded terminals on the new wall plate.

STEP 5 Attach the wires to the matching mounting screws of the new unit. Ignore any wires that were not connected to the old thermostat. Push extra wiring back into the hole. If the hole in the wall behind the wall plate is larger than necessary, seal it with insulation to prevent air from entering the thermostat and affecting its temperature reading.

STEP 6 Use a torpedo level to make sure the new wall plate is plumb, then screw the plate to the wall. Drywall mounting requires first predrilling the

124 UPGRADE YOUR THERMOSTAT

Programmable thermostats automatically adjust your home's temperature settings several times a day to fit your lifestyle. These units contain no mercury, are more accurate than manual thermostats, and can also save you money each year in energy costs.

Programmable thermostats include four default periods per day. They maintain accuracy within two degrees to keep the temperature steady. The newest programmable thermostats also have digital backlit displays, touch-pad screen programming, voice and/or phone programming, and other helpful features.

You'll find three types of programmable units, each of them equally easy to install.

TYPE	DESCRIPTION
7-day models	The best choice if your daily schedule changes often. These offer the most flexibility by allowing you to set different programs for different days.
5+2-day models	Use the same schedule every weekday and another schedule for weekends.
5-1-1-day models	Keep one schedule Monday through Friday, another schedule on Saturdays, and a third on Sundays.

anchor holes with a 3/16-inch bit and hammering in drywall anchors to house the screws. You may get lucky, as in the installation shown, if the pre-existing drywall anchors from the old thermostat happen to line up with the screw holes on the new unit. If no new drilling is required, simply line up the mount holes and drive in the screws.

STEP 7 Fasten the thermostat to the wall plate. On the unit shown, the thermostat attaches using press-release tabs at the top and bottom of the unit. Be sure the thermostat is set to OFF and the fan switch is set to AUTO. Insert the two AA batteries. Switch on the main power to the furnace.

STEP 8 Program the thermostat according to the manufacturer's guidelines. You'll soon be saving energy and money, and helping the environment.

PRO TIP

HAVE A SMART HEATER
One new advancement in thermostat technology is a model that learns the temperatures you like and programs itself in about a week. The thermostat turns itself down when no one is home to help you save energy, and you can even connect it to Wi-Fi for remote control. The new tech even alerts homeowners when temperatures drop to help avoid frozen pipes.

Outdoor light systems are wired up using either line-voltage or low-voltage power. Heavy-duty line-voltage wiring plugs into GFCI outdoor outlets, and the wires should be buried in a conduit. The more common low-voltage systems plug into a transformer. The wires of a low-voltage system are thin and can be buried discreetly in the soil.

Home centers sell multi-fixture DIY kits for low-voltage systems. Or purchase individual fixtures, wiring, and transformer separately and customize a system. Small plastic fixtures cost as little as a few dollars. More durable metal fixtures are about twice as expensive.

STEP 1 Choose a transformer, or power pack, that offers a wattage output greater than the total wattage of all the light fixtures in the system. For example, let's say a system includes four 7-watt fixtures, two 11-watt, and two 35-watt fixtures:

$7 + 7 + 7 + 7 + 11 + 11 + 35 + 35 = 120$ watts total.

In this case, you would need to have a transformer that offers a capacity of at least 121 watts. (Some are also equipped with built-in timing and/or photocell devices—popular features for many homeowners.)

STEP 2 Determine the number and style of fixtures you need. Walk the perimeter of your home, noting areas to illuminate. Sketch the plan on graph paper, noting key features such as trees, shrubbery, paths, decks, and patios. (Space path lights a minimum of 10 feet apart. Depending on wattage, flood lamps will cast light 20 to 40 feet.)

STEP 3 Locate a 120-volt GFCI outlet for your power pack. Certain manufacturers offer "weatherproof" outdoor power packs. Professionals still do suggest keeping the transformer inside to avoid the elements, which requires you to drill through a wall to run the cable. The transformer should be mounted within 3 feet of the outlet and at least 1 foot above the ground.

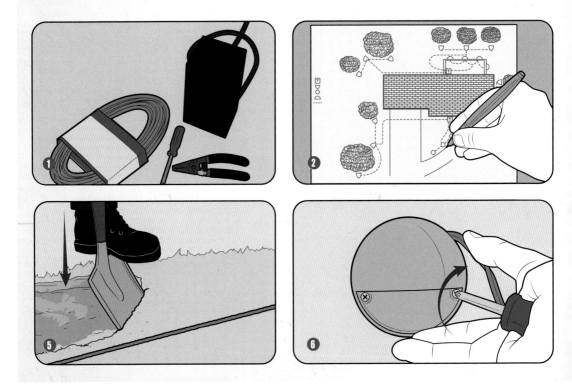

STEP 4 Determine the length of cable you're going to need for this project by measuring the distance from the outlet to the farthest fixture location. Include the length of cable that branches off the main line. Allow for several feet of extra cable. Cable for low-voltage systems is available in 8-, 10-, 12-, and 16-gauge sizes. The appropriate cable size depends on the maximum length of run from the transformer and the total wattage of the lights in the run. Check the cable manufacturer's recommendations.

STEP 5 Dig a narrow channel for the cable at least 6 inches deep from the transformer to each fixture location. At each fixture location, create a loop of cable (about 2 feet) for the attachment of the fixture.

STEP 6 Place each fixture at its desired location, attaching the fixture to the proper mounting device. "Surface mounts" are used for placing

fixtures on trees or structures. "Ground mounts" are stakes or spikes driven into the ground to support the fixture.

STEP 7 Connect the lead wire of the fixture to the cable run by splicing the wires together using wire nuts (apply a sealant and electrical tape to prevent corrosion, or solder the wires to ensure a strong connection). Cable connectors are a quick way to splice a fixture's lead wire to the cable run; some manufacturers even supply the connectors along with the fixtures.

STEP 8 Plug in the transformer, connect all of your cable runs to the transformer terminals, and turn on the system. If there's any trouble, recheck all wiring connections. Once the system functions properly, fill in the cable trench that you dug in step 5, and you're ready to light up the night.

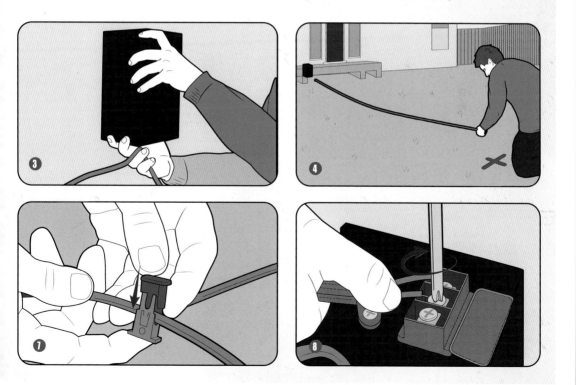

126 FIGHT THE FUNGI

Mold is a top concern for indoor air quality in homes nationwide. Mold and mildew are both fungi and share many traits. They thrive in warm, moist, and humid environments and on surfaces. They can blacken the grout lines in your shower, discolor the walls, darken your decks, or rot wood anywhere in or around the home. From causing musty smells to serious allergic reactions, indoor mold and mildew can be a pesky nuisance or a health hazard.

KNOW THE DIFFERENCE Mold is typically fuzzy in appearance ❶ and can be seen in many colors, including blue, green, yellow, brown, gray, black, or white. Mold can cause structural damage to homes over time and lead to health problems, including respiratory problems, migraines, and more. Mildew will usually grow in a flat pattern ❷ and may be powdery or downy. Powdery mildew usually starts out white and then might later turn to yellow, brown, or black. Downy mildew usually starts out yellow and later turns brown. Like mold, it can also lead to respiratory problems and allergic reactions.

TELL BY SMELL Musty odors can be a sign of mold growth, but such a smell may also indicate an infestation of mice. Microfungal growth of mold and mildew can sometimes be difficult to spot. Try shining a flashlight nearly parallel to the lower portion of wall or leg of furniture. Look for any fuzzy white, pale yellow, or blue-green spots. These are likely mold colonies; when disturbed, the spores can become airborne and emit a musty odor.

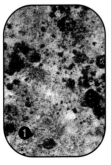

127 SPOT CLEAN

When you're cleaning up mildew and mold, ventilate your work area; several cleansers can give off fumes that are harmful to breathe. Wear rubber gloves, and use a face mask to avoid breathing in spores and any fumes given off by the cleaning product.

For a simple household solution, mix ¼ cup of bleach per gallon of water, spray on surfaces showing mold growth, and let dry for 10 minutes. Never mix bleach and ammonia, which creates toxic chlorine gas.

Bleach is often used to kill spores and clean surfaces, but it has harsh fumes and can be toxic, and the mold can return. Also, when it attacks the surface mold, it leaves a residue that prevents other antimicrobial products from penetrating to the mold roots or hyphae. If you've treated an area with bleach, clean the area with warm water and detergent; once the area is dry, apply a commercial antimicrobial product to the surrounding area as well as where you actually see the mold and mildew, to ensure you remove all traces.

Remove any items that cannot be thoroughly cleaned, such as insulation, carpeting, and drywall, and replace those with new mold-free materials.

128 TACKLE MAJOR DAMAGE

If your home has suffered any water damage from flooding, sewage backup, or plumbing problems, it will be prone to a mold infestation. The worst part of this is the speed with which mold develops—from only 24 to 48 hours of water exposure.

DRY OUT Set out fans and dehumidifiers, and move wet items away from walls and off of the floors. Find out the source of moisture and then prevent it from worsening the problem.

TOSS THE TRASH Items that have absorbed moisture and have mold growing on them need to be thrown out. If there has been flooding, remove the sheetrock a level above the high-water mark. Any kind of porous material that shows visible signs of mold should be thrown away.

CLEAN UP Surface mold growing on any nonporous materials can usually be cleaned. Thoroughly scrub contaminated surfaces using hot water, non-ammonia soap, detergent, or commercial cleaner. Use a stiff brush to scrub out all contaminants. Rinse with clean water, and collect the excess rinse water and detergent with a wet/dry vacuum, a mop, or a sponge.

DISINFECT Apply a bleach solution or antimicrobial cleaner to surfaces that show any mold growth. An effective way to eliminate mold and musty smells in large or inaccessible spaces is to use a "cold fogger." A fogger will create a mold-control mist that distributes the cleaner evenly throughout the living space, even into hard-to-access areas, crushing the mold spores as it dries.

LOOK OUT Be alert to the signs of mold returning to the areas of past infestation. If it does return, repeat cleaning steps or, in cases of heavy infestation, seek professional help. Regrowth is usually a sign that the moisture has not efficiently been controlled.

PRO TIP

SPOT THE PRIME SUSPECT To prevent growth on paint film, newer mold-killing primers now contain an EPA-registered antimicrobial agent. You can apply the primer directly to any problem areas without extensive preparation, and paint over and kill any surface mold, mildew, and odor-causing bacteria. This water-based primer can be used on nonporous interior and exterior surfaces and is recommended for bathrooms, basements, window frames, and more.

As we've discussed already, water can be your home's worst enemy, causing cosmetic and structural damage, and leading to mold and mildew infestations. Water can seep in a number of ways, so be sure that your home's exterior is well sealed.

1 ROOF Replace any missing or damaged shingles. Look for any exposed or protruding nails; replace them with larger hot-dip galvanized types if the flashing is galvanized sheet metal, or stainless steel nails if the flashing is made of stainless steel. Remove moss and lichen growth anywhere on the roof using a broom or garden hose that has a spray nozzle. Remove debris buildup in valleys and at wall-to-roof intersections. Inspect flashing around chimney and penetrations. If flashing is cracked or pulled off, call for expert repairs

2 GUTTERS AND DOWNSPOUTS Clean gutters with a blower, hose, or broom. A hose can help pinpoint leaks and other trouble spots. Use gutter cement on cracks, or replace the gutter sections according to the manufacturer's instructions. Replace rusted screws and ensure downspouts drain away from the house.

3 WINDOWS, DOORS, AND SIDING Inspect and recaulk siding, windows, utility penetrations and doors. Place a foam backer rod in any seams more than ½ inch wide or ¼ inch deep. Check that all of the weatherstripping around doors and windows is sealed tightly to prevent moisture from entering. Inspect all stucco and brick surfaces for cracked mortar; repair it with patch kits from your hardware store. Keep a minimum 6 inches of clearance between the siding and the ground.

130 KEEP THE WATER OUT

Your yard is a prime suspect in water damage. Check the following area to be sure the water stays where you want it: outdoors!

4 SPRINKLERS Water your plants, not your house. Redirect lawn sprinklers so they do not wet the siding, windows, or foundation walls. Overwatering your lawn or plants can create moisture and mold problems even in summer.

5 LANDSCAPING Trim plant life away from the siding. Large shrubs or vegetation may need to be moved if the foliage persistently contacts the house's siding, windows, or utility penetrations such as dryer vents. Tree roots can interfere with perimeter footing drain systems, disrupting the flow of water away from the

131   LOOK FOR MOISTURE

Once you've checked ways that the exterior of your home might be letting water in, it's time to move indoors and investigate these common problem spots.

7 **VENTILATION** Install timers on bathroom and laundry fans, and run fans for 20 minutes after showers. Your bath/kitchen/laundry fan ducts should vent outside and never terminate in the attic. Do not vent your dryers inside the home. Use an approved aerosol foam sealant to seal around any ceiling penetrations that may allow moist air to flow into the attic space. Place foam rubber insulation gaskets around attic space access panels.

8 **ATTIC** Be on the lookout for water stains on the underside of the roof, rusted nails, and discolored moldy sections on any surface. If you find any of these warning signs, look for the source of the moisture, possibly a faulty vent that isn't directing air to the outside. Also check that there is room for air to flow from the eaves (soffit vents) into the attic space and out the upper roof vents.

9 **KITCHEN AND BATH** Inspect plumbing fixtures under sinks and toilets and around shower and tub enclosures. Look for stains, cracks, and mold on caulk and repair as necessary. Use tile and marble sealers annually or as recommended by manufacturers.

10 **BASEMENT** Check your basement and crawlspace for any moisture problems: standing water, mold on floor joists, or rust on metal fasteners. Replace loose or missing batt insulation. If the crawlspace is not insulated, install a 6-millimeter polyethylene vapor barrier over exposed ground. If you find serious moisture damage or standing water in either the crawlspace or basement, call a contractor to repair and correct the source of the problem.

house and causing dampness or flooding along the foundation and into the basement. Design your landscaping to minimize potential root blockage of underground pipes.

6 **DRAINAGE** Make sure that the perimeter ground is sloping away from the foundation. If any downspouts dead-end near the foundation, add some splash blocks to redirect water away from the home.

Inspect the outdoor deck connection to the house. This is a major source of water intrusion that often goes unnoticed. This ledger connection should be flashed and have sufficient space between the ledger board and the deck boards to allow drainage away from the house.

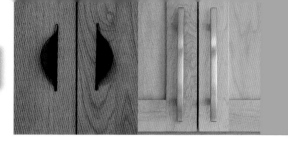

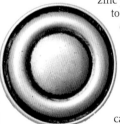

Knowing how to "accessorize" is the way that many fashionistas describe their penchant for flaunting jewelry; some interior designers have that same outlook on household hardware. If you consider the vast number of knobs, pulls, hinges, handles, and even heating registers that permeate the home, you may realize that hardware makes up a major component and can really make a visual statement. Classy cabinet knobs and pretty drawer pulls can make an old piece of furniture look decades newer and help focus the overall design of a room.

GO CLASSIC A traditional rule of thumb has been to match materials to the existing décor, for example, by choosing granite knobs to match the countertops, or purchasing pulls with the same metal and finish, such as stainless steel with stainless steel, and copper with copper. However, that idea took hold when there was less of an assortment of decorative options. With such an amazing array available today, all those old rules are taking a backseat to a more intuitive approach in which anything goes, as long as it looks good.

MAKE IT MODERN Modern options not only include crystal, ceramic, and wood but also a wide range of metal finishes such as brushed nickel, antique brass, zinc plate, and many more—too many to list. Hardware stores and home centers offer plenty of choices for inspection, but the widest selection and best cost savings for major house purchases are often found with online retailers. Style is a personal choice, but size is not, and your selection of cabinet and drawer hardware will of course be limited in size. When you remove a piece of hardware, the replacement should fit the same mounting holes, or cover them. For paint-grade furniture pieces, you may get away with filling the old holes, repainting, and drilling new locations, but this isn't recommended where woodgrain is exposed.

133 COME UNHINGED

When ordering hardware for cabinets, you'll also need matching hinges. The finish should match the décor, and new hinges should match the size and shape of the old ones. Face-frame cabinets have a frame over the top of the opening and need face-frame mounted hinges; other hinges have a recessed overlay. Check how much overlay the hinges need. Cabinet doors completely on top of cabinet faces require a full overlay hinge. If there's only a partial overlay, use a $^3/_8$-inch inset hinge door that completely conceals the hinge from sight when the door is closed.

To change hinges on a cabinet (or when replacing a door), remove the lower hinges first to keep the unsecured weight of the door from stressing the lower hardware or tearing the wood. Fasten the new top hinge first, and store old hardware until the swap is complete. If the new bolts aren't right, you may be able to use the old ones.

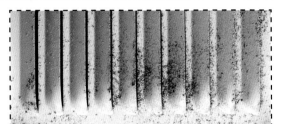

134 PAINT YOUR REGISTERS

Replacing an old, ugly metal HVAC register can rid the room of an eyesore. However, replacing a whole house full of them can get pretty expensive. Over time, metal HVAC registers accumulate rust and grime. You have three options: leave them as is, replace them, or paint them.

Painting is definitely a cheaper improvement, and companies are making some very cool new spray-paint formulas that mimic the look of antique hammered metal, namely copper, bronze, and silver (although more colors are available). The register shown here was thoroughly cleaned and then given a coat of Rust-Oleum's "Hammered Bronze" paint. Afterward, it looked brand new and stylish—for a fraction of the cost of replacing it.

PRO TIP

MOUNT UP Whenever you need to make new mounting holes in hardwood, always predrill the fastener holes to prevent splitting the wood. To tighten a loose hinge screw, remove the screw and tap pieces of toothpick into the screw hole. Cut the toothpicks flush with the cabinet face. Reinsert the screw, and the toothpick material should tighten the connection.

135 HANDLE IT

Most cabinet door handles have two mounting holes that you need to match precisely when replacing; spacing is not universal. Measure the handle or pull at the point between the pair of holes to the closest $1/8$ inch. Removal (along with replacement) will require only a screwdriver, usually one that has a Phillips-head tip. You might still, however, come across an escutcheon—a plate behind certain types of drawer pulls—but these can be removed with a small cat's-paw tool or (carefully) pried up with a putty knife.

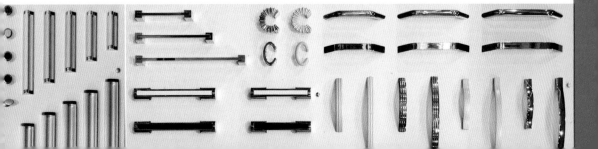

136 INSTALL CUSTOM CLOSET SHELVES

Organizing a closet by adding shelves supported by 1x2 wood cleats is a fairly simple procedure and can add much-needed storage.

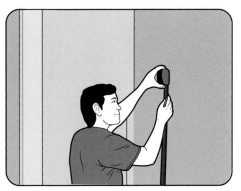

STEP 1 Mark the elevation (top surface) of each planned shelf on the back wall of the closet. When you're marking the elevation, take into account the thickness of each shelf (often   inch) as well as the height of the cleats (1¾ inch).

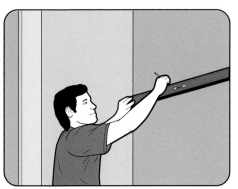

STEP 2 Mark level horizontal lines along the wall to indicate the tops of the shelves. Then mark out secondary horizontal lines that indicate the bottom of each shelf.

STEP 3 Cut 1x2 wood strips into cleats that fit flush between the side walls of the closet. Position each cleat along the lower line that indicates the bottom of the shelf and fasten it into the wall studs using an air nailer.

STEP 4 Level and fasten the side support cleats to the side walls, which intersect flush with the rear cleat. The side cleats can be cut to match the depth of the shelves, or they can extend all the way to the opposite wall if you plan to install full shelves on three walls of the closet.

STEP 5 Cut the shelf material to fit over the support cleats and flush against the three walls. From the bottom, tilt the shelves to install them over the cleats, and fasten them into the cleats with 1½-inch nails. Shelves are often built from ¾-inch MDF stock or other paint-grade wood product, which you can then finish to your preference. For wraparound shelves mounted to three walls of the closet, consider adding vertical partitions to compartmentalize the storage space for increased organization.

137 MOUNT SHELVES

The easiest way to mount a shelf on a wall is by using the right-angle shelf brackets commonly sold at home centers and hardware stores. They're available in a wide array of styles, finishes, and weight-bearing capacities. These L-shaped brackets mount into wall studs using strong screws, and the shelf is then screwed to the bracket.

SMALL SHELVES You can first locate the stud centers with an electric stud finder. Measure the distance between the studs where you'll mount the shelves. On the bottom of the shelf, center and then mark the corresponding bracket locations. Screw the brackets to the shelves with the rear arms flush with the back of the shelf. Level the shelf on the wall and screw the brackets into the wall studs.

LONG SHELVES You might find it easier to mark a level line on the wall to indicate the top of the shelf brackets. Line up the brackets along the line and screw them securely into the studs. Center the shelf over the brackets and mount with screws from below.

PRO TIP

FLOAT YOUR SHELVES
Floating shelves are made to hover on the wall with no visible brackets or mounting hardware. There being no brackets to contend with, the shelves can often be situated more closely together, thus granting more room for more shelves. Floating shelves are basically made of flat, hollow boxes. Depending on the method of construction, the hollow shelf mounts to either metal rods or a wooden cleat that fit inside the rear of the box and supports it from within. The rods or cleat are fastened securely into the wall studs for the strongest holding power.

138 JOIN THE INDUSTRY

You can make rugged "industrial style" shelves using support brackets made from ¾-inch threaded galvanized pipe, floor flanges and end caps. Assemble the brackets from the pipe components and coat them using a black spray paint with a hammered finish for a wrought-iron appearance. The shelves can be cut from 2× lumber and stained to your preference. Fasten through the flanges of the brackets into the wall studs using heavy-duty wood screws for sturdy holding power.

Removing wallpaper is sometimes a necessary evil if you plan to give your walls a pro-quality paint finish. Painting over wallpaper will not conceal seams or keep the paper from peeling in corners. Plus, any paint can cause the paper to wrinkle or bubble. For the best results, you should remove the wallpaper before painting.

Look for any loose corners or seams, and if you don't find one, make one. Give the loose tab a slow, controlled yank. You might be able to peel away large sections of paper by hand with little effort. Move along the wall, pulling off all the paper you can, because the follow-up methods require more time and work. Use a drop cloth to catch the debris.

The paper won't always completely come away from the wall while pulling it off by hand, however. The adhesive on the back can be stubbornly fused to the paper face of the drywall. To remove the paper without damaging the wall surface, you will need to weaken the chemical bond of the glue. There are two ways to do this: a liquid wallpaper stripper, or a steam-powered stripper.

PRO TIP

PREP BEFORE PAINTING
After removing wallpaper, wash the wall several times to remove glue residue. Use fresh water and a sponge. Otherwise, the residue will impair the bonding of the paint and cause it to peel. Use a box fan to hasten the drying process. Once the wall is completely dry, apply a coat of primer, then paint.

140 KNOW THE SCORE

Before you remove wallpaper, you should first use a perforation tool to abrade the paper so that it can absorb liquid (whether chemicals or water). This tool is sold at most hardware stores; it's basically a palm-size handle that houses wheeled spurs. Apply just enough pressure to perforate the paper without damaging the drywall. Alternatively, score the paper with the edge of a wall scraper in a crisscross pattern with 6-inch spacing.

141 USE A CHEMICAL STRIPPER

Using a chemical wallpaper stripper is one of the easiest and least expensive methods to do the job. Here's how to do it right.

STEP 1 Mix the liquid wallpaper remover with hot water, according to the manufacturer's instructions.

STEP 2 Use a paint roller or spray bottle to apply the remover to the perforated paper. Wait about 10 minutes for the remover to weaken the adhesive, and then peel off as much as you can with your hands.

STEP 3 For stubborn swaths of paper, lightly use a 3-inch scraper at a shallow angle to scrape the paper without nicking the wall.

142 STRIP WITH STEAM

If you frequently remodel or redecorate, consider investing in a steam-powered wallpaper stripper. These tools eliminate the need to use chemicals and can be reused over and over. The simplest steamers require only that the user fill the tank with water and plug the cord in an outlet to start the heating element. Once the water heats up, the steam that is generated escapes through a hose. At the end of the hose a steam plate collects the steam over a targeted area.

Just hold the steam plate flat to the wallpaper for about 10 seconds. The steam will heat and dampen the paper, which loosens the glue. Move the plate onto the spot immediately next to the one just steamed, from which the paper should easily come off with a little bit of encouragement from a wall scraper. This pattern should allow you to continuously remove paper. Don't forget that steam is hot; water will boil at 212 degrees Fahrenheit, so be careful when using a steamer.

143 SILENCE A SQUEAKY FLOOR

Floor squeaks are caused by flexing of materials in the flooring or subfloor, which usually rubs against a nail or adjoining floorboard to create the noise. A loose board is a common culprit.

USE A SHIM The easiest way to fix a floor is from below. If the floor is above a basement or crawlspace, you might have exposed floor joists; the simplest solution is to tighten the connection between the squeaky floor and the joist. Wedge a shim between the top of the joist and the subfloor. Use a hammer to tap in just enough material to close the gap and tighten the joint. Construction adhesive can hold the shim in place when the wood contracts.

SCREW IT If you know which boards have come loose, you might be able to tighten them from below with a screw and a large washer. Drill a pilot hole up through the subfloor using a drill bit slightly narrower than the screw. Consider the thickness of the subfloor, along with the finished flooring, and use a short enough screw that won't penetrate through the finished floor when driven in; its point should remain ¼ inch below the floor surface. Insert the screw and washer into the hole, driving it up through the subfloor into the floorboard, pulling the layers together against the washer.

ADD A CLEAT For larger areas that have multiple loose boards, wedge a wood cleat beneath the subfloor and fasten it to the floor joist. Position a 1x4 or 1x6 cleat against the joist and the subfloor and prop it in place with a 2x4. Hammer-tap the 2x4 to wedge the cleat to the subfloor. Fasten the cleat to the joist with 2- to 3-inch nails or screws.

BRIDGE THE GAP If the floor squeaks across a large area, the floor joists might be shifting as the house settles. To reinforce them, nail diagonal bridging between joists in an X pattern. You can cut your own pieces to fit or purchase precut wooden or metal bridging from a home center.

144 STABILIZE A FLOOR

A floor may be solidly constructed and adequately supported but still have a degree of "bounce" or vibration when people are moving throughout the room. This is usually not a major problem, but should be addressed if your plan to install a tile floor, because any minor amount of deflection within the subfloor could result in cracked grout or flooring. If you can gain access beneath the subfloor, you can construct a perpendicular girder and piers to help level the joists and stabilize the framing with additional support that connects to the ground.

145 REPAIR A CARPET BUBBLE

A "bubble" in a wall-to-wall carpet is an area of the rug that lifts above the subfloor and creates unsightly hills or ridges in the finished surface. It can be expensive to have the carpet professionally restretched to eliminate these bubbles. However, there's a simple and low-cost method to repair the carpet that takes only a few minutes to complete. All you need is a bottle of carpet-seam glue, a large syringe, pliers, and a towel.

STEP 1 Analyze the lay of the carpet throughout the room to locate all the areas of loose carpeting that need to be repaired. Purchase enough carpet-seam adhesive to address the square footage that you require.

STEP 2 Using a large syringe, just like the ones used to inject marinade into your Thanksgiving turkey, draw glue into the syringe.

STEP 3 Use pliers to gently lift the carpet off the subfloor/padding at the midpoint of the bubble. Pierce the carpet with the syringe and angle the tip toward the edge of the bubble.

STEP 4 Depress the plunger and then rotate the syringe so the glue is applied in a circular pattern, covering as much of the loose carpet area as possible. As you empty the syringe, draw the needle partially out of the carpet so the glue contacts the center of the bubble as well as the periphery.

STEP 5 Working from the center outward, press the carpet firmly into the adhesive and spread the glue beneath the carpet. If you have a laminate roller or rolling pin, put it to work.

STEP 6 Place a flat weight over the repaired area to provide clamping force while the adhesive is setting. Heavy boxes or books will work so long as they press the carpet flat into the glue. Keep pressure on the glue according to the adhesive manufacturer's recommended drying time.

Repeat all steps of this process for any areas of the floor that show signs of bubbling and, with any luck, your carpet should eventually stay down and bubble-free.

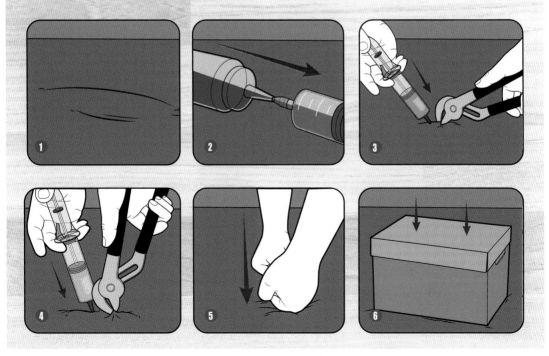

Screws often come loose because the wood that surrounds the threads has been worn out, often due to the wear and tear from movement over time. To tighten a screw, the threads need more material to bite. To fix this, simply add wood to the hole.

1 Depending upon the size of the hole worn in the wood, you can fill it using a wooden golf tee, barbecue skewers, or toothpicks; in the event of a sizable hole you can even try using a wooden chopstick. In a pinch you could even whittle some scrap wood slivers using a pocketknife.

2 Insert the wood pick into the hole as deep as it will go, then cut it flush with the mouth of the hole. Repeat this step until the hole is packed.

3 Reinsert the screw and tighten with a screwdriver. The threads of the screw should crush against the new wood fibers with outward pressure to mount securely inside the hole.

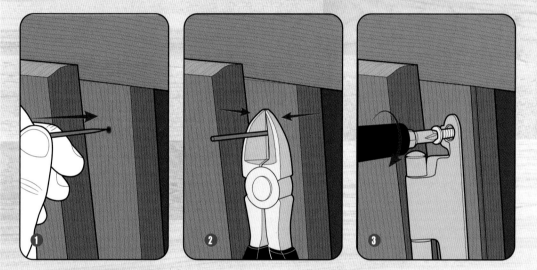

147 FIND PARTS ON THE WEB

Sometimes a simple repair won't be enough to fix the problem, and you need a replacement part. When it comes to furniture, those various parts—sofa legs, metal brackets, caster wheels—often have unique shapes that aren't so easy to find at the local hardware store. For a specific component, try looking online for furniture-part suppliers who offer a wide variety legs, clamps, adapters, mirror supports, daybed parts, sleeper sofa mechanisms and many other specialty items. In some cases, you can even email the supplier a picture and description of the item you need, and a product specialist will help you find the right part.

148 USE WOOD FILLER

Fixing larger dings and dents might require the use of wood filler. Also called wood putty or wood patch, this substance usually comes in two varieties: water-based and solvent-based. The product is perfect for restoring any damaged areas in wood to like-new condition. Solvent-based fillers have long been the mainstay in woodworking, but new water-based fillers perform as well as solvent-based.

Keep more than one color of filler on hand. If you're trying to match the wood closely, having a variety of colors allows you to mix up the right shade to match the item. Water-based and solvent-based filler are both easy to mix.

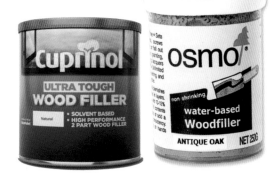

TYPE	PROS	CONS
Water Based	Free from solvent fumes and easy to handle. No acetone or turpentine. Won't dry out in the can. Easy to handle and clean up.	Not as many color choices. Dries more slowly.
Solvent Based	The choice of most professionals. Works better in larger areas. Larger selection of grain colors. Looks more natural.	Chemical smell. Difficult to dispose of. Can't work it in smaller spaces due to fumes.

149 HIDE SCRATCHES

Scratches are a drag, especially when visible in a nice piece of stained wood furniture. Use a permanent ink felt-tip marker to color the bare wood. If you don't have a set of colored markers handy, home centers and hardware stores usually stock felt-tipped stain pens made by popular wood-stain companies in colors that match the most popular furniture tones. This technique doesn't actually repair the scratch so much as hide it, but it's the quickest fix you'll find for concealing unsightly nicks and dings.

150 STEAM IT OUT

In the event that you dent or scratch finished wood of furniture, flooring, a picture frame, or such, you can often make a repair by dampening and heating the area to raise the wood grain. To do this, use a very small brush to apply a small amount of water to the scratch or dent. Then use a hot laundry iron covered with a soft cloth to heat the area, which should cause the fiber of the wood grain to swell and refill the dent.

151 TAKE CARE OF YOUR ROOF

An older roof may develop black streaks or stains, usually caused by algae. Chlorine bleach or sodium hydroxide solution that is applied using non-pressure methods will kill black algae and generally remove stains with the rinse phase, but this will not prevent the algae from returning in just a few months. These methods can also accelerate the corrosion of metal gutters, flashings, and fasteners;chlorine can also be harmful to surrounding plant life.

Try a cleaner designed for roofs, such as Defy Roof Cleaner, a blend of detergents and a nonpolluting chemical made of sand and soda ash. With spray-on/rinse-off application, this cleaner will remove algae without damaging the roof or harming any of the surrounding vegetation.

You can then follow up on cleaning with a stain-blocking agent to inhibit new growth, or install zinc strips at the roof line. When rainwater flows over the zinc, it generates zinc oxide, a harmless, invisible substance that coats the roof surface and inhibits the growth of fungus, moss, and algae. To install zinc strips, start at either end of the roof peak and then install a continuous row under the ridgeline. Apply roofing cement along the sealant edge and slide the strip under the shingle, leaving the lower half exposed to treat the rainwater.

152 DO AN INSPECTION

At least twice each year you should fully assess your property to make sure no major maintenance issues have gone unnoticed. Here are key spots to check.

LANDSCAPING Check that all irrigation paths are clear and unobstructed to divert runoff away from the house. Pull weeds and shovel away brush, leaves, or other organic matter that block drainage.

DRAINAGE Inspect all gutters and downspouts for drain blockage. A putty knife or even a spatula makes a good tool to scoop away the debris.

FOUNDATIONS Remove any dead wood near the house foundation—it's dinner to termites, luring them to your home. Even mulch (which termites can't eat) should be kept 12 to 14 inches away from the home to avoid providing the moist, dark environment they like.

PROTECT YOUR WOOD Dead leaves, downed limbs, and other organic matter can threaten any wood structures around the home. Shovels, gloves, rakes, and wheelbarrows will likely be the only tools you'll need to remove it. A powered blower can make quick work of clearing rubbish. Keep your decks and porches clean from leaves to reduce mold and mildew staining.

For similar reasons, you also need to clean the bottoms of deck posts and fences. Accumulated organic matter can retain water and transfer it to the wood, which may wick moisture into the end grain, contributing to rot and providing a pathway for pest infestation.

153 APPLY SOME PRESSURE

Pressure washers can work wonders on metal, masonry, and concrete. The PSI (pounds per square inch) rating of a power washer refers to the pressure that the washer unit is capable of producing. Pressure washers rated up to 2,200 PSI are generally used only for light-duty cleaning of mud and dirt from sidewalks and lawn equipment. Washers rated 2,200 to 3,000 are intended for more frequent use or larger jobs, such as cleaning siding.

Choosing the right nozzle can make a world of difference. Most manufacturers offer a range of options that attach to a washer wand with a standard quick-coupler. Some nozzles spray a fine fan of water for easy coverage when spraying a cleaning agent. When you need to blast away tough stains on concrete, switch to a zero-degree nozzle, which shoots a concentrated jet that can cut through stubborn dirt and discoloration.

154 SLUICE THE SIDING

Metal, concrete, and masonry siding can be cleaned fairly easily with a long-handle scrub brush or a pressure washer. Many of the recent spray-on bleach products are designed to clean on contact, requiring only a rinse coat to do the job without the work of scrubbing. (It never hurts to scrub, though.)

PRO TIP

CLEAN STUBBORN STAINS To tackle tough stains marring your brick masonry, try scrubbing with a wire brush. The harsh abrasion will often remove the stain by actually scraping away the material's surface.

155 WATCH YOUR WOOD

When wood is exposed to sunlight, it can damage the fibers, causing the surface to turn gray over time. When it's in the shade and exposed to moisture, mold and mildew can become a problem.

POWER CLEAN The most direct way to renew the appearance is to sand or pressure-wash the surface. However, sanding can be very difficult and time consuming for large areas, and pressure washing must be approached with caution, because too much pressure can damage the wood surface, removing the gray and green but causing the surface to fuzz or splinter. When using a power washer, limit your pressure to no more than 1,000 or 1,200 PSI, and carefully work in the direction of the grain—never against it.

SCRUB IT DOWN A less aggressive but effective method of cleaning is to scrub outdoor wood with a long-handled, stiff-bristle nylon brush. Some brushes even attach to a garden hose and feature nozzles that direct pressurized water right in front of the broom head for the most efficient scrubbing action.

Wood rot is the result of a type of fungal infection that destroys wood. It is as damaging as termite or other insect infestation, and it can wreak havoc on wooden windows. If the windows aren't maintained with paint, caulk, and glazing, then wood rot can take hold and completely ruin the casing.

However, in some cases you can catch the rot and make repairs before a complete window replacement is necessary. Try Durham's Water Putty, a powder product that has been around more than 80 years. The powder is mixed with water on site and can be used to repair damaged wood if applied properly. The putty is also easy to use and easy to clean up.

STEP 1 Remove damaged material and wood rot with a screwdriver, chisel, shop vac, and so on.

STEP 2 In a mixing container, add a little water at a time to the powder and then stir with a paint stick until you achieve a consistency similar to thick pancake batter.

STEP 3 Apply the product in layers up ¼ inch thick at a time. Allow each application to dry before adding more product.

STEP 4 Once the damaged area is completely filled and dried, sand the area smooth. It is also important to finish the repair by sealing it with a waterproofing product such as exterior primer and paint.

157 PERFORM SURGERY

In some cases, the best solution may be to cut out the damaged section of wood, carefully cut a replacement piece of pressure-treated wood to the same shape and dimensions, and then glue the piece into the window casing with a high-quality, exterior-grade adhesive that accepts paint. An oscillating multi-tool equipped with a plunge blade is an excellent device for cutting out the problem area.

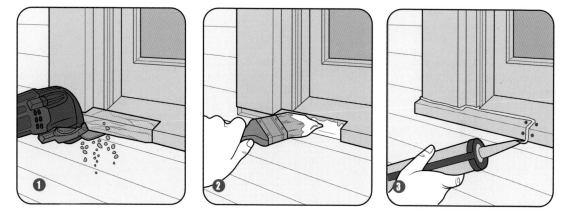

STEP 1 Remove all loose wood, dust, and debris. A clean work area will mean clean repairs as well.

STEP 2 Coat all sides of the replacement piece of wood—and do the same with the damaged area—using an exterior primer before fastening in place, in order to add an extra measure of moisture protection.

STEP 3 After gluing and nailing or screwing in the replacement piece, fill every holes and seam with exterior-grade wood putty, and then sand the joints smooth. Apply paintable waterproof sealant, primer, and matching paint to complete the repair. For extra protection, coat all sides of the wood replacement with exterior primer/paint before installing.

158 USE TWO-PART EPOXY

Another great fix for painted window casements relies on a two-part polyurethane-based wood repair filler. It's sold as a kit including a resin and hardener, which are mixed together to create a light tan epoxy. The filler is thin enough to fit into small gaps and cracks but thick enough that you can mold it. And, unlike some other wood fillers, it does not shrink or crack. The downside to the epoxy is that it's very sticky, which will make it tricky to work with and difficult to clean up. However, the upside is that the material can be molded into a three-dimensional wood replacement that can be cut or routed into shape. If you need to replace a damaged sill corner or chipped molding profile, you can form the repair from the epoxy and cut the final shape once it's dry.

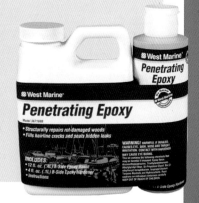

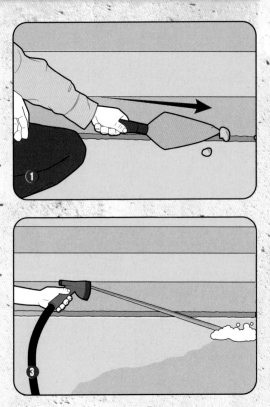

To patch up larger holes or cracks, you can try Vinyl Concrete Patcher, a self-bonding mix that's made for repairing any broken, chipped, or loose concrete and masonry, as well as filling cracks up to 2 inches deep. The material is available in tubs or a 40-pound bag. It will adhere to all properly cleaned surfaces and can be troweled to a feather edge of $\frac{1}{16}$ inch.

STEP 1 Chisel away cracked or crumbled materials, squaring off the edges. Even better yet, you can undercut the edges with a chisel and hammer.

STEP 2 Use a wire brush to scrape away crumbling materials and to roughen the surface if it has been finished smooth. The repair product should not be applied over painted surfaces. Clean away all debris and rinse with water.

STEP 3 Before application, dampen the area with clean water.

STEP 4 Apply the mix with a trowel, using heavy trowel pressure to force it into the crack. Overfill it slightly and then trowel it smooth to match with the surrounding concrete. If the cracks are deep it may be necessary to apply in a series of $\frac{1}{4}$-inch-deep layers, allowing the mix to dry for 2 hours between layers. Clean the tools immediately afterward with water.

160 TAKE THE TUBE

Some concrete crack-repair products fit into a caulk gun and are ready to apply. Sashco's Slab concrete crack repair caulk offers good adhesion and elasticity for a long-lasting fix. The product's water-based formula is also easy to apply and clean up. Just as with caulk, fill the crack level with the product and smooth the top of the bead. The formula even offers a heavily textured repair that matches the sand texture in the concrete. When used with a foam backer rod, the caulk will adhere to joints up to 3 inches wide.

A number of patching products come in easy-to-use squeeze tubes, such as Blacktop Crack, used for repairing cracks in asphalt driveways.

161 CARE FOR CONCRETE

Concrete is a very durable building material and can also be aesthetically pleasing. Over time, though, concrete can deteriorate. Most repair projects are fairly simple using some of the specially formulated patch and repair products available these days.

Various special concrete repair products are user-friendly and have distinct traits such as fast setting times, a high final strength, or an increased degree of resistance to cracking and chipping.

For most repairs you'll need a few tools: a cold chisel, ball-peen hammer or 8-pound sledge for larger areas, protective goggles, and a pair of gloves. Use a brush and broom for cleaning up, and a pointed trowel for application. If you're resurfacing steps and slabs, then you'll need an edger too. You may also need lumber for forming major repairs. Prep the repair area properly before applying the concrete product. Remove all cracked and crumbling areas. For larger areas, use a sledge and cold chisel to break away thin or loose edges. Sweep, vacuum, or hose away dirt and debris down to a solid base.

162 GO TO REFORM SCHOOL

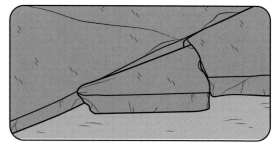

Larger repair jobs, such as broken corners or slabs of walkways, usually require re-forming. The first step is to remove the broken area down to the gravel fill. If the gravel fill has deteriorated, dig down a couple of inches below ground level and add a new gravel base. Use 2x4 or other material to re-form the area. The tops of the form boards should be even with the top edges of the adjoining concrete surface. Forms should be level and should follow the natural grade. Stakes should be driven into the ground to support the forms every 4 feet. They should also be cut off even with the top of the forms.

Packaged, ready-mix concrete can be used. Mix the concrete product, then trowel or shovel it into the form. Roughly smooth it up with a trowel, then cut around any forms with an edger. Allow the concrete to stiffen slightly until all water has evaporated from the surface. Once the surface turns dull, smooth and compact the concrete with a trowel. Keep the trowel pressed firmly down on the surface and flat. Use the edging tool around the edges to smooth them up. For a textured, nonskid surface, use a wood float or broom for finishing.

Cover the repair with a plastic sheet, or periodically spray with a garden hose to keep the concrete damp for 5 to 7 days, which helps the hardening, or curing, process. Concrete that has been moist-cured will be approximately 50 percent stronger than that exposed to dry air.

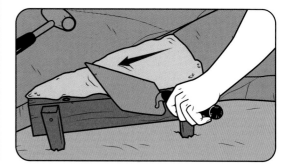

163 TREAT YOURSELF

You will be sadly disappointed in your outdoor construction project if you try to build it using any manner of wood products that were not meant for exterior use—your work will more than likely end up swelling, twisting, rotting, hosting a colony of insects, or any combination of these various tragic outcomes in a very short amount of time.

For many, if not most, outdoor projects, you will be looking at pressure-treated wood, which has been infused with various chemicals that help protect it from termites and other insects, as well as fungal decay.

Often made from pine or fir, treated lumber has a natural appearance, and its resistance to termites and rot is a major advantage for outdoor projects. Better yet, it is a plentiful and renewable resource, and is also usually the most economical choice available.

In addition, it can support more weight and span longer distances than cedar, redwood, or other woods. For this reason, many outdoor structures, such as decks, are framed with and supported by treated lumber, even if a different type of wood or other material is used for the finished surfaces.

Treated wood can be found in a variety of lumber grades, from knot-free, close-grain grades to lower grades that have more knots, splits, and wane (missing corners of the wood where the bark once existed). You can find the grade designation stamped on each piece of wood.

Generally, the higher the lumber grade, the higher the cost. Select the right board by one of three categories, which should be indicated prominently on the product label. They are as follows below:

ABOVEGROUND USE Best for decking, fences, and rails.

GROUND-CONTACT USE Great for posts, beams, and joists.

BELOW-GRADE Works for support posts that are partially buried below grade and for permanent wood foundations and planters.

164 TRY STURDY SOFTWOODS

For applications that don't require pressure-treated woods, or if you want to minimize the chemicals you're using, there are a good number of attractive hardwoods used for outdoor projects that possess some natural protection against insects and other damaging factors. Here are some of your options.

❶ WESTERN RED CEDAR This wood's natural fibers contain natural compounds that make it naturally insect- and moisture-resistant without chemical treatments. Plus, the even, consistent grain and low density make cedar less likely to swell, warp, cup, and twist than other woods. As a result, it lies flat and straight. Cedar is also free of the pitch and resin found in other softwoods—a quality that makes it ideal for a fairly wide range of finishes, whether you choose a lightly tinted semi-transparent stain or a two-coat solid-color finish.

❷ REDWOOD Not only is redwood strong and

beautiful, it is naturally resistant to insects, rot, and decay; it can also withstand high heat and pressure. It shrinks and swells less than other woods when exposed to water, which means that it's less likely to warp, split, or check (crack parallel to the grain), making it highly durable for building. It is one of the most pliable softwood species, making it easy to saw, nail, and drill. Redwood is also lightweight and has little to no pitch or resins. It is extremely easy to paint, stain, and glue, and a redwood deck can be restored repeatedly with minimal effort and cost.

❸ CYPRESS While actually a softwood, cypress grows alongside hardwoods and is usually grouped with them in manufacturing. Its natural durability is a great benefit for exterior applications. Cypress generates cypressene—its own preservative oil—which makes its heartwood naturally resistant to insects, decay, and chemical corrosion. These inherent strengths make the wood an ideal choice for long-wearing outdoor projects such as fences, decks, docks, and siding.

165 SIZE IT UP

Check local building codes for specific minimum lumber sizes required in your area. Depending on the size of the structure, support posts are usually made from 6x6 or 8x8 beams. Railing systems require 4x4 posts. Deck boards are often sold in 4x6-inch sizes, or you can use 2x6 lumber. Avoid using any boards wider than 2x8 for the flooring because of their tendency to cup. The length of deck boards will depend on the structure's design, and in some cases you can purchase boards long enough to install over the joists with no end joints between them. The sizes of joists and beams will depend on the size and joist span of the structure.

166 GO EXOTIC

Some lumberyards have begun specializing in bringing exotic woods to the market, such as mahogany ❶, and less familiar rainforest hardwoods such as ipe ❷ and Pau-Lope ❸. These unusual woods can offer a rare beauty, as well as hardness and durability that far exceed that of conventional lumber. The durability is a great advantage for outdoor projects but can also present a variety of challenges. Typically, these types of woods are very dense, making it difficult for stains to be absorbed. Their high amount of natural oils also make them resistant to penetration and require special steps for finish application. And of course, "exotic" also means you can expect to pay premium prices.

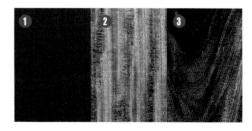

You should give your deck a full close annual inspection and fix anything you find. This will ensure years of function and beauty outdoors.

① CHECK THE BOARDS Look out for damage such as splitting, warping, and major checking. Replace entire boards if you should find any severe deterioration.

② TIGHTEN UP Make sure no fasteners are coming loose. A good way to do this is to walk the entire deck, back and forth along the joists, while being alert for any weakness or instability. Check for nails that have lifted or screws that show signs of significant weakening. Replace fasteners with any significant rust or corrosion, because they can deteriorate the surrounding wood. Replace with quality decking screws or spiral/rink-shank nails.

③ PUSH IT Inspect railings and banisters by pushing them to make sure there is no give.

④ FLASH IT Flashing is a metal or plastic guard that directs water out and away from sensitive areas that are prone to holding moisture and therefore being weakened. A piece of properly installed deck flashing should be somewhat L-shaped. One leg of the L runs up behind the siding, the other over the top of the ledger board. Be sure that the flashing at the ledger board is still sound, and be prepared to replace it if necessary. Also, make sure the proper ledger fasteners are used. Acceptable fasteners include through-bolts, ½-inch galvanized lag screws, or heavy-duty structural screws—but not nails.

⑤ CHECK CONNECTIONS Check the framing connections. Where the joists meet the ledger board there should be metal hardware (joist hangers). Nails driven at an angle ("toe-nails") are not a sufficient structural connection. Bolts in post-to-beam connections should be ½-inch in diameter and galvanized.

⑥ STEP UP Make sure stairs are of proper rise (height) and run (depth). The combined rise and run of a code-approved stair should be no more than 17 inches: ideally 7-inch rise, 10-inch run.

⑦ BRACE YOURSELF The posts, beams, and angle bracing should be the appropriate size and spaced properly. Your local building inspector can to tell you what's the expected standard where you live. Generally speaking, deck posts should be a minimum 6x6 and spaced 6 feet on center.

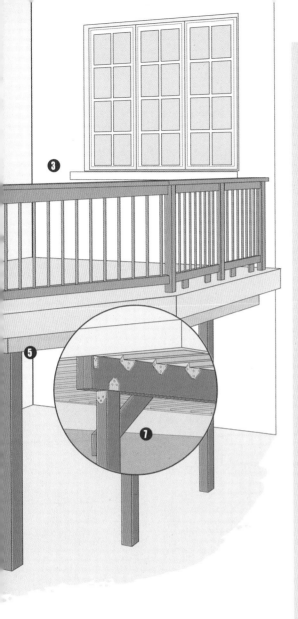

168 KEEP IT SPARKLING

With regular maintenance, the weathered look of decks usually can be revived with the application of the right deck cleaner. Even if your deck is several years old, it's easy to restore the original color and beauty of the wood by applying a cleaning solution and wood brightener. (Follow the manufacturer's guidelines for proper use and to make sure you're using the right product for your deck's wood species.)

CLEAN IT UP Deck cleaners and restorers generally fall into one of three categories—chlorine bleaches, oxygen bleaches, or oxalic acid-based formulas. Chlorine bleaches are especially effective at killing mold or mildew spores—a common cause of discoloration and staining. Oxygen bleaches are effective at removing mildew stains and weathered gray residue from sunlight-degraded wood decks. Oxalic acid products are useful brighteners for a wood deck but not very effective for removing mildew.

CONTROL MILDEW If you do have a mildew problem, treat your deck using an oxygen or chlorine bleach and water solution (typically 1:3, bleach to water) and follow up by using an oxalic acid-based product to brighten the wood color. Products with oxalic acid and bleach are also available. They will work on deep stains, mold, and mildew, but these are commercial-grade products and should be handled very carefully (pre-rinse and/or cover plants, and shield siding and doors, to protect finish). Mold and mildew may require an additional round of scrubbing and application of both a bleach/water solution and oxalic acid.

PRO TIP

KEEP THE PRESSURE OFF Should you use a pressure washer to clean your deck? You can, but first you should check the industry association website of the wood species (pine, redwood, cedar) to determine if power-washing is recommended. Always use as low a pressure as possible, and try to never spray closer than 12 inches to the deck.

WEEKEND
PROJECTS

GET IT DONE BY MONDAY

They call you a "weekend warrior" because you're not only fiercely fighting the many obstacles of a home improvement project, you're battling time as well.

The clock is ticking, and the job has got to be completed because Monday morning will be here soon, and then you'll have a different job to do (sheesh). But you take a stand. You stare the clock in the face with steely eyes and you spit on the ground to show you have no fear, because you're a warrior. On the weekend.

You've gathered your tools, you've mastered the quick fix and you're ready to conquer new frontiers. Well, now is the time to study up, because as your home projects grow more complex you'll find a greater likelihood for error.

And errors aren't your style.

But you're up to the challenge. Power tools are your weapons, and your strategy is sketched on notepad with a lot of chicken-scratch measurements. The shabby door that needs to go; you've got a replacement. The room that needs to be painted; you've got it covered. Need to pour a concrete slab? No sweat (well, maybe a little). Your living room and connecting hallway will soon be lined with beautiful crown molding, and maybe even a chair rail.

With the right supplies and a little know-how, you can knock out these projects and more. Nobody's going to stop you, and neither are the time constraints. Because this is the weekend. This is your home. And you're at war.

Paint sprayers can speed up the job and get into all the cracks and crevices that are hard to reach with brushes or rollers. This is especially important when working with rough surfaces such as brick or stucco. Here are some options.

1 HANDHELD For small to mid-size jobs, an electric handheld sprayer can do the work four times as fast as a brush, with easy cleanup. Some of the latest models offer adjustable spray patterns, variable speeds, and flexible suction tubes that let you spray at any angle.

2 HVLP High Volume/Low Pressure technology can put a very fine finish on small to medium jobs. The low pressure condenses the paint for controlled coverage with minimal overspray, and the sprayer easily disassembles for fast cleanup. This type works best with stains, sealers, urethanes, varnishes, lacquers, or thinned paints.

3 AIRLESS For both large jobs and small, applying paint with an airless sprayer is a quick and efficient method that also has the advantage of offering up a consistent, uniform coverage on a range of textures. The downside is that the cleanup for larger-volume models can be arduous and time-consuming. Some newer airless sprayers, however, have a pump and paint cup built into the spray gun, which offers less paint capacity but easier cleanup.

4 TEXTURE For adding texture to walls or ceilings, the right tool for the job is called a texture sprayer, or "hopper gun," which utilizes a hopper set above the nozzle to load the material (for example, drywall compound or popcorn texture). Simply fill the hopper and select your spray nozzle depending on the texture you desire.

170 PICK THE RIGHT PAINT

You're at the paint store, faced with endless choices. What do you do? Your first decision is based on what you're painting—an inside or outside surface. You don't want to use the wrong paint here, as exterior paints often have a fungicide or UV blocker to give better outdoor performance, but these chemicals may pose adverse health effects to the home's occupants when used indoors, where an interior-grade paint would be a better choice.

Next think about the substrate—that is, what material you're applying the paint to. Wood and drywall are easy to paint, but some plastic materials, metal, concrete, and masonry might require special primers and paints to ensure the best adhesion. Furthermore, the choice of paint color can impact the material's performance. For example, vinyl siding will warp from heat buildup, so very dark colors are not recommended. As a general rule, don't paint vinyl siding or trim any darker than the color of the original siding. (Make sure your paint is formulated to stick to vinyl siding, considering vinyl's tendency to greatly expand and contract. Recent advances in paint composition offer new options that work well on vinyl.)

OIL-BASED PAINTS Oil-based paints are usually composed of pigments dissolved into a mineral spirit such as paint thinner. These also require mineral spirits for cleanup and take longer to dry, but the trade-off is a harder finish.

LATEX-BASED PAINTS An emulsion suspended in water, these products typically will dry faster and are easier to clean up, requiring only water. Today's improved latex products can be used in nearly all applications that traditionally called for an oil-based paint.

ENAMEL A broad classification for any finishing materials that dry to a smooth finish; the term once referred only to oil-base coatings, but some new latex products are also referred to as enamel paints.

Whatever you choose, refer to the manufacturer's recommendations for specific usage instructions.

PRO TIP

TONE IT DOWN If you're planning a bold color for a big project, consider going a couple of shades lighter. Viewing colors on a small paint swatch can create a different visual impact than seeing them on the walls of a room. Large surfaces intensify color, and you might end up with a louder color than you intended.

171 GET THE RIGHT SHEEN

How glossy do you want to go? A few things to consider in the paint aisle.

FLAT PAINTS These pigments can conceal imperfections in walls and other surfaces, making them a good choice for ceilings and rooms that aren't exposed to much moisture or heavy soiling (bedrooms, home offices, and living rooms).

HIGH GLOSS These paints tend to highlight imperfections in walls and woodwork, but they are durable, stain-resistant, and much easier to clean than paints with less gloss. A high-gloss sheen is ideal for baseboards, windows, moldings, and playrooms.

SEMI-GLOSS A compromise between the two extremes, this option provides some of the benefits of each. Semi-gloss can be used on the walls and cabinets of bathrooms and kitchens. Additional sheens include eggshell and satin, which are less shiny than semi-gloss paints. They highlight nicks and imperfections less, but since they have a little gloss, they're still easier to clean than flat paints.

172 FILL A HOLE

Over time, walls are often damaged from accidental impact, and cracks can also develop from the house settling. Pictures and artwork are rearranged to update the interior décor, leaving behind fastener holes. Minor drywall damage can be easily repaired with a putty knife and vinyl spackling or lightweight joint compound. Clean the holes and recess the edges below the wall surface with the blunt handle of a putty knife. Use the blade of the knife to fill the hole with repair compound flush with the wall. Allow to dry overnight and reapply as needed if any shrinking has occurred. Lightly sand smooth if necessary. Coat the repair with two coats of primer before painting. Some of the new spackling pastes are formulated with primer already in the product, which eliminates the extra step.

For any larger holes, you can try an aluminum screen patch sold at hardware stores in 4-, 6-, and 8-inch sizes. Use one that is larger than the damaged area on all sides by at least an inch. Trowel on the first coat of drywall compound so the screen is barely visible, then allow to dry overnight. Follow with a wider coat of compound, feathering the edges smooth 8 to 12 inches outside the patch. Allow to dry, then add a third coat, sanding as needed to blend the repair with the surrounding wall.

173 MAKE A PANEL PATCH

For big repairs where you need to replace a sizable section of drywall (for example, from water or mold damage), try using a panel patch.

First, cut out a rectangular area of drywall around the damaged area, aligning its edges along the center of the wall studs **1**. This should give ¾-inch of solid nailing surface on two edges of the repair (plus the 2x floor plate if the repair extends to the floor). To provide a nailing surface at the unsupported edges of the hole, toe-nail 2x blocking between the studs.

Next, measure and cut a repair panel slightly smaller than the hole and fasten it in place by driving drywall nails through the panel and into the solid framing **2**. Apply fiberglass tape to the seams and finish the repair by filling up the nail holes and finishing all joints with successive applications of compound **3**.

174 REPAIR PLASTER

For plaster repairs, you can use a powder-based product called plaster patch, which has adhesives that bond to the existing plaster. Before applying the first coat, remove any loose plaster and undercut the edges of the hole as it approaches the wood lath to better anchor the patching. Prepare the damaged area by soaking with water, then mix the patch product smooth. Apply the first coat with a putty knife, in a thin layer (⅛ to ¼ inch). Score the wet compound with a nail for better adhesion of the second coat. Allow to dry completely to avoid cracking, and apply the next coat in a similar manner. Continue until the hole is filled, feathering the edges of the final coat. Sand lightly to smooth the patch.

175 BATTEN DOWN

A batten patch is great for larger repairs or for working on your ceiling, where gravity tugs at the repair before the mud sets. The key to this repair is to install battens behind the drywall, as fastening backers. For these battens, use thin strips of 1x lumber or thick paint mixing sticks (thin ones will split).

YOU'LL NEED: Drywall • Setting compound • Drywall tape • Cordless drill/driver • Screws • A wood-cutting saw (possibly)

STEP 1 First square up the hole as necessary.

STEP 2 Cut a couple of battens at least 2 inches larger than the hole. Work a batten into it and position the ends along the back of the drywall. With a firm grip on the batten, grab your drill and drive a drywall screw through the wall into the end of the batten. Drive the screws into the ends of each of the battens, pulling them snug against the rear side of the drywall and creating a sturdy wooden nailing surface behind the damaged area.

STEP 3 Measure and cut the repair section of drywall to slightly smaller than the hole, then install it. Fasten with drywall screws into the wood battens. Apply fiberglass mesh tape to the edges of the hole. Trowel on successive coats of compound, spreading the mud, feathering the edges smooth, and sanding as needed.

176 BITE THE BULLET

The bullet patch is an easy option for large holes. Here's how to use it.

STEP 1 Clean out the hole, then give it a rectangular shape using a utility knife or drywall saw.

STEP 2 Cut a blank of drywall bigger than the hole. Expose a "plug" of drywall ¼-inch smaller than the hole by scoring the back of the blank in a tic-tac-toe pattern of cross-cuts. You should cut through the core of the drywall, but not the paper face. Carefully peel the gypsum (chalky, white material) away from the paper. Be sure to leave the paper flange surrounding the plug intact, to serve as integrated tape when you mud it.

STEP 3 Apply a thin coat of mud to the wall around the hole, then place the patch on the wall and lightly press the paper into the wet compound with your fingertips. Don't press on the plug directly.

STEP 4 Apply a small amount of drywall compound to lubricate the edge of a 6-inch putty knife, and press it over the paper to squeeze the mud out at the edges. A couple of passes ensures a tight bond. Then, wipe a light feather-coat on the front of the paper and smooth down all rough spots.

STEP 5 Let the first coat dry, then apply the second with a 10-inch broad knife, spreading the compound and feathering the edges to blend with the wall.

STEP 6 After the second coat dries, lightly sand with 100-grit abrasive and apply a third coat of compound as necessary.

177 GET READY FOR PRIME TIME

Starting with a good primer will ensure the truest color for your top coat, no matter the surface you're working with—walls, cabinetry, or trim. Beyond the truer color, primer offers stain- and odor-blocking properties and also provides a more enduring top-coat finish. If you've done any drywall patches, it's essential that you prime before painting.

One thing to consider is that priming will never hurt anything. If in doubt, prime it. And it definitely helps to use a primer if you're painting a lighter color over a darker one. For darks over lights, you can use a tinted primer to reduce the number of topcoats you'll need to achieve the desired color.

178 BRUSH IT RIGHT

To load a brush, dip it only 1 to 2 inches into the paint. Gently tap the brush against the side of the container, first one side, then the other. The extra paint will stay in the container and leave you with a loaded brush for field painting or cutting in.

"Cutting in" is the art of drawing a straight line to separate two colors using only a paint brush— no masking tape or other aid. When cutting in, always keep a fully loaded brush. Using it parallel to the area to be cut, let the brush open up into a semi oval and then bring it into the line you are cutting. Follow the line until the paint begins to break up. Repeat this procedure, working into the previously painted area.

If you find cutting in free-handed too difficult to maintain a crisp line, simply mask off the lines with painter's tape. However, avoid pushing paint beneath the tape with the brush, which can cause the paint lines to bleed.

Also, don't paint by dipping the paintbrush right into the can. It will pick up debris that makes its way back into the source can and ends up creating specks and lumps in the paint. In addition, the air interacting with the paint in the can will dry it prematurely. Instead, load the paint into a separate lightweight container, working with a ½-inch pour of paint. Refresh the paint often to keep it in a fluid state.

179 BE A HIGH ROLLER

Rollers get the job done quickly with a consistent surface texture. Here's how to do it right. Always start with a fresh roller cover—worn out ones may fray and leave debris in your paint. Have a stash of extra covers on hand in case you need to replace one.

PRECONDITION This often overlooked step is crucial to proper performance. Every synthetic cover requires some form of preconditioning. Before use in latex paints, rinse the cover under running water, then spin it to remove excess water. Before using oil-based paints, the cover should be lubricated in the solvent used to thin out the paint. Any mohair covers should also be preconditioned in the solvent used for paint thinning. (Lambskin roller covers have natural oils and don't require any preconditioning.)

PAINT Fill the paint tray no more than one-third of the way. Load the entire surface of your roller cover with paint, rolling it slowly down the tray, then back several times so the cover absorbs. Use the tray's grid to prevent any overloading. When painting walls, start at the top and work downward. Roll a large "W" in a space about 3 by 3 feet. Then fill in between the gaps, blending

into your initial strokes. Always work from the unpainted into the painted surface. Repeat this process when you start a new area.

After your project, clean all rollers, brushes, and related paint equipment immediately and store in a clean, dry place.

180 TAPE AND PROTECT

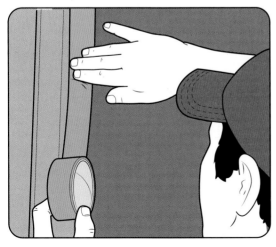

While doing priming and painting, DIYers can use painter's tape to mask off all areas where one color meets another, such as window or door trim, accent walls, etc. When applying tape, use a roller or putty knife to burnish it to the surface you're masking for the best seal. Always remove the tape right after you've finished painting, to prevent paint from bridging over the tape and peeling when you remove it, thus messing up the crisp paint lines.

Cover up everything you don't want painted with a plastic or canvas drop cloth, and pass on the cheapest, thinnest plastic sheets. The thicker the plastic sheets, the more durable they will be and the better they will remain in place without wadding up beneath your feet and exposing the floor or furniture. If you're painting a large room, cover the entire floor with thick plastic and seal the seams with tape.

Preparing a surface before applying a topcoat is the first critical phase of any paint project. Exterior jobs require extra steps to battle outdoor exposure. Paint is designed to form a film, so it peels if it can't adhere to a surface. It does, however, stick well to substrates that don't shift beneath the paint. Just about any metal is an excellent substrate. Aluminum siding is a good example; paint can last for years on aluminum. Wood and other "moving" surfaces that contract or expand due to moisture or temperature change may require some extra preparatory steps to minimize peeling.

CHECK THE WEATHER Weather conditions can have a great impact on how well paint holds up. The worst conditions are extreme heat or cold. The paint has to chemically bond to the surface that it is covering, and this bonding will only occur if the solvent (water or mineral spirits) in the paint is evaporating at a slow or medium pace. Plan your painting days for cooler temperatures and try to paint any areas after direct sunlight has left them for the day.

CLEAN WELL Before priming, make sure the exterior surface of your material is free of dirt, grease, mold,

mildew, or any other debris. Remove any loosened, peeling paint already present. Flat putty knives or "pull" scrapers work well for this.

SAND IT Some substrates can be sanded smooth where the old paint meets the bare surface. For best paint adhesion on any glossy surfaces, scuff-sand the surface before painting. But keep in mind, there are some situations where sanding won't always be the best idea. Some older exterior house paints contain lead, and sanding off this type of paint will end up creating toxic lead dust.

WASH UP Your next step is to wash off the surface. Regular liquid dish soap may work fine, although it does produce a lot of suds. You may opt for a non-soapy detergent such as trisodium phosphate (TSP) to get rid of dirt and grease. Clean the entire surface with a sponge or scrub brush. If any mold or mildew is present, use a mildew-removing solution. Quickly rinse and allow the surface to dry thoroughly before priming. Allow porous surfaces such as wood or brick to dry for a minimum of two days before continuing.

182 SPIFF UP SIDING

To prepare aluminum siding, scrub it with detergent, rinse thoroughly, and let it dry for several days. Pressure washers work well for this job. Remove all mildew and residual chalk from the old finish; paint will not stick to a chalky surface. Replace any loose caulk. To prime aluminum siding, use a thinned metal priming paint. Try a mixture of one pint of paint thinner to one gallon of high-quality oil-based primer. Consider having the primer tinted to half the strength of the color of your finish paint for easier top-coating.

Clean vinyl siding the same way as well. An oxygen bleach solution does a good job of removing mildew from vinyl and won't harm the vinyl or the plants in your yard. Priming vinyl is not necessary, but do remove any rust from metal areas and coat those with a good rust-inhibitive primer.

183 PAINT CONCRETE FLOORS

Before you start the whole process of painting your concrete floor, you'll want to test to be sure you don't have any moisture issues in the area, because if you do, the concrete won't take paint properly, and your effort will be wasted.

To test this easily, just tape a 2-foot-square piece of plastic to the floor and wait 48 hours. If after that period you see discoloration or moisture under the plastic, skip painting.

Otherwise, you can clean the floor off with a degreaser and then roughen it using a wire brush and an acid-based solution (a good example is one part each hydrochloric acid and water) to help the paint bond to the concrete. Rinse your floor thoroughly, let it dry for two to three days, and then paint.

184 PREP METALS

Start by cleaning away any corrosion with a wire brush and sandpaper. Metal should be primed on the same day it is cleaned. Oil- or alkyd-based metal primers that contain high quantities of rust-inhibitive pigments give the best results when priming rusty steel.

Unfinished galvanized metal or aluminum should be wiped down thoroughly using a degreasing cleaner, then rinsed off and dried. Lots of both water- and oil-based paints work well for metals, but be sure to use the paints that are compatible with your primer. Most manufacturers indicate what type of primer should be used for a particular finish coat, and vice versa.

Special paints designed to stand up to high temperatures are available for painting central heating pipes and radiators.

185 WORK WITH WOOD

Outdoor wood can be the toughest material to paint. Its tendency to expand and contract can take a toll on the strongest of paints. With paint as its only line of defense, if any exposed edges or seams aren't painted, severe wood rot can develop within just a few years. Every wood surface must be primed first, using an exterior wood primer.

PREP IT Paint will adhere well to wood if all the wood has been primed before installation. Sealing the wood completely requires painting and priming all cut edges as well as the board faces. The cut ends are often where end grain is exposed; this is where it is easiest for water to enter the wood. Absorbed water can migrate 5 or 6 inches in from the end of the board, which is why you see the edges or bottom portions of trim boards flake.

SEAL IT Use exterior-grade caulk to seal the end grain. Wipe the caulk with a moist sponge as soon as it has been applied to produce a clean, smooth joint. If painting siding, caulk all joints between the siding and trim boards, but do not caulk the bottom edge of clapboard siding. (The small crack on this type of siding allows it to move and allows vapor to escape.) Apply a rust-inhibitive primer to any exposed nails. Countersink the nails and fill the holes with exterior spackling compound.

PRIME IT Oil-based primer is a great choice for wood projects because it penetrates deeply into wood fiber. This seals wood such as cedar and redwood that can produce "bleed" stains when coated with water-based products.

PAINT IT To accommodate for the movement of wood, it helps to use paint with some built-in flexibility. Acrylic resins (paint glue) offer the greatest amount of flexibility. These paints will resist becoming brittle like older oil-based paints, and they can also withstand many years of substrate movement.

Adding texture to a wall is a popular way to add character to a room. Knockdown texture is a popular option that has an aged, stucco-like appearance. It's sprayed onto a primed surface with a hopper gun and, after the texture has completely dried, coated with white-pigmented shellac primer and a satin or semi-gloss finish coat.

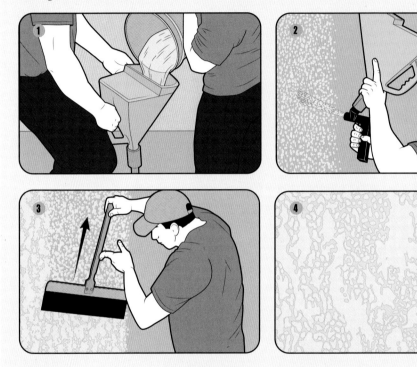

STEP 1 Load the hopper gun with powder-based drywall compound mixed to a consistency similar to pancake batter (you can also employ a special texture compound that's formulated to inhibit mold growth).

STEP 2 Test your spray pattern on scrap material until the mud mix is at the consistency you want. Different nozzles and adjustable tips enable you to use a variety of spray techniques. Adjusting the air compressor's output pressure may also help fine-tune the spray.

STEP 3 Spray the texturing compound onto the wall, moving over it in big, even strokes to cover the entire surface from the top to bottom with a fairly consistent amount of splatter. The largest dollops of the compound should each be about the size of a penny.

STEP 4 Now it's time for you to "knock down" the sprayed dollops. You'll need a broad knife or large drywall trowel. If you're not skilled with a trowel, use one that has rounded corners (or grind them yourself) to keep from damaging the wall surface. After the compound sets for 15 to 30 minutes and becomes tacky (but not completely dry), hold the trowel at a very shallow, flat angle and work it from top to bottom, bottom to top, in vertical strokes over the dollops of compound. The objective here is not to smear or displace the dollops, but to remove any peaks. The vertical motion of the trowel will pull the mud upward and downward, thus giving the wall that rough, textured finish.

STEP 5 Allow the texture to dry completely (for at least 24 hours), then apply a shellac primer and paint with your color of preference.

187 APPLY FAUX FINISHES

Faux finish techniques can add depth and character to the interior décor. Paints blended with complementary colors and glazes can create artistic effects and textures to distinguish the look from standard paint jobs. Begin with a non-porous base coat of acrylic eggshell or satin finish paint. The finish paint will be your base color, and most effects are created by applying a translucent glaze of a different color over the base (although some effects require solid colors).

The glaze modifies the appearance of the base coat by partly concealing it with a translucent filter. The glazing technique can be "positive" or "negative." With a positive technique, you methodically add glaze to the wall to enhance the décor of the base coat. With a negative technique, you cover the base coat with glaze and then use a tool such as a sponge or rag to remove it, revealing the base color beneath.

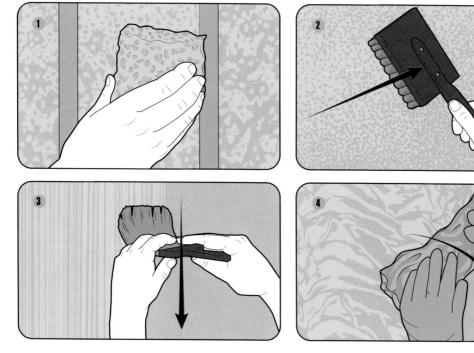

1 SPONGING This positive technique utilizes a sea sponge to apply two to three accent colors to a base coat for casual to elegant looks. Sponging can create a soft, mottled look on anything from walls to trim, and even furniture.

2 STIPPLING Another technique similar to sponging uses a special brush to create the pattern. Pounce the brush over the base coat lightly, using just the tips of the brush, to apply the translucent color. The brush should be continually rotated to develop a random pattern with no visible square edges.

3 DRAGGING This popular negative technique is great for both walls and furniture pieces that have large flat surfaces. First apply the glaze with a roller, and then create the pattern by pulling a special, dry "dragging brush" downward through the wet glaze, removing streaks of glaze to reveal the base coat.

4 RAG ROLLING A positive or negative technique, rag rolling creates dramatic patterns through either rolling on or rolling off the glaze. In both techniques a ragging cloth, roller, or pad is used to create the effect. To roll on, apply the glaze to the rag, twist it into a cylindrical shape, and then roll it across the surface to create the pattern. To roll off, apply the glaze with a roller, and then dampen the rag with water, roll it into a cylindrical shape and roll it over the wet glaze to remove some of the top color.

188 KNOW TRIM BASICS

Trimming out a room is a hot project for a DIY homeowner who wants to dramatically accent otherwise lackluster ceilings, walls, or windows. Along with traditional baseboards, chair rails, crown moldings, and casings, a homeowner can also consider options such as fireplace mantels, cornices, medallions, and more. Here are some terms you should know before you start.

BASEBOARD MOLDING This border of trim decoration hides gaps and imperfections at the floor-to-ceiling transition. Various sizes and profiles are available. The baseboards are generally attached to the wall studs, footplate, and wallboard with finish nails.

CHAIR RAILS This horizontal molding type is usually placed above wainscoting or used to divide two wall colors. Usually set near the height of chairs, its original purpose was to protect the wall from the scuffing of chair backs, but today it's commonly used as a decorative element.

CROWN MOLDING This option covers the transition point between the wall and ceiling. Available in many different shapes and sizes, it can be installed as a simple trim profile or combined with other pieces of molding to produce elaborate architectural displays.

CASING The trim that surrounds windows or doors is available in options ranging from simple craftsman style trim to multi-piece moldings and crossheads for a more elegant appearance to the frame.

189 FINISH THE ROOM

When coping the molding, follow the installation sequence shown here for the best appearance. Begin on the wall that is opposite the door and install a piece that is square at both ends, flush between the two adjacent walls. This way, anyone walking into the room sees the best side of the joints. On the two adjacent or "side" walls, cope the joints where they meet the installed molding, but cut the opposite ends square and butt them against the "door wall." The fourth wall molding should be coped in both corners, but the joints on the "door wall" are the least noticeable in the room in case of any minor imperfections. All moldings should be fastened securely into solid framing with two nails driven at offset angles per stud location.

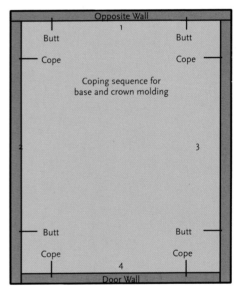

Opposite Wall
1
Butt — Butt
Cope — Cope

Coping sequence for base and crown molding

2 — 3

Butt — Butt
Cope — Cope
4
Door Wall

PRO TIP

GET PRIMED You might consider priming and painting all the trim pieces for your project before you install them. This will reduce the time you spend working on your knees (for base) or a ladder (for crown) and limit your post-installation painting to touch-up work.

190 LEARN TO COPE

When installing trim, it's tempting to cut 45-degree miters at the corners and hope for a sure fit. The problem is that most walls aren't 90 degrees. Joining two 45-cut molding pieces may give you a square joint, but a square joint may not work for your crazy corner. Even the perfect miter joint can end up developing gaps when the wood dries and contracts in winter.

Unlike miter joints, cope joints have one trim piece butted against the adjacent wall at the corner. The joining trim piece is carefully cut to nest against the profile of the first. These joints eliminate the problem of out-of-square corners when installing trim, and they're less likely to reveal a gap when the wood shrinks. To do it right, follow these steps.

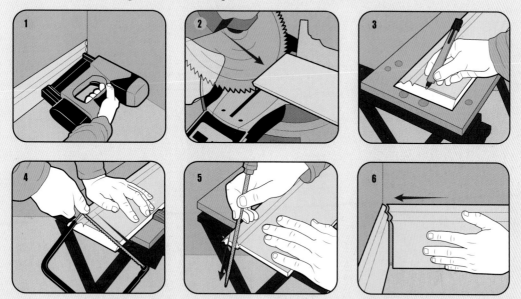

STEP 1 Butt the first piece of molding into the corner and fasten in place.

STEP 2 Cut the second piece of molding just a few inches longer than its final length. Then, on the intersecting end of the second piece, cut a 45-degree inside miter.

STEP 3 Run a carpenter's pencil along the edge of the mitered profile, which does the job of marking the shape for better visibility.

STEP 4 Clamp the second piece of molding to a work surface securely and use the coping saw to cut along the pencil line. It may help to angle the blade to back-cut the molding. Keep the blade about ⅟₁₆ inch to the waste side of the cutline.

STEP 5 When most of the wood is removed, use a file to finish the cut and clean up the profile, revealing a shaped edge that will be the only point of contact between the intersecting pieces of molding. Remove all the wood forward of the profile to create a socket that fits over the face of the first piece. A rattail file, which has a round, slender shape works well for fine-tuning small curves and edges. A flat file will work well on square edges.

STEP 6 Test-fit the molding against the first piece. Check for any gaps and sand or file away any high spots to ensure a good fit. Nail the molding into place and finish off by caulking the seam. Proceed around the room to complete the installation.

Upgrading trim can be a fairly simple and relatively inexpensive way to upgrade a room. And there are some tips and tricks to make it even easier.

MATCH IT UP Ensure that each length of the crown molding you purchase has precisely the same spring angle, width, and thickness. This is very important because building supply stores purchase their own trim from several manufactures, with each using their different fabrication standards/tolerances, and any dissimilar pieces won't fit together correctly.

GET SQUARE Always check the square of your saw before you begin. For every degree your saw is out of alignment, you will get twice that error in each joint that you cut.

BEEF UP For optimal strength, be sure to use adhesive in every single joint.

FILL IT Caulk all joints and the top and bottom of your crown and trim. Use a shrink-free spackling for nail holes. (Caulking nail holes will leave visible dimples.)

GO LONG Do not nail any closer than 6 inches to the joint for long pieces of crown or trim. For short pieces, you can glue the joint and/or use adhesive under the trim piece.

BE CAREFUL When cutting the molding or trim to your desired length, it is best to make the first cut at least a half inch into the waste side of the crown or trim, and then make small cuts until you reach your length mark.

TRY TEMPLATES Try building a set of crown molding or trim templates to help guide your blade orientation when making the cuts. Make templates for right-hand and left-hand cuts for both inside and outside miters.

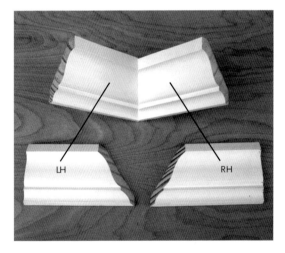

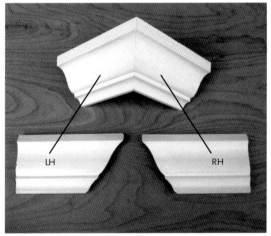

PRO TIP

THINK BEYOND THE WALLS Fireplace mantels, built-in bookshelves, bar areas, and more make great candidates for decorative trim enhancements. Instead of crowning a wall, use molding to create skirting for a mantel shelf. Use a piece of baseboard turned upside down to line the upper portion of a bookcase. Think outside the box when designing and selecting your trim packages, and don't feel limited by the traditional use of the materials.

192 GET HIGH

A ceiling medallion is an easy trim upgrade that adds elegance to a hanging light fixture. Some ceiling medallions come in two halves for simple application over an existing fixture. Others are single-piece products that require removal of the fixture. Some medallions are made of thin plastic and install with two-sided tape, but we prefer the solid urethane versions that can be securely glued to the ceiling. To install, all you'll need is a power drill/driver, a handful of trim-head drywall screws, wood filler, and some construction adhesive.

To begin, test-fit the medallion and make note if it needs to be centered, in case the base of your light is slightly smaller than the medallion's inside diameter. When you're satisfied with its position, mark the ceiling around the medallion's perimeter for easy replacement after you add the adhesive. Liberally apply beads of adhesive to its back side ❶ (use polyurethane glue for urethane medallions). Replace the two halves around the base of the light, interlocking the joint ❷.

Countersink a few trim-head drywall screws through the medallion and into the ceiling joists to hold the trim piece while the glue sets ❸. Conceal the small screw heads with plastic wood filler. Caulk the seams and paint if desired.

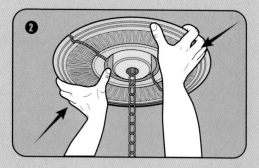

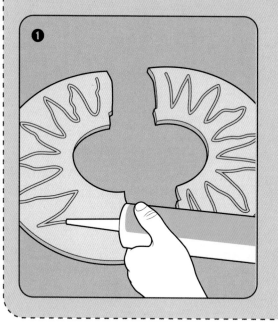

193 INSTALL CROWN MOLDING

Crown molding can add greatly to a room's overall décor. Here's how to successfully complete the job in a standard square room. One nice thing about ceiling trim is that there are generally no doors or other room openings to contend with. This simplifies the layout somewhat, but you should plan the installation according to the locations of the coped joints (see item 189).

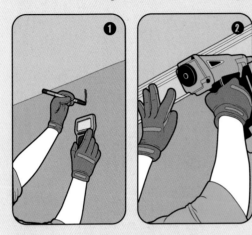

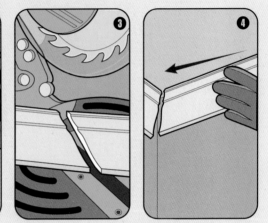

STEP 1 Start by using a stud finder and pencil to mark the wall studs and ceiling joists around the perimeter of the room ❶. Mark just outside the molding location so you'll know where to drive the nails.

STEP 2 The first piece of molding requires no angled cuts, thus making it the easiest to install. Measure the wall, then make a 90-degree cut to trim the molding to length. Use a powered miter saw or a handsaw with miter box.

STEP 3 Fasten the molding into the wall and the ceiling framing with finish nails ❷. A hammer and nail will suffice, but it's pretty easy to dent the molding this way. A better (and much faster) tool for the job is a pneumatic nail gun, such as a brad nailer or finish nailer.

STEP 4 Here's where you begin the coping part of the job. Measure the wall and then mark your measurements onto the intersecting end of the second strip of molding. Cut a 45-degree inside miter at the mark ❸.

When cutting crown molding on a miter saw, you will typically have to cut it upside down and backward, so the saw's base represents the ceiling and the saw's fence represents the house wall.

With 45-degree inside corners, the cut should be made so the lower, longer point of the molding (when positioned on the wall) meets the mark you made for the molding's overall length.

STEP 5 Cope the miter cut and check for fit on the wall. Cut the uncoped end square to fit against the opposite wall. Butt it against the far corner to meet another coped piece ❹. Repeat this process for the molding strip that intersects the other end of the first piece. Complete the rest of the room according to the installation sequence for coped joints.

STEP 6 The final molding strip on the fourth wall, above the door, is coped at both ends. Admittedly, it is difficult to successfully fit a piece of molding that has been coped at both ends. To make this easier, you can fit each coped corner on a separate piece of molding and cut a scarf joint to join the two pieces in a continuous run (see item 195).

STEP 7 With all the molding solidly fastened into place, fill up the nail holes and seal seams with a high-quality caulk or wood filler. Sand the caulk after it dries and then "spot" prime the seams and nail patches. Once the primer dries, mask off the molding and finish up with a couple coats of your favorite semi-gloss or high-gloss paint.

194 INSTALL OUTSIDE CORNERS

To install molding at an outside corner, first cope the end of the molding opposite the outside corner. Hold that strip along the wall, nesting the cope up against the preceding piece of molding so that the other end runs long over the corner. Mark the cut line where the molding overhangs the corner **1**. Do the same for the intersecting piece. Cut miters at the marks on both pieces.

To cut outside corners on crown molding, position the molding upside-down and face up on the miter saw. Ideally you'll need to make a 45-degree cut on one end of one piece, and another 45 on the intersecting piece **2**. However, walls are often out of square, so first check the angle with an angle gauge and then cut it accordingly.

Install the pieces by applying a bead of carpenter's glue to the joint and securing with finish nails. You can then smooth the joint by running the rounded edge of a nail set over it to press the fibers closed **3**. For thick, heavy moldings or problem gaps, drill pilot holes at the top and bottom of the joint, and drive 4d finish nails perpendicular through one molding into the end of the other.

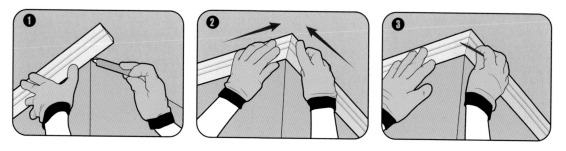

195 SCARF IT UP

Use a scarf joint anytime you need to join two pieces of molding along a straight run of the wall. To make this joint, cut opposite miters on the two molding pieces and nail the joint securely over a wall stud. Make the cut so it angles away from the doorway to better conceal the joint. After fastening the first half of the run over the stud, cope the corner end of the second piece. Then, cut a supplementary miter on its opposite end, leaving the strip just a little too long. Test-fit this last piece and then cut way the excess on the miter until it fits snugly into the scarf joint with no visible gap.

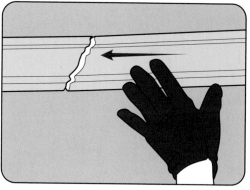

196 TOOL UP

A few simple tools can make your trim installation much easier.

LASER RANGE FINDER A precise set of wall-to-wall measurements are critical for installing crown and base molding. Although a tape measure will work, a laser range finder will make the task easier. Just aim the device from one corner to the other. With only a push of a button you'll have the exact measurement recorded in digital readout, and you're ready for a trip to the saw to cut the molding to match.

CROWN MOLDING HANGERS If installing crown molding by yourself, check the local hardware store for these handy time-savers. To use them, tack in a couple of nails about 6 feet apart just below the ceiling. Hook the Crown Hangers on the nails—they're sold two per set. Then, hang the stick of molding on the two brackets. After that, you can adjust each of the hangers by sliding the brackets upward and finger-tightening with a lock nut, which positions the molding against the ceiling, ready for fastening.

197 GET A COMPLEX

Crown molding and casing are both available in simple geometric profiles as well as elegant, intricate profiles that mimic complex classical designs. DIYers can purchase these moldings preformed at the factory or they custom-build their own from individual trim strips sold at home centers.

Dentil molding, for example, is composed of a series of repeating rectangular blocks that add depth and character to millwork such as fascia trim and crown profiles. This particular molding style has been popular for centuries, but traditional installation was often a time-consuming and labor-intensive process that required combining all the individual pieces.

Today, wood moldings are available with all of the dentil molding pre-attached to the profile by the manufacturer. For paint-grade trim, synthetic moldings offer similar design advantages. You can purchase single-piece polyurethane foam or vinyl molding, which weighs less and resists shrinkage, peeling, and other problems associated with built-up wood molding. Plus, with paint-grade projects, minor errors in the installation can be repaired with caulk and painted over.

Some of the larger, more elaborately crafted moldings have a gap at the rear that can make it tough for the nails to penetrate fully through to the house framing. To create a solid nailing surface on which to hang the molding, you can

198 GO MITERLESS

Skipping the mitering process is a big time-saver, and you can do it with crown molding systems that use corner blocks instead of miter cuts at each joint. You just make square cuts on the molding; there's no need to measure angles or think "upside down and backward," and each cut can be made with the molding flat on the base of the miter saw.

Begin by drawing a layout of the room and determine what materials you need. Pay attention to corners; when ordering you must specify the exact number of corner blocks, and whether they are oriented outside or inside.

With the materials ready, apply urethane-based adhesive to the rear and upper surfaces of the corner block. Press the block into position at the wall/ceiling transition ❶ and nail it securely through the recessed areas of the corner piece. Proceed around the room, installing all of the corner blocks the same way.

Next, measure how long you'll need each piece of molding to be to fit between the corner blocks ❷. Cut the molding to fit, erring on the side of too long. Check fit before installing ❸; adjust as needed. (For urethane moldings, add ⅛-inch to every 5 feet of linear run.)

Position the molding on the wall so it closely follows the profile of the corner block, which is slightly larger than the molding for a uniform reveal at the transition. Each block should appear as a slightly larger accent piece at each corner of the layout. Position the first end against the corner block and fasten in place, moving from one end toward the center. Nail the molding into the wall studs every 16 inches ❹.

If two lengths of molding have to join in the middle of a wall, the miterless system also comes with divider blocks. The lengths of molding can be cut square and installed right against the flat surface of the dividers.

install wooden blocks along the perimeter of the ceiling. Measure the angle of the molding profile using a combination square, then cut triangular blocks from scrap wood to fit behind the molding. Nail the blocks every 16 inches into the wall studs. Then, nail the molding into the blocks.

Don't be afraid to get creative and develop your own moldings from any of the range of shapes and profiles on the market today. Practice the assembly on a workbench and make sure to keep your reveals consistent. (The "reveal" is the exposure of one trim piece beneath another.) Make sure your molding is securely attached with nails and glue (if necessary), and the sky will be the limit on the designs you can come up with.

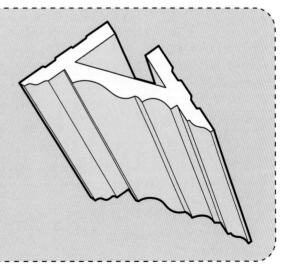

The term "wainscoting" refers to nearly any sort of treatment you give to the lower portion of a wall in contrast to the upper portion. This will often involve a system of panels capped by a chair rail that lines the lower wall as a decorative enhancement. One traditional type, bead board (shown below), is popular with DIYers because of its narrow repeating pattern, which makes it easy to hide a cut between panels.

Plan the installation so that the full panels are most prevalent, with cut panels located in a less conspicuous areas. Make strategic cuts in order to continue with a full repeating bead-board pattern from one panel to the other until the wainscoting meets a corner.

Apply construction adhesive to the back of each panel and fasten them into the wall studs with brad nails. (The rule of thumb is that the wainscoting panels are usually one-third the height of the wall.) Install all the panels perfectly level. Gaps at the floor can be concealed with base or shoe molding. Finally, nail the trim profile of your choice on top of the paneling to serve as chair rail.

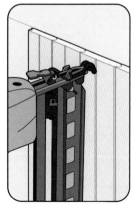 

Raised panel wainscoting gives a room a more formal appearance, popular in dining rooms, foyers, and hallways. Assembling these panels from scratch, however, will require some careful measurement and shrewd carpentry skills, plus a lot of time and labor.

One way for a DIYer to cut the labor in half is to order customized wainscoting that is shipped to your home as large, single sections with all the decorative patterns routed into the MDF panels. Rather than piecing together every rail (horizontal piece) and stile (vertical piece), these large panels can be installed directly to the wall so that the job progresses as much as 8 linear feet at a time. The single panels are also less prone to paint cracking, because there are no rail or stile joints, which are prone to expansion and contraction.

Wainscoting America is a supplier that helps streamline the selection process with an online design tool. First step is to select your preferred style and the height of your panels, and then you choose from a number of other parameters. Based on your careful measurements of each wall, the web tool will produce a visual representation of

201 FAKE IT

Faux wainscot paneling has made its way into today's homes because it's easy to install and saves time and material. Installing faux paneling basically entails attaching moldings to the walls to create the look and effect of solid wainscoting panels. The moldings are mitered to create a square or rectangle, and the wall and moldings are painted one color to look like solid wainscot.

For curved walls, flexible molding can be applied to simulate curved panels.

your panel design. Make adjustments until you're satisfied. The panels then ship to your home.

The panels are installed over the wallboard using a combination of construction adhesive and brad nails driven into the wall studs. The seams between panels are concealed with an overlapping rabbet joint. The chair rail is installed with glue and nails, and the entire project is finished with caulk, spackling, primer, and paint.

202 GET FILLED IN ON FRAMING

When replacing windows or doors, DIYers will have to understand the basics of wall framing. It's usually easy to replace a new window or door matching with the size and design of the existing unit. If the new unit is larger, major framing reconstruction will be required to accommodate the installation.

The walls of a house consist of bottom plates that are nailed to the subflooring, or possibly attached by anchor bolts onto a concrete slab. Studs are then nailed to the bottom plates, and the top plates are nailed to the studs. The studs carry all the weight of the structure above them, so any time there is an interruption in those studs, such as the rough opening of a window or door, the overhead load must be distributed and well supported by a header and trimmer studs.

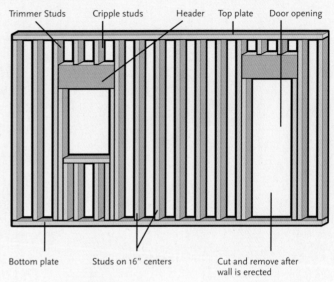

Trimmer Studs   Cripple studs   Header   Top plate   Door opening

Bottom plate   Studs on 16" centers   Cut and remove after wall is erected

203 KNOW YOUR LIMITATIONS

The rough opening defined by the wall framing means that replacement windows and doors are limited to matching sizes unless you want to reconstruct the wall frame. In some cases you can install windows that are taller than the original windows by removing and reconstructing the height of the sill plate. However, to increase the width of a window or door—or to add a window or door where one does not exist—will require temporarily supporting the overhead structure while you open the wall and reconstruct the headers to accommodate the larger units.

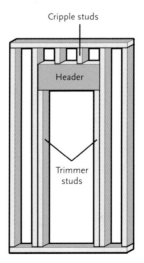

Cripple studs

Header

Trimmer studs

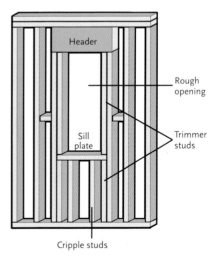

Header

Rough opening

Sill plate

Trimmer studs

Cripple studs

204 WRAP YOUR HEAD AROUND HEADERS

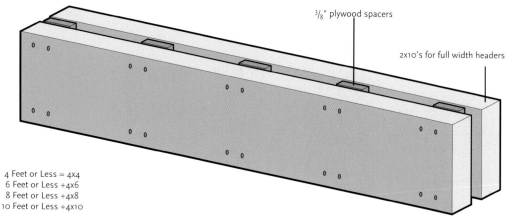

³/₈" plywood spacers

2x10's for full width headers

4 Feet or Less = 4x4
6 Feet or Less +4x6
8 Feet or Less +4x8
10 Feet or Less +4x10

Headers are structural framing members made from doubled 2-inch lumber that bridge the rough opening of a door or window, supporting the overhead weight that would otherwise fall on the missing studs. The lumber's size depends on the span of the opening and whether or not it is a load-bearing wall.

For load-bearing walls with an opening of 4 feet, a 4x4 (doubled 2x4) should be adequate as long as the wood is Douglas fir or stronger. Openings between 4 and 6 feet require a doubled 2x6. The required size of the header increases as the span gets wider; they can be larger than necessary, but not smaller.

The header should be exactly as thick as the wall studs. Because a doubled 2x4 (nominal) measures only 3 inches, and a 2x4 (nominal) wall stud is 3½ inches, blocking between the 2x members of a header is required to increase the thickness of the header. Half-inch plywood or drywall is usually used as a middle board to carry the load and ensure the header has a flush nailing surface with the drywall (inside) and sheathing (outside) on both sides of the wall. Rigid polyurethane foam can also add insulation to the header. For smaller headers, the distance between the header and the top plate may be taken up by partial, or "cripple," studs.

For non-load–bearing walls, the header simply serves to define the rough opening of a door or window and provide a proper nailing surface for jambs, drywall, and sheathing. Headers made of doubled 2x4 are adequate for non-load–bearing walls up to 72 inches, but use 2x6 for longer spans to avoid sagging.

205 PUT IT ON A PLATE

The bottom edge of the rough opening of a window is defined by a sill plate. The sill plate is a horizontal framing member the same size as the wall studs, which the window sits on. Cripple studs are installed beneath the sill plate to support the window and to create a flush nailing surface for the wallboard. Always make sure that the rough opening is plumb, square, and true for doors and windows.

206 GET A TRIM

Trimmer studs are installed under the ends of the header to support its weight and help define the sides of the rough opening. These studs are nailed flush against full-length wall studs (called "king" studs) and run beneath the header to the bottom plate to transfer the overhead load to the ground or lower level of the home. Trimmer studs must be the same thickness as the wall studs and header.

Windows are available in many styles and operating types. Your lifestyle and decorative preference will help determine which type will match your long-term expectations for your home.

SINGLE HUNG The top sash of the window stays fixed, while the bottom sash lifts open and tilts in for easy cleaning.

CASEMENT The sash is hinged on one side of the window, and opens like a door by turning the crank handle at the base.

SINGLE SLIDER One sash that is fixed and doesn't move, while the other sash opens and closes by sliding from side to side.

GARDEN These extend outward from the house and feature functional casement sidelites. They are designed to showcase plants or collectibles.

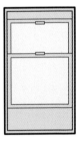

DOUBLE HUNG Both sashes on double hung windows lift to open fully and tilt inward for easy cleaning.

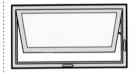

AWNING The sash has hinges at the top and it opens outward when you turn the crank handle at the base.

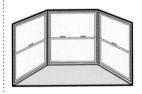

BAY A trio of windows mulled together at either 30- or 45-degree angles that extend outward from the frame of the house.

GEOMETRIC Fixed windows that do not open or close, but are available in a variety of stylish shapes.

PICTURE These large windows are fixed and don't open or close.

DOUBLE SLIDER Paired sashes that are opened and closed by sliding from side to side.

BOW Similar to a bay window, bow windows are even more rounded in appearance because each of the 3, 4, or 5 lite windows are mulled at a 10-degree angle.

GARDEN DOOR Garden doors operate like normal doors—they swing open. Garden doors can have one fixed door, or both of the doors can swing in or out.

208 GET A GREAT LOOK WITH GRIDS

When ordering windows you're going to have to make a decision on grids, which can affect the overall look of the home's exterior as well as its interior. Here's what to think about.

CONSIDER THE SIZE If a window looks a bit large for a room or you want to accent the unit, it's time to think about grids. Basically, grids (which can sometimes be called grills, grilles or muntins) divide a large window into smaller viewing units, called "lites."

PICK AND CHOOSE The grids themselves can be thin, flat, sculptured, grooved or even round. Different window manufacturers offer a variety of selections.

KNOW YOUR TERMS Vertical grids go in an up and down direction on the glass of the window. Horizontal grids go side to side. You don't necessarily need to have both vertical and horizontal grids in a window.

MATCH PATTERNS Grid patterns should match in all the windows on the same floor and on the same side of the house for a unified look on the exterior.

VISUALIZE A GRID Take a sheet of notebook paper and then fold it in half. The resulting size shows the average size of glass surrounded by grids. Generally, lites in grid patterns should be no smaller than 8 inches wide and 6 inches tall. The larger the window size, the more lites can be created using grids. Consider making a mock-up by applying masking tape to the windows where you think you'd like to have the grids. This way you can see where the grids would be, and you can make changes.

209 BE ENERGY EFFICIENT

When looking for new windows, consider those with energy efficient designs for year-round thermal performance. Single-pane windows have poor insulation and result in cold spots in a room. New windows with double-pane Low-E glass, filled with harmless argon or krypton gas, can reduce a home's power bill. The gases are a great thermal barrier, reducing heat and cold transfer. Low-E coatings reflect infrared light to keep the heat in during the winter and outside in the summer. These coatings can also reduce fading in carpets, artwork and photos by helping block damaging ultraviolet rays.

210 PICK YOUR MATERIALS

Windows take lots of weather abuse; their material makes a significant difference in durability and performance. Wood windows generally require repainting and re-glazing every 2 to 3 years.

Aluminum windows don't generally have the same maintenance problems as wood, but painted aluminum can pit and the metal has poor thermal performance. In summer they can conduct unwanted heat from outdoors into the room. In winter, aluminum transfers cold the same way. This heat transfer leads to condensation and related issues. Modern aluminum windows often use thermal breaks, made of vinyl, to help with the condensation problem and increase energy efficiency.

Vinyl replacement windows are popular for remodeling since vinyl minimizes heat transfer from the outside to the inside. They are energy efficient, need little maintenance, and there is no need to repaint or re-stain them since they're a solid color throughout.

The easiest method of changing a window is "pocket replacement," wherein you just swap the existing window for one of the same size. This allows a homeowner to keep the trim intact around the windows. Depending on the window's construction, it may help to remove the old interior trim for a more correct measurement of the rough opening. If a window manufacturer offers specific measuring instructions, defer to those guidelines.

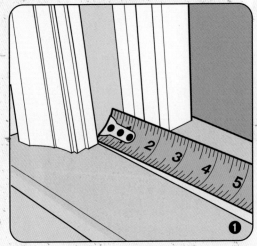

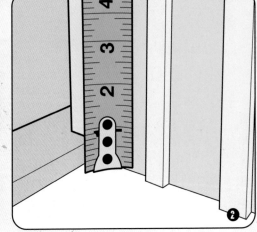

When measuring the existing window for width, place the tape against the jamb and measure to the other jamb ❶ (not the stop molding or the parting bead—the wooden strips attached over the jamb). On double-hung windows, the parting bead that separates the sashes is removed from the jamb when the new windows are installed. Replacement windows are all sold in a standard thickness to fit the 3¼-inch pocket between the outside and inside stops after the parting bead has been removed.

Measure the window's width in three places: the top, middle, and bottom. Use the smallest of these measurements to determine the final width around the window.

Next, measure the height of the window, placing the tape on the very top of the sill ❷. (Be careful to not confuse it with the stool—a section of interior molding at the bottom of the window that helps to give it a finished appearance.) On a double-hung window, the sill is the board the sash closes onto. The sill is usually sloped to divert water away from the house, so it is important to measure from the uppermost point of the sloped sill, down to the top jamb (not a stop or parting bead).

Measure the window's height in three places — right, center, and left—and use the smallest of these measurements to determine the height.

Once you have taken all of the existing window measurements, consider deducting slightly from them so the replacement window is easier to install. Some professionals suggest deducting ¼ inch from the width and ½ inch from the height, to make sure that the installer won't try to force the new window into place, potentially damaging it. The replacement window can be adjusted using shims, and the extra space can be filled with insulation.

Remember that the replacement window must fit into the opening plumb, level, and square, even if the opening may not be any of these.

Most manufacturers will offer standard sized windows; you should order one that most closely matches those measurements unless you plan to change the size. (Some manufacturers customize their windows to the exact measurements that are requested, so all the standard sizing issues don't apply.) If the window is slightly smaller than the window frame, it can be shimmed to properly fit, but if the window is too large, the wall will need substantial reconstruction to fit it.

212   REPLACE METAL WINDOWS IN BRICK HOMES

Metal windows are generally fastened with a flange inside the wall behind the brick. To measure height and width, follow the same three-step measuring guidelines (see the previous item) but strike the tape from brick to brick to measure the window's width, and measure from the brick at the bottom to the metal lintel at the top of the opening for the height. The brick opening may be larger than the window opening; always use the smaller measurement to determine the size of the replacement.

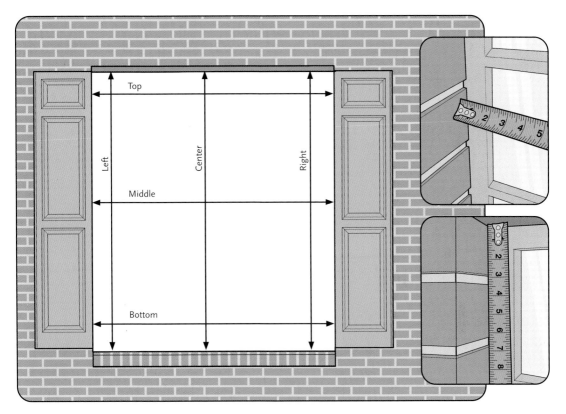

213   DO IT YOURSELF (OR GET HELP)

A homeowner with the right tools and carpentry experience can install a replacement window. However, we strongly advise that first-timers enlist the assistance of an experienced professional to show them the ropes. If the window is installed improperly and is not plumb, level, and square, a number of problems might occur. The double hung and slider sash may be difficult or impossible to remove. A casement sash may not operate properly due to excessive drag on the sill. The sash pivot bar on double-hung windows could bind and cause the sash to become inoperative, or the weather stripping may not seal properly—allowing air and water infiltration, even if the sash is locked. And remember: Products vary by design, so all window installers—both professionals and DIY—should always consult the manufacturer's guidelines for installing their specific units.

214 TRIM YOUR WINDOWS

Architectural trim can define your home's interior décor. The majority of today's home-improvement stores offer a wide variety of the most popular trim and molding profiles for doors and windows.

These trim pieces are available in a wide variety of lengths and sizes, and they are often made of paint- or stain-grade pine. Several of the selections are also available pre-primed and ready to paint.

A basic trim package has casing mitered at the corners and applied around the window, but it can be more elaborate or decorative with a few enhancements.

The window shown here features jamb extensions, curved fluted casing, rosette blocks on the corners, and a keystone in the center

215 JAMB ON

Jamb extensions line a window's interior frame to provide a decorative shadow line against the casing. The front ends of all of these extensions should all be installed flush with the face of the wall, thus providing a continuous flat surface on which to nail your casing. The rear sides of the jamb extensions should not interfere with sash operations. The extensions are attached to the sides and the top of the window opening using finish nails.

It's common to encounter a few framing imperfections when installing the extensions. Wood shims can be used to make sure they're square in the opening.

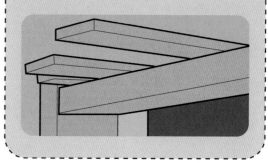

216 GIVE YOUR WINDOW AN APRON

The trim piece below the stool is called the apron, and it's often made of a simple, flat painted board. For this project we used brick-mold, which has a decorative profile. We also cut mitered returns for each side of the apron for a finished look, and then fastened those to the ends with nails and wood glue before installing. We then completed the window-trim job by filling all fastener holes, caulking the seams and painting.

STEP 1 Mitered returns give the ends of the apron a finished look.

STEP 2 Nail the apron flush beneath the stool plate. It should be sized so the stool extends beyond the sides of the apron.

STEP 3 Fill the nail and screw holes, caulk the seams, and add primer and paint where needed.

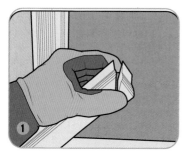

217 CASE THE JOINT

For the casing pieces, consider a fluted wood profile with 3½-inch rosette blocks at the corners. Before installing, carefully measure out and test-fit the leg pieces and corner blocks. For this style, the head and leg pieces should be centered on the rosettes. Once everything is level and plumb, the legs are fastened in place, followed by the corners and the top. Finish nails are used for all the casing and corners, driven into solid framing.

When installing casing, each piece should bridge the edge of the underlying jamb extension, not completely conceal it. A trim gauge (or combination square) is a good layout tool to keep reveal consistent throughout.

STEP 1 Cut the casing to length and nail it over the jamb extensions.

STEP 2 Keep a consistent reveal where the casing laps the jamb extension.

STEP 3 Center the rosette blocks over the casing and nail in place.

STEP 4 Fasten the head casing flush between the corner blocks.

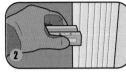

218 PUT YOUR WINDOW ON A STOOL

For the stool plate, we measured the window width and added twice the width of the casing (to account for both sides of the window). We then cut the stool 2 inches longer than the measurement in order to allow a decorative overhang on the window sides. The stool should also be deep enough to extend slightly beyond the face of the window casing, so that the casing pieces can sit on the stool with no overhang. A good choice of wood for trim applications is 1x (3/4-inch) poplar, which is easy to cut and rout, and is relatively inexpensive.

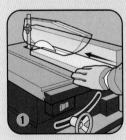

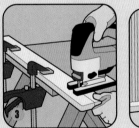

STEP 1 Rip the stool plate to width.

STEP 2 Rout a decorative profile on the front and sides of the stool plate.

STEP 3 Use a jigsaw to cut out square notches in the rear corners, measured to fit snugly around your window frame and wall.

STEP 4 Install the stool onto the windowsill using countersunk wood screws and wood glue. Make sure it is level; if it is not then adjust it with wood shims until it is, and then fasten securely. There should still be plenty of clearance left between the stool and the window latches.

219 CHECK THE EXTERIOR

Also called entry doors, exterior doors have a solid core and are typically wood, fiberglass, or steel. Most modern entryway doors are insulated and sold as pre-hung units with the jamb already attached, or as slab doors with no framing. Common styles include panel doors, windowed doors, carved wood, and more—the decorative possibilities are endless. Entry doors often have a transom (window above the door) and/or sidelites (windows at the sides).

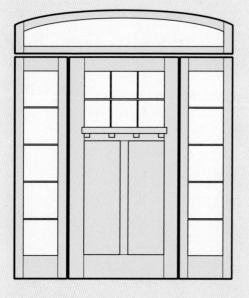

Left Hinged Active Outswing

Interior

Exterior

Right Hinged Active Outswing

Interior

Exterior

Left Hinged Active Inswing

Interior

Exterior

Right Hinged Active Inswing

Interior

Exterior

220 GET ANCHORED

There's not much wood in a hollow-core interior door, so screws will usually tear out of one as soon as any weight is applied to them. This complicates mounting items such as pictures, mirrors, and hooks, to the door. Mounting anything into a hollow door requires special hollow-core door anchors ❶. These plastic anchors fold down flat to fit inside a pilot hole drilled into the door ❷. Once inserted, a small key is used to open up the anchor ❸, which spreads side brackets to clamp the front collar of the anchor against the door face, like a toggle bolt. The screw is then driven into the anchor (❹, ❺) until tight.

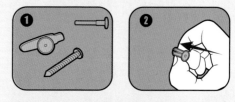

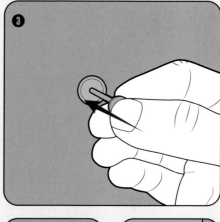

221 GO INSIDE

Interior doors usually have a hollow core, weigh and cost less, and have no need for insulation. Also sold as slab or pre-hung versions, these doors also come in many different styles. Flush and paneled doors are popular, and the way the door opens varies beyond the standard side hinges. Pocket doors slide into a wall to be concealed when open. Barn-style doors roll on an exposed overhead track. Double doors are often used for closets or to partition rooms, and can be configured as bi-fold doors, bypass doors that slide over one another, or fresh doors with inset window lites.

Panel door

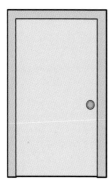

Flush door

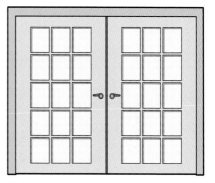

Fresh doors

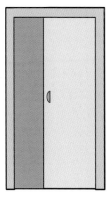

Pocket door

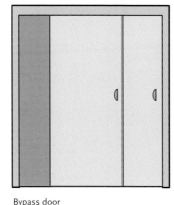

Bypass door

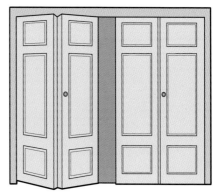

Bifold doors

222 ADD ANOTHER DOOR

Storm and screen doors are secondary exterior doors mounted to a metal frame that allow light and/or air into the home when the main entry door is opened. Storm doors are sold in a wide range of paint colors, handle options, and glass designs. Installation requires little more than a screwdriver to fasten the frame flanges to the casing of the doorway.

223 KNOW YOUR DOORS

If you take a moment to think about the number of doors you pass through each day, you'll realize what a major component of a house they are.

Doors are usually sold in standard sizes, although custom orders are also available. When selecting a door, pay particular attention to the direction the door opens, which greatly affects the flow of traffic in and out of the doorway.

224 PULL OUT THE STOPS

Most manufacturers offer their windows in standard sizes to provide a close match to existing window units. Once you have the new windows, double-check all of the measurements for fit before removing the existing units.

Most windows are "clamped" in place with stop molding on each side of the wall. The first step to pulling out the old windows is to remove stops. Exterior stops can be removed to install the window from the outside. For indoor installations, you will have to remove the interior stops.

Use hammers, putty knives, and pry bars to dislodge the old stop molding. With the stops gone, the old windows can then be carefully pushed out of the frame.

225 PUT IN A NEW WINDOW

Once your old window is out, you will have some cleanup to do. Remove and replace any rotted wood in the window casing, sill plate, or framing.

Next, refer to the manufacturer's instructions for specifics on assembling your model. The windows may include various accessory pieces, such as vinyl sill extenders to help fit the window into the opening, which should be attached before installation.

If the window is to be installed on a sloped sill, wood blocks should be installed along the sill as well, to help support the window and keep it level. When installing, tilt the new window into the opening with the sash closed and locked, setting the bottom on the sill (or wood blocks).

226 CHECK THE FINAL FIT

Your replacement window has to be level, plumb, and square, otherwise it won't open or close properly and air and water could infiltrate around the edges. Check both sides for plumb ❶ and the bottom for level ❷. To check for square, measure both window diagonals from corner to corner to make sure they match ❸. Adjustment can be made with shims ❹, which should be installed at all anchor points and anywhere necessary to keep the unit correctly in place.

Once the window is plumb, level, and square, drive the installation screws (included with the window) into the prefabricated holes in the jamb ❺. Don't over-tighten, or the window might bow and not function properly. Check the sash for proper operation once the screws are in place.

If there are any gaps greater than ⅛ inch between the window and frame, loosely pack insulation in the interior. Spray foam is acceptable if the product is designated for windows and doors, so it won't expand to the point that it could prevent proper operation.

Reinstall new stop molding then caulk and paint to your preference ❻.

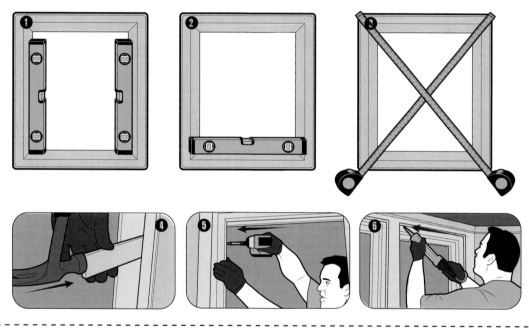

227 BRICK YOUR WINDOW

Metal-framed windows in brick walls have a nailing flange behind the brick. After removing the sash, you will have to cut away all caulk and pry out the flange. You shouldn't have to alter the brick unless you want to change the size of the windows. Apply flashing tape on all exposed wood framing before installing new windows.

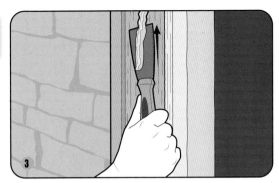

Need to make a great first impression? Upgrade the entry door to your home.

STEP 1 Take the old door off of its hinges and back out the long hinge screws that hold the jamb to the framing. Remove the screws from the sill and the bolts of the door strike. Cut loose all caulked joints around the jamb with a razor. Pry off the casing on the inside or remove the brick molding outside to remove the jamb; if it isn't loose in the framing, run a reciprocating saw with a long blade between the jamb and framing to cut through any remaining fasteners. This should free the door so you can tip it out of the rough opening for removal.

STEP 2 Pull the jamb out of the rough opening.

STEP 3 Prepare the rough opening by checking all corners for square. Double-check by comparing the diagonal measurements. The rough opening should be frame height plus ½ inch, and frame width plus ½ to ¾ inch. Use a 6-foot level to confirm the framing

and walls are plumb (front to back and left to right). Fix any problems using shim boards or by adjusting the studs. Also, ensure the subfloor is level and solid. Scrape, sand, or fill the opening as required.

STEP 4 If the door includes a transom that needs to be attached, lay the door down on a flat work surface (covered with a blanket to prevent scratches). Liberally apply flexible, exterior-grade sealant between the door top and transom bottom.

STEP 5 Position the transom onto the door and flush with the jamb on all sides. Hold the seam closed with clamps or an assistant while you screw the two pieces together using metal nailing plates. For a more solid connection, fill all holes in the metal plates with short screws into the mating jambs.

STEP 6 Liberally apply sealant to the subfloor. (Caulk the rear of the brick molding if it's pre-attached.) For an extra layer of moisture protection, install a sill pan in the rough opening beneath the new door.

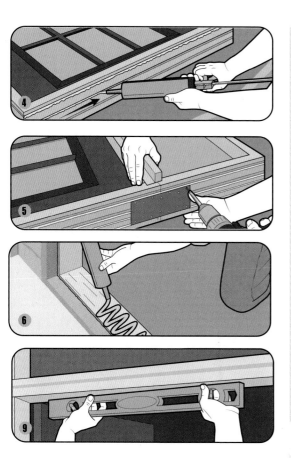

229 LEARN TO USE SHIMS

The best way to use wood shims is to insert them in pairs between the surfaces you're trying to move or support. When shimming a door, for example, the shims are inserted from each side of the jambs so that their thin ends meet and overlap. By sliding the shims further into the gap, they push the shimming surface outward, creating the thickness of two shims. This method also provides a flat surface to work with; using a single triangular shim from one side creates a "teeter-totter" effect against the surface being shimmed.

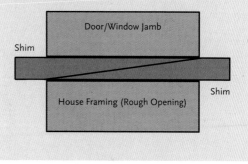

Door/Window Jamb

Shim

Shim

House Framing (Rough Opening)

STEP 7 Position the door's threshold over the sealant and tip it into the rough opening. Temporarily secure the unit in place by installing screws in the center on both sides of the door jambs. Use 3-inch screws, but don't tighten them fully yet.

STEP 8 Plumb the hinge-side jamb first (in both directions) so the door swings properly. Check and make adjustments using a 6-foot level. Place screws at each hinge location. Insert the shims behind the hinges and above the screws (so the screws prevent them from falling down while adjustments are being made). Slide the triangular shims into or out of the jamb to adjust spacing until the hinge side is plumb and straight. Finish driving the screws tight (the middle first, then top and bottom).

STEP 9 Check the door's weather strip reveal and points of contact. Adjust the frame so the weather strip contacts the door surface equally at the top, center and bottom.

230 DOUBLE UP

To install a double door, have an assistant help to center the jamb in the frame. Drive one 10d finish nail or 3-inch screw through the mid-point of each hinge jamb into the framing studs. Hold the door in place with nails or screws while you plumb and square the jamb, using shims as necessary. Place the shims at the hinge locations between the jamb and the studs, and any other locations needed to square the opening. Check for square by measuring the diagonals of the jamb in an X pattern (corner to corner) to confirm they match. Make sure the door panels are also even across their tops and bottoms, and that the reveal between them is even as well.

Doorknobs are often overlooked, but a handle-set can highlight the decorative appeal of the door hardware. Upgrading a simple design or replacing an old handle with a modern style can spruce up an entryway.

Installing a new door handle-set can be a quick and simple project, especially if there are precut knob holes. However, in some cases, the precut holes are located too low for comfortable use of a latch handle. Compare the hole's height with the recommended installation height of a handle-set; a knob may be a better choice. Designs may vary, but this replacement procedure will be similar for most handle-sets.

STEP 1 Unscrew and remove the old door handle. Test-fit the new handle to the existing hole

STEP 2 Some handle-sets include paper templates to help align and mark placement of the handle and dead-bolt holes. Otherwise, measure according to the manufacturer's instructions.

STEP 3 If there are no holes available for a handle-set or deadbolt, drill them out with a hole saw. Double-check the handle manufacturer's instructions for the recommended diameter. Use a 1-inch spade bit to bore holes in both the jamb and door for the deadbolt.

STEP 4 If you're cutting new knob holes, you'll also have to cut mortises for the faceplates of the latch or deadbolt. Trace the faceplate perimeter with a pencil, and then use a wood chisel and hammer to chip out

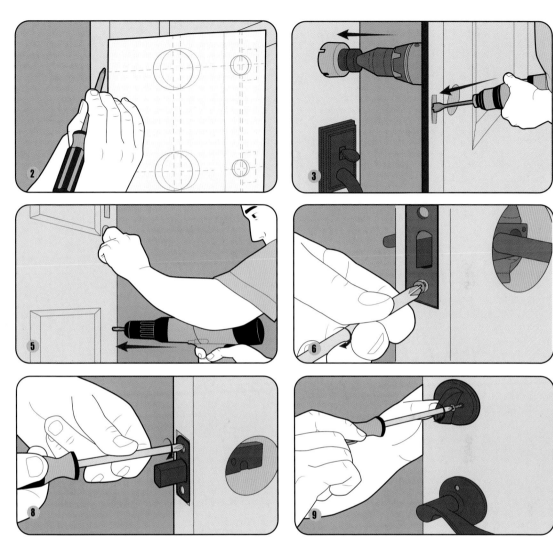

a recess in order to set the faceplate flush with the wood surface.

STEP 5 If the handle-set includes a through-bolt used to anchor the bottom of the handle with the door, use a spiral or brad-point bit to drill out the mounting hole. For wooden doors, you should start by drilling out the hole from both sides of the door in order to prevent tear-out.

STEP 6 Install the handle mechanism inside the door holes, and align the spindle with the latch. Secure the faceplates into the mortises that you've previously cut in Step 4, using a pair of screws so that they are flush with the door edge.

STEP 7 Add the interior lever to join with the exterior handle. Two screws are all that's required to fasten most handles together.

STEP 8 Mount the deadbolt and strike plate. The strike plate (which will receive the deadbolt) comes with two 3-inch screws to drive into the door jamb and house framing. This design will provide extra holding power for the deadbolt.

STEP 9 The deadbolt housing is simple to install, as it requires only two bolts to join the halves over the deadbolt. Finish the handle-set by installing the lower through-bolt (if included) and cover cap to conceal the interior bolt head for a finished appearance.

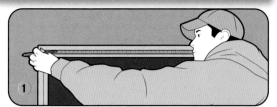

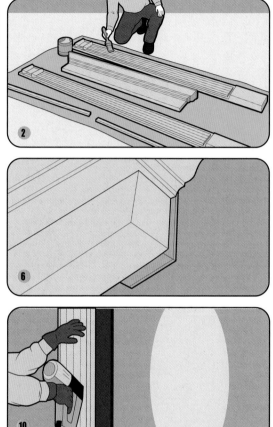

You can easily and dramatically enhance an entryway with elaborate trim packages. You can build up all of the trim piece by piece, but it's easier to use a pre-assembled door-trim kit. The 4-piece kit that's shown contains a pair of urethane fluted pilasters and a crosshead. Architectural details (the backing trim, fluted casing, crown molding, and plinth blocks) are extruded in manufacturing so you don't have to install them individually, saving lots of time and hassle. And, unlike wood, urethane is lightweight and won't rot.

STEP 1 Before purchasing the trim, first measure your doorway. Crossheads look best when their breast-board is the same width as the window or door, plus any side trim. If your door is too narrow, you may have to trim the crosshead in the middle and reassemble the two halves with adhesive. If it's too wide, you may have to combine two crossheads to bridge the distance.

STEP 2 The kit is factory-primed, but pre-painting the trim will make it easier to access all the edges rather than trying to paint after installation.

STEP 3 Mark the center point of the crosshead for alignment. Do the same for the door jamb, and then hold the crosshead in position and align the marks. When aligning the crosshead, work on achieving a consistent reveal between the new trim piece and the existing door jamb or casing. Once positioned, pre-drill and countersink all fastener holes. Mount the trim with appropriate fasteners. Concrete screws were used on the stone wall shown, requiring pilot holes made with a hammer drill.

STEP 4 After drilling out the pilot holes, remove the crosshead, flip it over, and run a bead of polyurethane

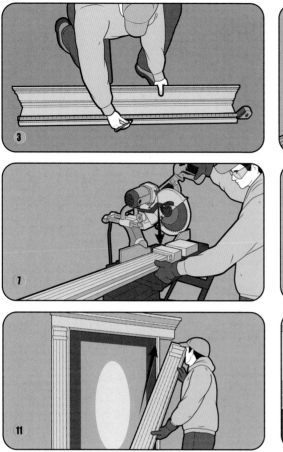

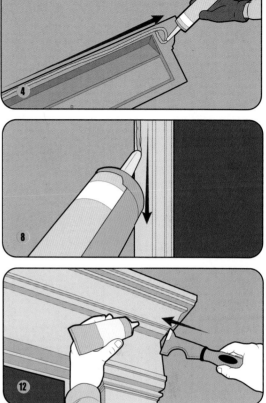

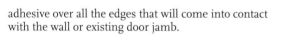

adhesive over all the edges that will come into contact with the wall or existing door jamb.

STEP 5 Carefully reposition the crosshead above the door, aligning the centers and the reveal, and then screw it to the house wall.

STEP 6 Shim the rear of the crosshead as necessary at all screw locations for an even and secure installation.

STEP 7 Measure the distance from either end of the crosshead down to the ground and then trim the two pilasters to fit. Each pilaster is manufactured with a plinth block at the bottom, where cuts can be made to accommodate different doorway heights. You can make the cut with a miter saw, or even a standard hand saw.

STEP 8 The pilasters install in a similar manner as the crosshead, with a combination of polyurethane construction adhesive and screws.

STEP 9 Keep all trim reveals consistent to ensure a uniform-looking installation.

STEP 10 To close the seam, tack down the inside edge of the pilasters using finish nails while the bead of adhesive sets.

STEP 11 The basic trim kit you purchase will almost certainly come with the option of a center keystone. The keystone is a decorative element that helps to cover up a crosshead seam when you have to glue two pieces together. You can always leave the keystone off if you have limited clearance above the door, and should always feel free to alter the decorative package to suit your situation.

STEP 12 Fill all fastener holes with a color-matched plastic wood filler. Sand as necessary and caulk all the joints with a paintable exterior sealant. Complete the project with a fresh coat of touch-up paint.

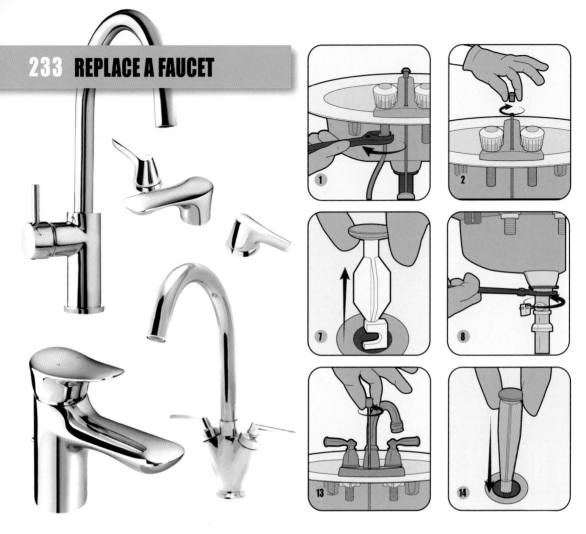

New faucets can add style to interior décor; newer ones even conserve water for lower utility bills. Choose from such finishes as chrome, oil-rubbed bronze, brushed nickel, and more, in a modern design or traditional styling. Faucet installation is fairly straightforward, but cramped space and poor visibility beneath a sink can be confusing for first-timers. Here's an example, using the parts of a faucet designed for 4-inch center sets.

STEP 1 Shut off the water supply, then use a wrench to unscrew the supply lines and wing nuts beneath the faucet levers.

STEP 2 Unscrew the cap of the drain's lift rod so the faucet will slip over it.

STEP 3 Remove the faucet; it should pull right out, but you may need to break the seal of old caulk.

STEP 4 Scrub away any remaining old sealant or putty with a degreasing product.

STEP 5 Place a bead of plumber's putty along the edge of the plastic gasket that fits between the sink and faucet. Apply the gasket to the sink.

STEP 6 Insert the shanks of the faucet through the sink and secure them with new wing nuts.

STEP 7 Unhook the old pop-up drain cover from the lift lever in the drain pipe and pull it out.

STEP 8 Remove drain by unscrewing the retaining nut from the drain assembly with a wrench or pliers.

STEP 9 Apply plumber's putty beneath the lip of the new drain cap, and seat the cap into the sink.

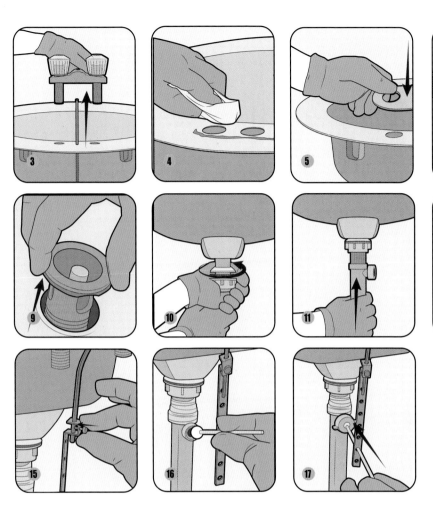

STEP 10 The drain assembly mating component is installed from beneath the sink with a rubber gasket. Apply plumbing sealant to it before installing.

STEP 11 Connect the drain and gasket to the drain cap from below with a new retaining nut.

STEP 12 Position the drain pipe with the lift-lever hole facing the rear of the sink. Fasten the pipe into place with thread seal tape or self-fusing silicone tape.

STEP 13 Thread the lift rod in through the top of the new faucet.

STEP 14 Drop in the new drain cover.

STEP 15 Install the adjustable extension arm to the lift rod, which connects with a simple thumb screw.

STEP 16 Install the lift lever in the drain, and thread the short end of the lever (near the ball) through the hook in the new drain cap. The ball is secured in the drain pipe with a nut.

STEP 17 Thread the lever's long end through whichever hole in the extension arm that will allow easiest operation of the drain assembly. Reconnect the sink drain onto the P-trap with a coupling nut, and then reconnect the water lines. The new faucet is now ready for use.

When a tub or shower faucet leaks, the trouble often lies behind the handles, which turn valves governing water flow. These valves should be fixed quickly; aside from the irritating drip-drip-drip, a leaky shower can waste a small pond of water every day. Repairs are fairly simple, but you'll need a special set of deep-socket wrenches.

STEP 1 Shut off the water supply to the faucet before disassembling the handles.

STEP 2 Modern faucets usually have rubber washers that seal water; over time, these can deteriorate and leak. To get to these, first pry the decorative cap off the handles. (In some cases these caps are threaded.)

STEP 3 Remove the handle's retaining nut and pull the handle off the valve stem.

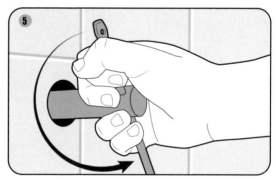

STEP 4 Remove the escutcheon, which is often held with a retaining nut. If not, then the escutcheon is threaded over the valve stems, and you can unscrew the entire escutcheon as one piece. Cut away any caulk that might be holding it to the wall. A strap wrench may help encourage a stubborn one to turn.

STEP 5 The bonnet nut that holds the stem in place is recessed behind the wall requiring a special wrench. A deep-socket shower valve wrench will fit over the protruding valve stem and reach the bonnet nut for removal. Unscrew and remove the bonnet nut.

STEP 6 Pull the stem from the wall to expose the seat washer and retaining screw. Remove the screw and worn seat washer. Replace with a new one, coated in heat-proof faucet grease. Use the correctly sized and shaped seat washer and press it firmly into the stem's retainer. If the stem is in good shape, you're ready to reassemble the shower handles and test your faucet.

STEP 7 Some metal stems may be worn out and need replacement. When purchasing the stems, note the model numbers, typically labeled with either H or C, indicating hot or cold. These determine the direction of handle rotation. Get one of each; be sure to keep them straight during installation. Coat the rubber seat washer with heat-proof faucet grease and install the stem.

If the junction of the shower head and the plumbing spout leaks, wrap the threads with thread-seal tape in the same direction as the head screws onto the spout.

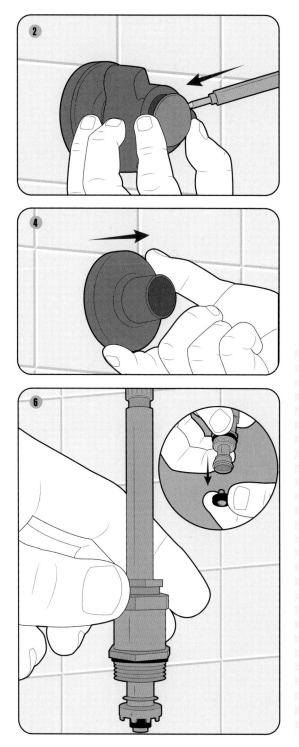

PRO TIP

FIX SINGLE-HANDLE TUB & SHOWER FAUCETS

The repair procedure for single-handle faucets is very similar. First, remove the handle and any stainless steel sleeve or escutcheon that may be in place. The valve cartridge is typically held in place by a U-shaped retaining clip; use needle-nose pliers to carefully take it out. Pull out the old valve cartridge and insert an exact replacement. Reinsert the retaining clip, then replace the sleeve and handle.

235 GET A VALVE SET

A shower-valve set provides the super-deep wrenches needed to remove tub and shower valves. The wrenches are each double-sided, accommodating the 10 standard sizes of plumbing fasteners to make virtually any residential shower or bath valve repair. The wrench sets are available at most hardware stores for $10 to $15.

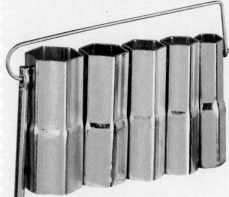

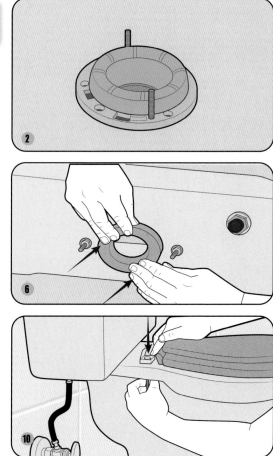

If your toilet is old or needs repair, it may be cheaper to install a new one than patch up the existing, especially if you do it yourself. Installing a new toilet is a rather simple procedure that can be accomplished in just a few steps. To install the new toilet, you'll need a new gasket and two ⁵⁄₁₆-inch bolts to mount the bowl to the floor flange; most of the required parts are included with the new toilet.

STEP 1 Shut off the water supply and flush the toilet. Use a bucket or cloth to remove any leftover water in the tank and bowl. Using a pair of pliers or small pipe wrench, remove the nut connecting the water line to the ballcock valve at the bottom left side of the tank. Remove the two nuts attaching the bowl to the floor flange with a crescent wrench. Once they're removed, lift off the old toilet. Scrape away old gasket material to expose the drain flange (the mounting base for your new toilet). Discard the old bolts.

STEP 2 Place the two new ⁵⁄₁₆-inch bolts in the holes located on the sides of the exposed flange, with the bolt heads inside the flange. Position the two bolts straight up and across from each other. Then put the new toilet gasket (wax ring) on the flange, with the flat side pointing up (if tapered).

STEP 3 Lower the bowl straight down, centered on the wax ring; Ensure the bolts come though the holes on each side of the bowl. Apply pressure straight down; pushing the bowl over the ring and flange squeezing the wax to create a seal.

STEP 4 Add washers and nuts to the protruding bolts and tighten them; be careful not to crack the bowl.

STEP 5 Push a pair of ⁵⁄₁₆-by-3-inch mounting bolts through the small holes on the tank's bottom. Place rubber washers just beneath the bolt heads for a

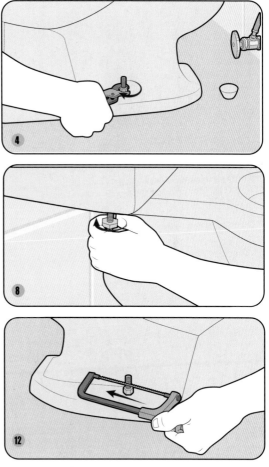

watertight seal. Add nuts and washers to the bolts on the underside of the tank and tighten until snug..

STEP 6 Apply the sponge-rubber gasket over the discharge tube where the tank sets on the bowl.

STEP 7 Set the tank on the bowl, threading the bolts into the bolt holes on the bowl and sandwiching the gasket between the tank and bowl.

STEP 8 Add metal washers and nuts to the bolts on the tank's bottom. Hold the tank level and tighten. Keep each bolt stationary with a screwdriver while backing up the nut with a crescent wrench. (Avoid over-tightening, which can crack the porcelain.)

STEP 9 Screw the flush handle to the lift arm through the hole in the tank. Connect the lift arm to the chain of the flushing ball/flapper in the tank.

STEP 10 Bolt the new toilet lid to the bowl.

STEP 11 Install a new water line from the wall or floor fixture to the feed valve on tank's underside. Turn on the water, check for leaks, and try a few trial flushes. If your toilet holds water, tighten the bolts that hold the bowl to the floor. Adjust minor spacing issues or instability between the tank and bowl, or bowl and floor, with hard rubber shims.

STEP 12 Once everything is in place, cut the ends off the mounting bolts to accommodate the plastic caps. Caulk the base of the bowl to create a waterproof seal, protecting the floor and providing additional stability. Replace the tank cover and your new toilet is ready.

237 INSTALL LAMINATE

A popular and economical choice for both kitchen and bathroom countertops is plastic laminate, available in many attractive colors and designs. Laminate countertops (often called Formica, although that is actually the name of only one manufacturer) come in just about every pattern imaginable. From contemporary patterns to styles that mimic popular stone looks, laminate is durable, affordable, and you can install it yourself

238 CLEAN UP A COUNTER

Before installing laminate on your countertops, you need to prepare the surface. First, remove obstacles such as sinks and faucets. If installing new sheet laminate over old laminate material, thoroughly sand and clean the old surface to remove all debris and contaminants. Sanding removes any glossy coating and roughens the surface for better bonding with the adhesive.

Plastic laminate is often sold in 4-by-8-foot sheets. Test-fit the laminate. In some cases, you can set the sheet in place using a marker to trace the shape of the countertop on the underside of the new laminate. Allow extra room outside the traced lines when rough-cutting a sheet.

The edges of these sheets are very straight, so plan for the edges to line up to the rear of the cabinet against the wall, when possible. The sheet cutouts should roughly mirror the shape of the final countertop, but add a few extra inches so the sheet edges will overhang the edges of the countertop. You'll go back later with a router and trim the edges flush.

239 MAKE CLEAN CUTS

There are special blades that let you use a utility knife to cut a sheet. You can also cut plastic laminate using a circular saw, jigsaw, or table saw with a fine-toothed blade. Put a strip of masking tape where the cut is to be made to prevent chipping and make the line easier to see. If using a powered circular saw or jigsaw, cut from the back side to help prevent chipping.

On a table saw, use a fine-tooth blade installed backwards. The rip guide of the table saw helps to make a straight cut, the blade peels a strip of material as wide as the kerf itself, and the cut is perfectly smooth. You will need to set up both outfeed and lateral supports to work with the big 4-by-8 sheets. (Return the blade to its normal direction after cutting.)

240 MAKE CONTACT PROPERLY

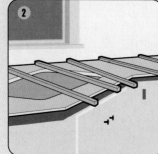

It's important for you to attach your laminate to the countertop the right way. Here's how.

STEP 1 Plastic laminate is generally applied with contact cement. Brush contact cement onto the old countertop surface in a smooth, even layer. Then, brush a layer of contact cement on the back side of the laminate cutout for the counter. Allow the adhesive to dry until tacky, usually about 5 to 10 minutes, but check the contact cement label for recommendations.

STEP 2 Place wooded strips or dowels onto the countertop roughly a foot apart. They won't stick, and will act as a temporary barrier between the sheet and countertop. They must be long enough to extend past the counter edge so you can pull them out later. Next, place the new sheet laminate face-up on the wood strips. Don't let these glued surfaces touch yet or they will bond together. The new sheet should be accurately positioned right above its final installed location with its edges flush against the surrounding walls.

STEP 3 Starting at one end of the sheet, remove the first wood strip or dowel and use a J-roller to press the new sheet down onto the counter, bonding the two pieces together. Use the roller to apply pressure to the sheet so the glue will have a strong bond and no air pockets.

STEP 4 Work toward the opposite end, removing each of the wood strips one at a time and rolling the entire surface thoroughly as you progress.

STEP 5 By the time you reach the other end of the counter, the entire new laminate surface should be securely bonded. Use a router fitted with a flush trim bit to trim away the excess laminate flush with the edge of the counter. Do not rush the router; let the tool do the work.

STEP 6 You may encounter obstructions such as sinks, faucets, and such, that require cutouts. You can use a jigsaw with a fine-tooth blade for the cutout, as well as a router or spiral saw.

241 COVER BIG COUNTERS

In some cases a countertop might be too long, requiring you to join two sheets. You can then bond the larger sheet in place like normal.

STEP 1 Put a narrow strip of wax paper down along the edge of the larger piece. Use some wooden strips to keep the second piece away from the cemented surface of the counter.

STEP 2 Along the seam, position the second piece flush against the first piece, on top of the wax paper. Tape the second piece to hold it in place. Roll the second sheet of laminate down as usual, removing the wood strips as you progress toward the seam.

STEP 3 Once the second piece has been fully bonded in place, lift the edge covering the wax paper. Remove the paper and use your J-roller to roll from the middle of the second piece toward the seam, bonding the seam tightly.

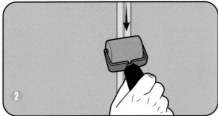

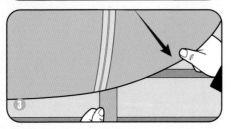

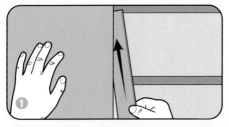

242 COAT A COUNTERTOP

One alternative to re-laminating is to give your old countertops a contemporary finish. Rust-Oleum's Countertop Transformations kit can create a striking new look that really does change the existing surface into any of a number of faux granite or stone finishes. You need to follow the instructions meticulously for best results.

STEP 1 Carefully tape off anywhere walls or other surfaces meet the laminate, as well as all fixtures.

STEP 2 Next, scuff-sand the existing laminate surface. Be sure to rough up everywhere that you're going to coat or the material may not bond evenly.

STEP 3 Apply the adhesive base coat with a roller. The adhesive dries quickly, so if your have multiple counters, do the adhesive and chip steps on each one before moving on to the next.

STEP 4 Use a seed spreader to coat the applied adhesive with the decorative chips, for a faux granite look. When the adhesive is fully dry, sand the surface and apply a clear topcoat.

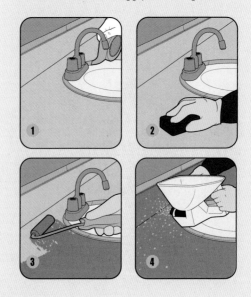

243 EDGE IT RIGHT

Replacing your countertop's edges is a straightforward, but important part of the job. Here's how to do it.

STEP 1 For the most part, edge strips install in much the same way as the surface sheeting. Cut the edge strips to size. Brush contact cement onto the back of the strip and the old countertop surface edge after prepping. Allow the glue to dry tacky, then install the edge strip and roll it in with the J-roller.

STEP 2 Use clamps to hold the edge strip firmly in place while it dries.

STEP 3 Don't break the edge strip at a curve. In some cases your edge strip may not be long enough to cover the entire countertop edge, and you'll have to join two edge strips. Ideally you can stop the edge strip at a corner and begin the second strip on the other side. If you have a sweeping curved edge, break the strips at a long, flat area, instead of a curve. The edge strips have a tendency to straighten out, and it'll be nearly impossible to get the edging to stay glued in place if you break it at a curve.

STEP 4 Once the edge strips are bonded, remove the clamps. Trim the edges using a router and flush trim bit. With bits that use a guide wheel, carefully set the guide so the bit cuts the edge of the laminate but not the adjoining countertop. Fine-tune the edges using a half-round file to slightly bevel the transition between the countertop and edge. Laminate filler can also help fix nicks, scratches, or other minor damage.

Cabinets greatly determine a kitchen's overall décor. Over time, peeling paint, nicks and scratches, or a dull, dirty finish, can detract from the look of kitchen cabinets, but adding on a fresh coat of paint can give them new life. Repainting also saves tons of money when compared to full replacement, which can easily cost several thousands of dollars.

Depending on the condition of your cabinets, the job might only call for a thorough cleaning and light sanding (220-grit to scuff the surface) to renew the existing color. This is a fairly straightforward procedure that requires you to remove the hardware and doors, and secure a dust-free location for painting and drying the doors; the carcass can be painted in place.

To change a cabinet's color, or for any heavily worn, stained, or water-damaged cabinets, the best practice is to sand and/or strip off all the paint and damaged surface to reveal the original wood. Complete removal of the old cabinet finish will guarantee a good bond for the new paint.

245 TAKE THEM APART

In order to refinish your cabinets, you'll need to prepare them first.

Unscrew all the hinges, handles, and knobs to remove the cabinet's doors and drawers. If you plan on reusing the old hardware, store all loose components and fasteners safely while you paint. Label the doors with painter's tape to identify location for replacement.

Fill any scratches or dents in the wood with non-shrinking putty. If you plan on using any new hardware on different fastener locations, fill the old screw holes with putty, let dry, and sand smooth.

Set up a work area with a large, flat surface to work on the doors. Use dropcloths to cover and protect anything you don't want exposed to wood dust or paint stripper. (Some paint strippers require open-air ventilation.)

246 SAND OR STRIP

Once you've dismantled your cabinets, you'll need to remove the old paint. Fortunately, there are multiple ways to do this.

STRIP DOWN Paint strippers vary in formula so get the right one. Brush on a coat according to the manufacturer's instructions; after just a short time, the surface should discolor as the finish dissolves. Scrape it away using a putty knife or furniture scraper, and discard it into a plastic bag. Stripping brushes work well to remove material from contoured edges. This is a messy job, so use drop cloths and rubber gloves; keep plenty of rags for cleanup.

SAND AWAY Clamp the door to the work surface and use a random orbit sander with a medium-grit sandpaper to get to the bare wood. Stock plenty of replacement abrasive discs. This is a messy job; work outdoors or use a sander with a dust-collection system.

COMBINE TECHNIQUES Thicker, gel-like strippers stick to vertical cabinet surfaces, but using a power sander in an upright position can be exhausting. Place doors on a workbench for comfortable sanding.

FINISH UP Once the original finish is all removed, finish-sand the wood to achieve a very smooth surface. Start with 150-grit sandpaper, then use 180-grit. The fully prepped surface should be clean, dry, dull, and smooth. Remove all wood dust with a tack cloth (don't use water).

248 PUT IT TOGETHER

Once you've finished with your repainting, it's time to put your cabinets back together. Replace all the old hardware, or install new hardware. To avoid splitting the wood, keep knobs and pulls less at least an inch from any edge of the door. A general rule of thumb is to locate them within one-third the height of the cabinet.

STEP 1 Use a combination square to keep the location of all handles, hinges or other hardware consistently spaced from door to door.

STEP 2 Drill pilot holes for all screws, then fasten all hardware securely.

STEP 3 The doors must be installed level and plumb. Ensure that your doors cover up their respective openings evenly; any offset to the right or left will be noticeable and will likely interfere with installing the next door in line.

STEP 4 Once all the doors are back in place, you'll have the look of new cabinets at a small fraction of the price.

247 APPLY NEW PAINT

With proper application and cure time, either oil- or latex-based paint will achieve a quality finish. If you opt for latex paint, make sure to use 100-percent acrylic formulation, which is much more durable than vinyl acrylic paints. A sprayed-on finish will achieve the smoothest finish coat. To avoid spraying indoors, you may want to brush-paint the carcass and then spray-paint the doors outside with an HVLP sprayer. Otherwise, you can paint the doors by using a smooth foam roller.

STEP 1 Begin with a coat of oil-based primer, covering all surfaces completely to ensure the adhesion of your paint coats.

STEP 2 After the primer has dried out, lightly sand it with 180-grit sandpaper to remove any imperfections before applying your topcoats. Use a tack cloth to wipe down the surface after you finish sanding.

STEP 3 Apply two coats of paint to the doors, drawer and carcass, allowing the paint to dry overnight between coats.

249 PRESERVE OUTDOOR WOOD

Whether pressure-treated, cedar, cypress, redwood, or even a high-end exotic hardwood, proper care and maintenance will protect exterior wood and keep it in sturdy shape for years. Staining and sealing outdoor wood is among the best ways to protect it from the elements and seasons.

The most commonly used outdoor wood coating is an exterior-grade penetrating stain. These water-repellent preservatives include a mildewcide; some products even contain ultraviolet light absorbers that protect from sun exposure. Available in both oil- and water-based formulations, the resins penetrate wood pores to provide pigment and block out the damaging effect of weather while allowing the natural wood grain and texture to shine through.

The second category is a film-forming sealant that bonds to the surface of the wood like paint or shellac. These products provide a high-gloss furniture look, while still allowing the natural grain to show through. Available in oil- or water-based finishes, they form a durable and beautiful satin surface, but they can only be maintained with another coat of film-forming sealant. Pigments are added to change the wood color and add UV protection. Film-forming sealants should be avoided in areas exposed to foot traffic, because the abrasion can wear through the film coating.

Outdoor wood coatings are typically formulated with either water or oil. Many water-based stain/sealants have tiny particles of pigment and resin that adhere to each other very tightly as the finish dries, similar to a patchwork quilt. With oil-based finishes, the tiny particles actually fuse together chemically into one large sheet-like substance, which achieves a harder finish and is less likely to develop an amber color tone. Examine the product's label for clues to the coating's quality, looking for any reference to "non-yellowing" properties.

Water-based finishes are generally heralded for their ease of use. Compared to oil-based formulas, they're easier to clean up, have a lower odor and are often less costly. Most water-based coatings require more coats, however, and they still will not last as long as their oil-based or "alkyd" counterparts, which generally can offer more long-term, wood-preserving durability for outdoor construction.

250 TREAT NEW WOOD

Allow new pressure-treated wood to dry before staining or sealing. The treatment of lumber with waterborne preservatives leaves moisture in the wood. This is why fresh PT lumber often arrives wet from the supplier, and the moisture can impede the penetration of stains and paints. For best performance of paint and stain coatings, allow the treated wood to dry for 2 to 4 weeks prior to application. Estimating exactly how long treated wood will take to dry is difficult, and a lot depends on how much time has elapsed since the treatment, the lumber's exposure to the sun, ambient weather, etc.

Wood that has its own natural preservatives, such as western red cedar, cypress, or redwood, do not require as much drying time because the wood was never pressure-treated using any sort of preservative.

Contrary to popular belief, new wood still needs to be cleaned to remove any "mill scale", which is a compression of the grain during the milling process that can cause the stain to float or run off without absorption. Clean the surface with an oxygenated bleach.

251 FIX WEATHERED WOOD

When wood is exposed to the sunlight the ultraviolet rays can damage the wood fibers over time, causing the surface to turn gray. The most direct way to renew the appearance is sanding or pressure-washing the surface. However, sanding can be very difficult and time-consuming, and pressure-washing can remove the gray but cause the surface to fuzz or splinter, posing a "touch" hazard for areas such as deck surfaces where people may walk barefoot. When using a power-washer, limit your pressure to no more than 1,000 or 1,200 PSI.

Some individual boards may be heavily weathered. Replace them completely, clean the existing boards, then stain them all to match.

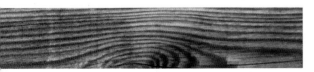

252 APPLY STAIN PROPERLY

For a good, long-lasting coating of stain on wood, there are some simple tips you can follow.

Always thoroughly mix the stain to evenly blend the solids and ensure a consistent color tone throughout the project. For both horizontal and vertical structures, brushing is the best way of stain/sealer application because the bristles push the product evenly into the woodgrain to increase absorption. Using a sprayer or roller can apply the stain more quickly, but both of these methods leave much of the stain on the surface without adequate penetration into the pores. This superficial product can wear away unevenly, so you should still back-brush it into the woodgrain for the most consistent appearance and best protection.

253 USE A CONDITIONER

An often overlooked step for outdoor staining projects is the application of a wood brightener. These chemical agents open the woodgrain to improve penetration of the stain and help restore the appearance of weathered wood to a like-new condition. The product can simply be sprayed onto the wood surface, given a few minutes to work its "magic" and then rinsed off, requiring very little labor.

After using any chemical treatment to clean and prepare the wood, use plenty of water to completely remove all traces of the products—and then allow it to dry fully prior to stain or sealer application.

254 IMPROVE OLD STAIN

Generally, it's best to remove old stain before applying new stain, especially when changing products or colors. Old stain will usually show through the new, leaving blotchy spots in the finish. Film-forming stains must be completely removed before applying a penetrating stain. If you plan to use the same color and type of stain (and your deck is in decent condition), you can probably get by with a thorough cleaning and a fresh maintenance coat. As always, refer to the manufacturer's recommendations for the best application and care practices.

If old stain is built up on the deck, you may need to use something stronger than oxygen bleach cleaner. Stain strippers are often more caustic, but they can remove most weathered stains in a single application. Small, stubborn spots can then be removed with a hand sander once the deck has dried.

255 INSTALL GUTTERS AND DOWNSPOUTS

Gutters and downspouts can protect your house from water damage. By collecting roof runoff and diverting it away from the building envelope, they help prevent wood rot, mold, and mildew. Professional installation of metal gutters usually involves the use of specialized equipment to form seamless gutters out of rolls of sheet metal at the job site. However, DIYers who don't mind working on a ladder can save considerable cost by installing gutters using sectional systems available at home centers.

Start by sketching your gutter system on paper to quantify the various components required. Measure your roof line and the wall height to calculate the number of 10-foot sections of gutter and downspout required. Account for end caps, seamers, inside or outside corner pieces, downspout elbows and end drops. You'll also need sealant or mastic for sealing the joints, downspout bands to fasten the assembly to the house, and sheet-metal screws to connect the downspout sections.

256 CHALK THE SLOPE

Before you place your gutters, you need to be sure they'll drain water properly. Attach a ladder stabilizer to the top of your ladder to prevent swaying. This also provides a 10-inch standoff from the roof line, which makes it easy to access the fascia and gutter without obstruction from the ladder.

At one corner of the roof, hook a chalk line at the point where you want the top edge of the gutter to terminate. At the opposite end of the fascia, first level the string, then drop it 1 inch per 40-foot run and snap the chalk line. This marks a slope that will help pull water to the downspout locations. If you have a long run with downspouts at both ends, slope the gutter from its midpoint toward both of the book-ending downspouts.

257 CUT IT DOWN TO SIZE

When assembling a gutter and downspouts, you'll likely have to cut some of the materials to length. One basic method is to clamp the material firmly to a bench and cut using a hacksaw. A good pair of metal snips can do the job as well. A sliding miter saw, with a fine-toothed blade turned backward, makes a nice, clean cut with very little effort. When cutting gutter material on a miter saw, turn the section upside-down so that the cut will enter the more stable underside instead of the top edges.

258 PREASSEMBLE YOUR GUTTERS

To ensure proper construction, build as much of the gutter system on the ground as possible.

STEP 1 Joining gutter sections requires a seamer, a 3-inch wide piece of gutter material in a matching profile. First, apply gutter sealant or mastic to the top side of the seamer piece.

STEP 2 Wrap the seamer around the butted gutter sections from beneath. The seamer's front hooks onto the front edge of the gutter; the rear extends above the back of the gutter, and this metal flap folds over its edge. Crimp the seamer's front and rear lip tightly to the gutter with pliers. Cover the visible seam with a generous bead of sealant.

STEP 3 Attach the gutter sections and end drops the same way. End drops are the short sections that drain into the downspouts, and should be located at the end of a wall.

STEP 4 Cut and seam gutter extensions to the end drops as needed to extend the entire length of the roof line. End caps fit onto the profile with sealant to ensure water exits through the downspouts.

STEP 5 Give the sealant a few hours to dry and gain some rigidity at the joints before installing the gutter section on the house.

259 HANG 'EM HIGH

Gutter sections are very lightweight, but they can be cumbersome for one person to carry up the ladder and install. Recruit help if possible.

STEP 1 Place the ladder on the roof about midway to where your first section will be installed. Position the gutter section so the end is about 1 inch beyond the roof line. Tilt it slightly so the top edge matches the slope of the chalk line. Zap a screw into the center fastener.

STEP 2 A single screw holds the section in place while you install the others.

STEP 3 Repeat the steps of this procedure for the adjoining sections. The only difference here is that you will have to seam together the separate gutter sections at the roof line rather than on the ground.

Once your gutters are installed, the downspouts are your final piece of the puzzle.

STEP 1 Use screws and sealant to fasten a flange outlet inside the hole of each end drop.

STEP 2 Duct-tape an elbow section onto each flange outlet. Use a straight edge to follow the path of the elbow to the wall where the second elbow will be located. Tape the second elbow in place on the wall. Measure the downspout section needed to install between the two elbows. Each downspout and elbow has one end crimped; the larger end fits over the smaller end to form a slip joint. Account for the overlapping slip joint when measuring—about 1 inch of downspout should overlap the elbow at each end.

STEP 3 Assemble your downspout at ground level, driving two primed aluminum screws into pre-drilled holes at each joint. Avoid any leaks by orienting the successive pieces so the upper elbow or downspout tucks into the lower section.

STEP 4 Nail or screw the downspouts snugly against the wall using two flexible downspout bands per each 10-foot section. Duct tape will hold the downspout stationary while fastening.

STEP 5 Attach a front or side elbow at the bottom of the downspout.

STEP 6 Finally, use drain extensions or splash blocks to direct water away from the building foundation.

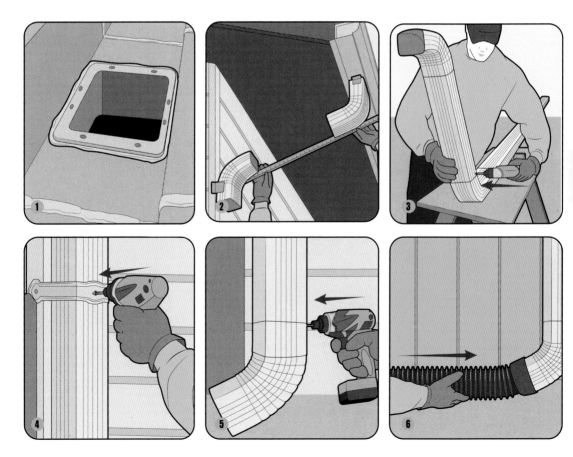

261 FASTEN IT YOURSELF

Gutter fasteners come in various styles and shapes. Some options include a screw and ferrule, fascia brackets, roof hangers with strap, or hidden hangers (the type shown here). The hidden hangers clip over the rear edge of the gutter and then hook beneath the front lip. Each fastener comes with a ¼-inch hex-head screw that is driven into the fascia board to hang the gutter.

Pre-attach the hidden hangers at ground level, clipping them on every 2 feet along the length of the gutter section. Locate a fastener near the end of each gutter section in order to minimize stress at joint locations.

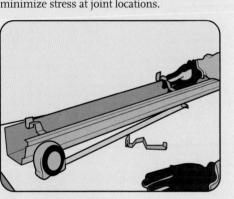

PRO TIP

COVER UP FOR EASY MAINTENANCE Gutter protection reduces the need to climb a ladder and scrape muck out of your gutters. The idea is to prevent leaves and any other debris from accumulating in the gutter system, which can result in blockage and in some areas lead to ice dams. A number of cover types are available, including hinged lids, foam-type fillers, and products that look similar to large pipe cleaners.

A concrete slab is one of the most basic components of modern construction throughout the world. Whether it's used as a building foundation, sidewalk, patio, or a footing for an exterior stairway, the construction is largely always done by the same method.

STEP 1 Mark the perimeter of the slab location with stakes and string.

STEP 2 Calculate the total depth of the finished slab, including the concrete and the gravel base. Concrete is typically applied at a minimum of two inches, but we recommend a thickness of at least 4 inches for more durability. With this type of application, both a fine and coarse aggregate are required. We used ready-mix bags of concrete available from the local home center.

STEP 3 Dig a level excavation to the dimensions of your slab, plus room for forming boards.

STEP 4 The first base layer will consist of 5 inches of gravel. Shovel in the gravel and compact the bed down to 4 inches with a hand tamper. Be sure to dig deep enough to account for the gravel base (about 4 inches after compaction) plus the concrete pour (another 4 inches).

STEP 5 Build a rectangular concrete form using treated 2x4s. Pros often use duplex nails to build the form, which are easy to pry out after the slab cures, but for a more low-profile form, heavy-duty screws can be even faster. The forms should frame the perimeter that you marked with the stakes and string. Depending on the application the form may not necessarily have to be level, but it should always slope slightly away from any structure so that it can shed water.

STEP 6 Anchor the form in place on the gravel bed every 12 to 18 inches by screwing in stakes driven in the ground outside the frame. These hold the forms securely so they don't bow or blow out when filled with the heavy concrete. With the stakes in place, cut the tops flush with the form, so you can use a screed board once the concrete is added.

STEP 7 Reinforce the slab with a grid of rebar on wire brackets that float the rebar about midway deep in the concrete forms. Tie the rebar intersections

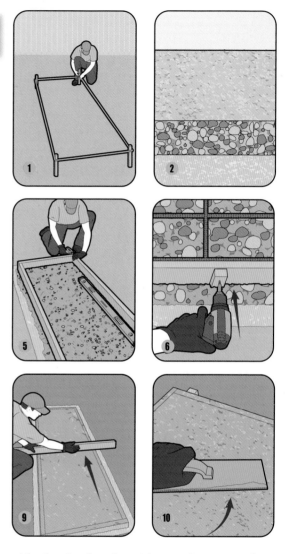

with wire. Cut the rebar with a grinder or a metal-cutting chop saw.

STEP 8 Mix up some quick-drying concrete and then fill the form. Work one bucket at a time or just rent a concrete mixer. Spray the form and the gravel with water when adding the concrete. Keep the entire work area damp throughout the installation of the concrete so the surroundings don't leach moisture out of the concrete before it has properly cured.

STEP 9 When the mix reaches the top of the forms, strike off the excess concrete level with the top by screeding it with a very straight 2x4. Move the edge

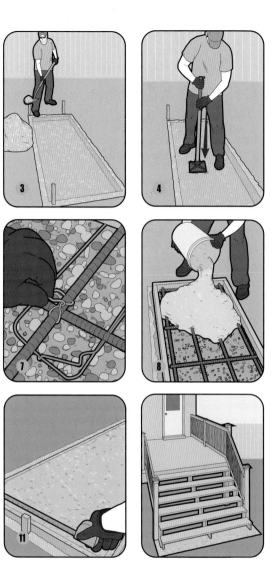

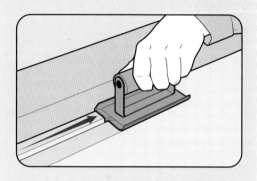

263 MAKE A JOINT

Large slabs, such as sidewalks and driveways, require expansion joints to prevent cracking. A jointer tool held against a straight edge will produce a nice, straight-line groove in the slab surface. Control joints are normally spaced at intervals that are equal to the width of your pour, but you should avoid exceeding 10 feet in any direction without a joint. The joint should be cut to at least one-fourth of the depth of the slab. Control joints in large slabs can also be cut after the concrete cures, using a masonry blade in a circular saw.

of the screed board in a side-to-side motion across the upper edge of the form to create an even slab.

STEP 10 Use a wood float in a circular motion to work the heavy aggregate below the concrete surface and bring the "cream" to the top. To give more traction to the top of the slab, roughen the surface with a broom as the concrete cures.

STEP 11 Allow the concrete to cure for a few days more before walking or building on top of it. Keep the slab covered in plastic to retain moisture longer for a slow, solid cure.

264 CURE YOUR CONCRETE

Concrete doesn't get its strength from drying, but from curing. According to the experts at the Sakrete company, "Curing is the action taken to maintain moisture and temperature conditions in freshly placed cement mixes, allowing the cement to thoroughly hydrate." This is done by misting the concrete, placing wet covers such as burlap on the concrete, or by coating with a product such as Cure 'N Seal.

Curing is necessary for the concrete to have its desired properties. Rapid loss of water from the surface of the concrete will cause the top of the slab to cure faster than the bottom. This can happen during periods of high temperature or wind. If the concrete cures at different rates, the slab can develop cracks.

BIG
PROJECTS

GO BEYOND THE BASICS

Here you venture into the world of construction craftsmanship. The trade professionals who do following projects daily make their living by applying hard-earned expertise developed through time and experience. As a DIYer, you probably don't have the luxury of that experience.

I know what that's like. I have a history of diving head-first into big projects and regretting it later. I've shingled roofs, built decks, erected fences, installed flooring, and knocked out walls. Some of those big projects I hope to never do again. Now that I have the benefit of experience, I know when I've bitten off more than I can chew. I didn't give up and I didn't surrender, but I hated every grueling minute of trudging all the way to the end of those projects. I also learned from my mistakes.

So, here's the best advice I can offer for large-scale projects: Proceed carefully, research the project ahead of time, and expect a lot of hiccups. You'll find some helpful advice in the following pages, but products vary, materials evolve, and entire books have been dedicated to parsing the details of some of the upcoming topics.

In general, I've developed what might appear to be a grim projection for major DIY home improvement projects: Expect multiple unforeseen obstacles. Expect the job to cost more than you estimated. And plan for the job to take at least twice as long as you think.

I don't view those rules as pessimistic, however, just realistic, and I base that on experience. Home improvement is rife with surprises. Forewarned is forearmed when you need to schedule a big project around your day-to-day life.

Look at it this way: If you prepare for the worst-case scenario and only the best comes to pass, then you'll be one happy DIYer with extra time on your hands to enjoy the fruits of your hard work.

265 WORK WELL WITH TILE

Tile provides hundreds of creative design options. Often made of ceramic or stone, tile is a durable material for flooring, walls and countertops. It's available in a vast array of colors, patterns, shapes, and sizes. Tile is durable enough to withstand heavy foot traffic and can feasibly last as long as the substrate that supports it.

TOOL UP You will need chalk line, an angle grinder and/or diamond-blade wet saw, a notched trowel, a grouting float, a carpenter's level, a clean sponge, a masonry bit, a half-round file, a dowel, a caulk gun, a broom, and (optionally) tile spacers.

GET YOUR MATERIALS You will (obviously) need tiles, along with thin-set mortar or tile adhesive, grout, caulking, and tile/grout sealant.

266 PLAN YOUR INSTALLATION

Sketch a floor plan to calculate how many tiles you'll need to purchase, including special border features or decorative patterns. Thick grout lines between joints will also impact how many tiles will fit on the floor.

Before installation, remove existing floor coverings and baseboard trim. Make any necessary repairs, such as re-nailing any loose boards that might squeak. Tile should generally be installed on a rigid underlayment, which resists movement such as the swelling and

contraction that occurs in wood, which can damage the installation. Tile can be installed over a cement floor that is structurally sound and dry.

Wood subfloors should be a minimum of 1¼-inch thick. In new home construction where traditional ¾-inch plywood is used as a subfloor, use additional sheets of ½- or ⅝-inch cement board to ensure rigidity beneath the tiles. Fasten the reinforcing sheets to the subfloor, spacing screws every 8 inches on center.

267 PREP YOUR TILES

Some tiles, such as natural stone, can vary in thickness, so sort those accordingly before laying the floor. Tiles that are notably thicker can pose a tripping hazard if the edges stick up above the normal plane of the finished surface. Start with the thickest tiles and use mortar or adhesive to build up the thinner ones.

Check the tiles for surface damage. Set aside chipped pieces to cut for edge tiles. Color varies as well; sort tiles according to the pattern you want, and stack them around the room strategically so they'll be within reach during the installation.

Lay out the tiles dry, filling the four quadrants created by the chalk lines until the whole floor, apart from the edges, is laid in place. Ensure the layout is square and symmetrical; correct any errors before installing with mortar.

Cut border tiles to fit around the room's edges, allowing at least ⅛-inch grout joint along the walls.

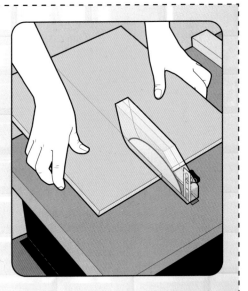

268 GET THE RIGHT LAYOUT

A standard tile layout procedure is the quarter method, wherein you divide the room into four quarters to help sequence the layout. First, measure and mark the midpoint of all four walls. Snap intersecting chalk lines at the center point of the site to form a cross. Check that the lines form right angles. Lay a row of tiles in a dry run along all four lines, all the way to the walls, creating a cross of tiles in the center of the room. Start laying the tile from the center and work your way outward.

Use tile spacers if you prefer visibly distinct grout joints. Insert the spacers so they stand up between the tiles like tiny handles. These can maintain uniform joint spacing during layout and installation. You may also opt to butt the tiles against each other and grout the resulting fine joint line between them, using no spacers.

Typically, the dry run will reveal that the last tile against the wall won't fit in the space provided. Here you will need to adjust your original chalk lines so that the border tiles of opposite walls will be the same size, resulting in a symmetrical tile layout. Adjust all the chalk lines and, once again, lay out a dry run of tiles to make sure the layout will be symmetrical. All of the cut border tiles should be the same size from one end of the room to the other. There should be no border space along the edge of the walls of less than a half tile in width.

For a diagonal layout, use the center point established with the quarter method and snap square lines across the two diagonals of the room, forming an "X" on top of the cross. Install tiles along the X, using the quarter method. Ensure the lines are at true right angles and that the partial border tiles are equal in width.

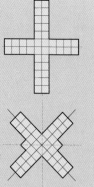

269 INSTALL YOUR TILES

The following steps explain floor tile installation, but the procedure can generally be applied to most tile projects.

STEP 1 Lift about nine tiles in the corner of the room furthest from the door. Using a trowel with ¼-inch notches, spread an even bed of thin-set mortar over a 2-by-3-foot area. Then, reposition the tiles from the walls inward. Reinsert spacers, if required.

STEP 2 Press each tile down firmly or tap it using a rubber mallet. As you progress, use a carpenter's level to ensure the tile surface is even and flush with surrounding tiles. Use mortar to build up beneath the tiles as needed. Immediately wipe the surface with a damp sponge to remove any mortar from the face of the tiles. Continue working outward from the walls, progressing toward the room's exit.

STEP 3 Allow tiles to set for at least 24 hours. Remove any spacers and fill the joints with sanded grout. (For delicate tiles such as marble or polished stone, use unsanded grout to avoid scratching the surface.) Work the grout into the joints with a sponge float, which has a dense foam pad on the base. Use the float tilted at a 45-degree angle to work the grout over the tile to

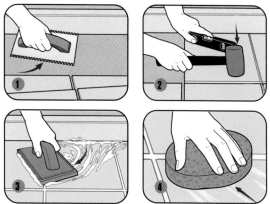

completely fill all joints. Wipe off excess grout with a damp sponge, rinsing it frequently with a bucket of clean water. Once the tile is fully grouted, shape the joints by running a dowel or grouting tool over the grout lines. Leave joints in floor tile as full of grout as possible to avoid dirt accumulation.

STEP 4 Allow the grout to cure overnight. On the next day, scrub the tile using a damp, abrasive sponge to remove grout residue. Repeat the scrubbing for the next three days. If grout haze remains, a solution of vinegar and warm water will usually remove it. Allow grout to cure for a week before sealing.

270 APPLY SEALANT

Most ceramic tiles are glazed at the factory, but some varieties of tiles (such as natural stone or terracotta) may not be glazed and will require a protective sealer once installed.

Regardless of your choice of tile, you should always apply sealer to the grout to keep it from absorbing dirt and grime. Doing so will protect against stains and make routine cleaning much easier. Work the sealant over all the grout lines using a small brush. Remove excess sealant and let it dry for at least four hours before use.

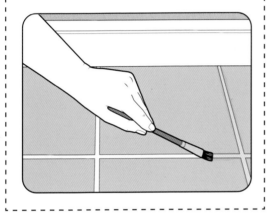

271 MAKE STRAIGHT CUTS

For small installations of glazed tile, you can use a small handheld glass cutter to score a straight line on the glazed surface. Place the tile over a dowel aligned beneath the score mark, and press down on both sides of the tile to snap it along the line.

For larger jobs, speed up the process with a snap tile cutter. First mark the cut line on the tile. Set the tile on the cutter's base plate, align the cutting line with the guide bars, and lower the carbide-tipped cutter onto the line. Draw the carbide wheel or blade across the tile surface to score it. Then press down on the handle to break the tile along the score line.

These tools only make straight cuts that extend across the entire tile. For curved cuts, partial cuts, or anything irregular, you'll need different tools

272 NIP IT INTO SHAPE

Tile nippers provide a simple way to make small partial cuts along the edge of a tile to fit around a pipe or other obstacle. Tile nippers look much like a pair of pliers but take small bites (⅛ inch) out of tile. The smaller the nibbles you make, the more control you have of the cut, and the less likely the tile will crack or shatter beneath the pressure of the blades. Practice on a scrap piece of tile before making any critical cuts in your installation.

The nipper's teeth usually leave a fairly ragged edge along the cut. This may not be an issue if the cut is going to be concealed with a plumbing escutcheon or similar device. In any areas where appearance matters, it may help to smooth the rough edges with a file.

273 WHET YOUR WET SAW

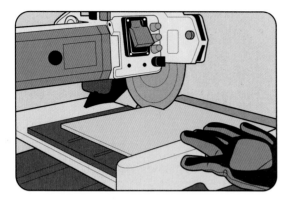

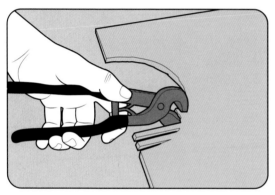

When cutting tile, professionals will often use a wet saw: a powered circular blade that has an integrated water reservoir (often with an electric pump) to cool the cutting action. These are available in a variety of configurations: the table-saw type (the blade protrudes from beneath the table surface and the tile is pushed over it); the bridge or sled-type (the blade is mounted at the top of the tool and cuts the tile from above); and portable handheld models. Overspray from wet saws can be messy, so they're typically used outdoors.

Wet saws are generally used with diamond-tipped cutting wheels to remove ceramic and stone material with great precision and minimal heat buildup. When equipped with a miter gauge, they can make accurate cuts at any angle.

The circular blade of a wet saw enables only straight cutting, but you can still use it for irregular cuts. To fit a tile against a post or molding, simply scribe the profile of the obstacle on the tile, first make a series of closely-spaced parallel cuts up to the profile line, and then use a set of nippers to remove thin strips of tile between the kerfs.

274 DRILL TILE AND GLASS

When you need to mount fasteners into tile, glass-and-tile bits have an arrowhead-shaped tip designed for penetrating brittle materials. Drill the pilot hole at a slow speed and use a spray bottle of water to cool the cutting surface, which helps drilling performance and extends the life of the bit. Gently increase speed and pressure as needed.

If you're going to be cutting larger holes, you can select from carbide-tipped masonry bits or diamond-tipped hole cutters. As with the smaller bits, carbide bits should be lubricated with water to reduce heat.

By comparison, diamond-tipped hole cutters are designed to drill at higher speeds and can even cut dry. They will allow you to create holes with larger diameters for pipe and cable access located in the center of a tile.

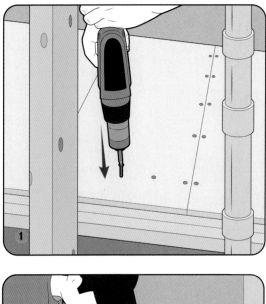

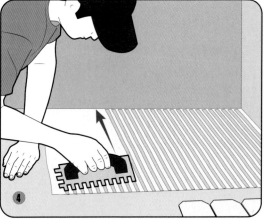

Mosaic tile is a combination of little colored tiles that are called "tesserae," and they can be used to make artistic or geometrical designs. Tiles of one color can be used for a plain layout. Complementary colors are a more popular option; multiple colors can be used for more complex patterns. With many small tiles the installer can use individual units like blocks of color in a painting. To skip the assembly of mosaic tile piece-by-piece, you can also use larger tiles that consist of tesserae attached to a backing in a prearranged pattern. The backing can be cut to size and lets the tiles easily adhere to the floor.

STEP 1 Install cement board over the plywood subfloor and screw it down securely.

STEP 2 If you're using tiles on a scrim backing, cut to size to fit the room's dimensions properly.

STEP 3 Start with a dry run over the cement board.

STEP 4 After planning your layout, spread tile adhesive onto the cement board with a notched trowel. It may help to use plastic tile spacers to keep grout joints consistent during installation.

STEP 5 Mix polymer-modified, sandless grout for mosaic tile.

STEP 6 Apply grout to the tile joints with a rubber float, then finish the job like a standard tile installation.

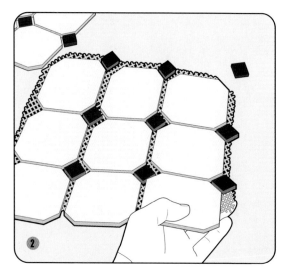

②

③

⑤

⑥

Floor installation is a big job due primarily to how disruptive it can be to an occupied living space. But upgrading a finished floor can dramatically improve a home and add to its value. Floor installation is also achievable by a savvy DIYer, although some methods are easier than others.

STICK WITH STONE Tough tile and stone floors stand up to water exposure, so they're popular in kitchens, bathrooms, and outdoor patios. Ceramic and stone tile can be purchased in a dazzling array of colors, sizes, and styles for virtually limitless design flexibility.

BE RESILIENT Flexible resilient floors are available in vinyl, linoleum, and rubber in many colors, styles, and patterns. Individual tiles are easy to work with, but sheet flooring can be more difficult to install, but is particularly water-resistant because it can be installed with no seams.

TRY CARPET For warmth and comfort, carpet is hard to beat, and available in a spectrum of colors, patterns, and piles. Keep it clean; dirty carpet can trap odors and stains. Carpet can be a bit difficult to install for a DIYer; you need a few specific tools—available for rent—but carpet suppliers generally price installation into the product cost. Renting the tools will not save you much money compared to professional installation. Carpet tiles, on the other hand, are easy to install and make a fine choice for targeted areas of the home.

LAMINATE IT A popular DIY choice is click-together laminate flooring, made from high-density fiberboard planks covered with decorative sheeting and a clear plastic wear layer. This flooring is available in a wide array of wood appearances—cherry, walnut, beech, oak, and tons more options. Some laminate flooring has realistic wood textures on the top surface; others have a high-gloss finish, and even tile patterns are available. These floating floor systems are typically installed with tongue-and-groove boards that connect along the edges and are "locked" together. No nails or glue are used to fasten the boards to the subfloor; instead, the completed floor floats like an assembled jigsaw puzzle, held stationary by weight and friction.

STUDY ENGINEERING Similar to laminate flooring, engineered flooring features a layer of genuine solid wood roughly ⅛-inch thick adhered to a fiberboard core. These engineered products offer the unique grain character of real wood, and they can be sanded and refinished (usually only once). These products are installed just the same as laminate floors but are also generally more expensive.

STAY SOLID A genuine solid wood floor can offer a traditional look, natural woodgrain character, and the floor can be sanded and refinished in the future. Real wood flooring is generally more expensive than laminate, and nailing, stapling, or gluing down the boards can be challenging to inexperienced DIYers.

277 PREP YOUR SITE

Before putting in a new floor, first remove any baseboards and shoe molding. If you remove the trim carefully, you can usually repair it and reinstall it over the new floor. Also, remove the old finished flooring. (In some cases, an existing vinyl floor can be left in place if in good condition because it can serve as an effective moisture barrier.)

Subfloors in a home refer to the structural floor material that is installed over the joists; examples include ¾-inch plywood and tongue-and-groove dimensional lumber. A visible finished floor is installed over the subfloor. The subfloor must be strong and completely level. Replace any sagging or rotten boards and set flush any proud nails.

Check for level and flatness with an 8-foot straightedge laid out across the subfloor. Most manufacturers will recommend no more than a ³⁄₁₆-inch difference in height between any two points in a circle with a 20-foot diameter. Smooth dents with leveling compound, and plane down any high spots. You can also help reinforce a subfloor or prepare a concrete slab by nailing or screwing down sheets of ¼- to ¾-inch plywood to ensure a level base.

After the floor is leveled, apply a moisture barrier and/or underlayment as required by the flooring manufacturer and the conditions of the jobsite. (Install the barrier beneath the plywood/OSB if you have installed a layer to reinforce the subfloor.)

PRO TIP

INSULATE A BASEMENT FLOOR
When making a basement into a living space, consider an insulated subfloor to increase the room's comfort level. This will not only control moisture in a basement floor; the flooring can also transfer cold from the ground below to the room. Some subfloor systems are sold as tongue-and-groove OSB panels with added closed-cell polystyrene for less heat loss.

278 USE BARRIER PROTECTION

Any floor installed over an unconditioned air space needs a vapor barrier to prevent transfer of moisture. For instance, wooden floors over concrete require an impermeable barrier, or else the wood will buckle and warp. For floating floors, most manufacturers often recommend rolled plastic sheathing in a 6-milimeter thickness, which should be laid across the installation area with taped and/or overlapping seams.

Another option for use on concrete floors is a liquid moisture barrier applied with a trowel, which works well with glue-down floors installed over concrete.

For wood subfloors, plastic sheathing should not be used because it can trap moisture which may lead to mold conditions at the subfloor. Instead, use 15- or 30-pound asphalt felt roofing paper, which can offer breathability and does not promote any mold growth. Recently, hardwood adhesive manufacturers have also developed sealers to be used in glue-down installations and nailed or stapled floors.

Note that upper floors are not affected by moisture and don't require a waterproof barrier. However, you should always check the instructions for your specific flooring because a barrier may still be required for the manufacturer's warranty.

An underlayment is a layer of material that installs over the subfloor but underneath the finished flooring. An underlayment can serve a variety of purposes. For example, in a tile floor, a cement-board or a flexible membrane underlayment can uncouple the wooden subfloor from tile and mortar, which prevents cracking in your floor when the wood expands or contracts. A foam underlayment beneath floating wood or laminate floors can help prevent any floor squeaks, pops, and echoes. The seams of an underlayment butt together rather than overlap to maintain a level surface.

279 INSTALL A FLOATING FLOOR

Installation methods for floating floor systems are the same for both laminate flooring and engineered hardwoods. The first step is to lay out your floor plan. Sketch the room on paper and mark the dimensions. Calculate the square footage required, and then order extra flooring material to account for unusable cut boards or any damaged boards that might require replacement in the future.

Also, make note of the different transitions in the room where the new floor will meet other types of flooring or exterior doors. The flooring supplier will usually have transition moldings for these areas.

280 BE READY TO FLOAT

To ensure a long-lasting floating floor, there are a few important steps you should follow before making the installation.

Once the flooring is on site, keep unopened cartons of planks in the room where they will be installed for at least 48 hours before actual installation. This allows the flooring to shrink or swell slightly, according to the climate.

Begin the job by preparing the subfloor for level and flatness. Be sure to eliminate any squeaks. Apply a moisture barrier and/or an underlayment if necessary. Manufacturers often recommend using foam underlayment beneath floating systems to reduce impact noise and add extra comfort. Some products even have the underlayment pre-attached to the underside of the floorboards.

Prepare the room by undercutting all of the doorjambs and casings in order to allow room for the thickness of your new flooring. Use a handsaw and pull saw, or try a power tool with a flush-cut blade. Determine the height of the cut by using a scrap of flooring as a saw guide. Leave an additional ¼ inch of space concealed beneath the door frame to allow expansion.

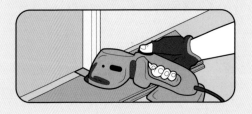

281 LAY THE FLOOR

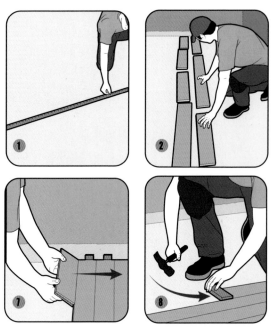

After all your prep work, it's go time! Here's how to install your new floor.

STEP 1 Measure the room's width to ensure that the last row of your flooring will be at least 2 inches wide when it's set lengthwise against the wall. Divide the width of the room by the width of the exposed face of the flooring. The remaining number will be the width of the last row. If the last row is less than 2 inches, rip the first row of boards narrower to allow more room for the last row, using a table saw and rip fence, or a handheld circular saw equipped with an edge guide. (If your baseboard or shoe molding won't conceal both the tongue and expansion gap, rip the tongues off the first row of boards.)

STEP 2 Some floor systems' boards have a standard length; others have random lengths. If you're working with floorboards that all measure the same, lay them out in a dry run. If you have a sliver of board at either end of the room, cut a third the length off the first board to make more room for the last.

STEP 3 Assemble the first three rows of the tongue-and-groove boards with the tongues on the long edge facing the nearest wall. You can assemble them a few feet away from the wall to allow some room to work.

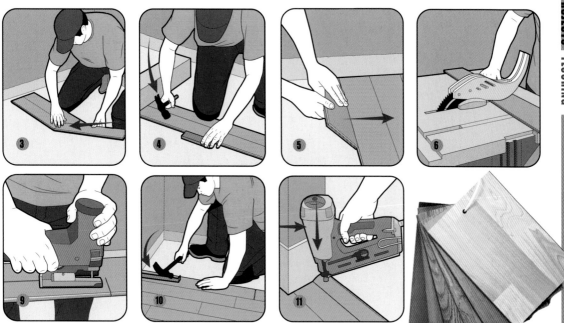

STEP 4 The shaped edges join together at an angle similar to a lock and key. You can use a hammer and a rubber block to tap these joints securely into place. If you don't have a helper, you can hold down all the previously installed floorboards with a box of flooring as you move down the first three rows. The weight of the box will hold them securely to the floor, so that they don't separate while you hammer-tap the new boards into position.

STEP 5 When possible, connect the long joints first and follow with the shorter joint on the end. The best way is to hold the groove board flat while you insert the tongue of the joining floorboard at an angle. Then bend the board downward, which pulls the tongue into the groove. Stagger the end joints of adjoining rows by at least 5 inches.

STEP 6 If the last board in a row will not fit precisely into the space against the wall, cut it down to length. You can then use the remainder of the cutoff piece to begin the next row.

STEP 7 Once you have gotten the first three rows fully assembled, place ¼-inch spacers against the walls to allow for expansion, and then push the three rows in place against it.

STEP 8 When locked in place, the weight and rigidity of the combined rows will have enough structural integrity to assemble the rest without your needing to weigh down the assembly. Continue working board by board and row by row, using spacers against all wall transitions.

STEP 9 In some cases, you'll need a jigsaw for making small cutouts, such as rectangular cuts around floor registers. For small, round cutouts around pipes, try a drill equipped with a hole-saw.

STEP 10 At the opposite wall from where you started, you won't have clearance to "push" or hammer-tap the final row into place. Hook the end of the board against the wall using an S-shaped pull bar, and then hammer-tap the striking plate on the pull bar to inch the board into the row and fasten the tongue-and-groove joint. When the floor is complete, take out all the spacers along the walls and reinstall shoe and/or base molding.

STEP 11 Nail the matching floor transitions along the bottoms of doors where the new floorboards meet other flooring types. Cut them to length and then nail them flush between the two floor areas to get a sleek, finished appearance.

Solid tongue-and-groove flooring is a classic option for homes. Available in hardwood and softwood varieties, tongue-and-groove flooring also comes in pre-finished or unfinished boards, the latter requiring application of a protective sealant/topcoat after installation.

Unfinished material is a less costly product, but it still requires money, time, and effort to sand the floor and apply urethane. Pre-finished floors have serious benefits that are worth considering. First, the installed cost of solid, pre-finished wood flooring can rival the installed cost of bare hardwood. Although the products cost more, they also have a bulletproof, factory-applied finish that will stand up to nearly anything. The trade-off is a bevel between each floorboard to hide slight discrepancies in board thickness.

283 READY THE NEW FLOOR

Before installing your floorboard, be sure to ready the room and materials first.

Wood expands and contracts with moisture and temperature changes; let the floorboards acclimate inside the room where they are to be installed for at least 48 hours. Depending on the size and design of your new floorboards, precutting them to random lengths may make them easier to maneuver and help to ensure a random series of staggered joints.

Prep the site the same as any floor project. Remove baseboards and shoe molding. Your subfloor must be flat, dry, and level. Build up minor flaws with building paper; a liquid floor leveler may be required for any bigger dips, as well as a belt sander for high spots.

For first-floor installations, you will require a moisture barrier over the subfloor. Apply a coating of liquid waterproof membrane over the subfloor or slab using a roller and let dry according to the manufacturer's instructions. Plastic sheeting is not suggested, since nails or staples can penetrate it. If you are working over concrete, use a construction adhesive to glue down ¾-inch marine-grade plywood over the waterproofing. Trim door jambs to the new floor height if needed.

284 LAY OUT THE BOARDS

Got supplies and room both ready? Then it's time to put in your new floor.

STEP 1 Measure the width of the room and divide the span by the width of the exposed face of the boards. If the final row is less than half the width of a full board, consider ripping your first row of floorboards narrower to split the difference.

STEP 2 Snap a chalk line along the longest, straightest wall in the room. With the groove side of the board facing toward the wall, predrill holes along its wall edge and nail it to the floor every 6 inches, following your chalk line. Predrilling isn't necessary if using an air-powered finish nailer. Maintain ½-inch spacing between the wall and flooring around the entire room to ensure an adequate expansion gap.

STEP 3 If your flooring has tongue-and-groove end joints, slot the second board into the first.

Otherwise, abut it closely to the next board and nail in place along the wall. Work to the end of the wall, cross-cutting the final board to size. Leave a ½-inch gap against the wall at the end of the row. You can then use the leftover cutoff from the final board to begin the following row.

STEP 4 Drive nails at a 45-degree angle through the tongues of the first row and into the subfloor (called "blind nailing"). Predrill holes if hammering the nails. Countersink any proud fastener heads with a nail set. Lay the following row by slotting the grooved end over the exposed tongue of the first row. Close the tongue-and-groove joint tightly with a hammer and rubber block.

STEP 5 Proceed down the second row, driving nails into the tongue every 6 inches. Keep the end joints between each row spaced at least 18 inches apart for a random appearance and to add rigidity to

the installation. Blind-nail the entire floor or, once you have laid enough rows to gain some working clearance from the wall, speed up installation with a flooring nailer or stapler. A jigsaw is best when you need to notch a board around a corner or make a cutout for a vent register. Use an electric drill for pipe or cable access.

STEP 6 To install the final row, you'll probably have to use a table saw (or circular saw with rip gauge) to cut off the lower edge of the groove so that the last boards easily drop over the exposed tongue of the preceding row. Close the joint along the final row of boards with a hammer and pull-bar (or Lam-hammer). Nail and glue the last row in place.

STEP 7 Remove spacing blocks and fill small gaps in the flooring with matching wood filler. After it dries, sand and finish the floor to your preference (if it is required), then reinstall baseboards and molding.

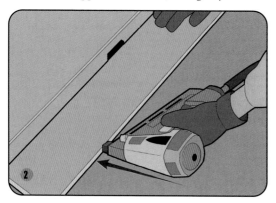

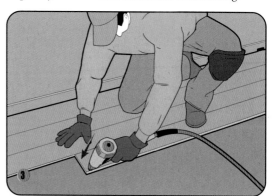

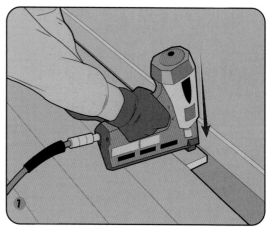

285 BE RESILIENT

Vinyl tile is the easiest resilient flooring option for a DIYer to install. Available in a rainbow of colors, textures, patterns, and appearances, the material can mimic other more expensive materials for a fraction of the price.

Although it's scratch-resistant, easy to work with, and can also easily be trimmed using a sharp utility knife, vinyl flooring does have its pitfalls. It's not as durable as laminate, and dog paws have been known to damage the surface. Adhesive-backed vinyl planks and tiles have been available for years, but some of the cheaper varieties are notorious for coming unglued after their installation and sliding apart underfoot, opening ugly joints in the floor. For this reason, speak to your supplier and research your options to find a quality product from a reputable manufacturer.

286 GET IT READY

Preparing to lay vinyl flooring is much like other flooring projects. Ensure the existing floor is completely clean and free of debris. Vinyl tiles are very thin, and any small objects that are trapped beneath the installation will be visible on the surface. Like wood flooring, the material should be stored on site at room temperature prior to installation. Any wood subfloors should be leveled using ¼-inch marine-grade plywood. Concrete slabs can be smoothed with leveling compound.

The method of installation varies among vinyl flooring products. Some systems have tiles that butt against one another and glue directly to the subfloor. Some products are glued to the subfloor, but the individual tiles are installed along with tile spacers to ensure a consistent grout joint. Other systems have adhesive edge strips that glue vinyl planks to each other rather than to the floor, creating a floating floor system.

287 FLOAT A VINYL FLOOR

For vinyl planks that resemble wood flooring, snap a chalk line along the straightest wall in the room, and install the planks along it as you would with a wood floor installation.

STEP 1 Some of these systems create a floating floor, but use double-sided acrylic tape at the first edge to help hold the first rows stationary during installation.

STEP 2 To install, just remove the paper backing from the adhesive strips, align the strips between one plank and the other, and press into place to close the joints.

STEP 3 The thin vinyl planks can easily be cut as needed with a utility knife. A pair of aviation snips works well for making any small cuts around trim. Some professionals recommend using a hair dryer to warm the adhesive edges along the newly joined seams to help melt the glue together, give the planks a tighter bond, and also make the vinyl tiles more pliable and easier to cut.

STEP 4 Complete the installation by rolling the surface using a vinyl floor roller, available at any rental outlet, which helps to press all the joints together to assist the adhesive bond while also ensuring all seams lay flat.

288 PEEL AND STICK IT

Stick-down tile is a type that has the appearance of genuine stone. With some careful planning and grouted joints, you can install a new vinyl floor with a classic look faster and easier than using thin-set mortar and ceramic or stone tile.

STEP 1 You can install vinyl tiles over existing flooring, but it's best to just install over a bare subfloor. Ensure that the surface is completely smooth. Sweep the floor several times and wipe with a damp cloth to remove all loose particles. For the best adhesive bond, coat the subfloor with multipurpose floor primer using a long-handled paint roller. Allow the primer to dry according to the manufacturer's instructions.

STEP 2 Snap intersecting square chalk lines and arrange the tiles into a dry test-fit installation as you would for a ceramic tile floor. Shift the layout to avoid small sliver tiles at the edges, and rotate tiles to avoid repeating patterns if they mimic the look of natural stone. Also, consider placement of the tiles in the doorway of the room. The majority of homeowners prefer a full tile in the middle of the entrance if possible.

STEP 3 Remove the paper backing from the tiles and install them in place one by one. Simply press the adhesive side firmly to the subfloor. Press down the installed tiles with your body weight or a roller to ensure firm adhesion. Fill in one quadrant of the cross pattern at a time. Use plastic tile spacers to keep all the joints the

same size. These come in different sizes, but small ⅛-inch joints provide less grout surface to collect dirt and grime.

STEP 4 Tiles at the end of the row will have to be fitted. Place the tile to be trimmed over the last full tile, flush with all four edges. Then, place another full tile against the wall and mark a cut line where the tiles overlap. Unlike ceramic or stone, no heavy-duty power tools are required to cut vinyl tile. All you need is a sharp utility knife and a straight edge to guide the cut. To fit around obstacles, make a pattern on paper or cardboard, trace its outline on the tile, and cut to shape.

STEP 5 Grout the joints as you would any other tile installation, with a ready-to-use, premixed sanded acrylic grout formulated for vinyl tile. Spread grout diagonally, holding a sharp-edged, rubber grout float at a 45-degree angle to the joint. Press firmly to completely fill the joint. Remove excess grout, using the edge as you would a squeegee. Angled strokes help prevent the float from digging into the filled joints and pulling out the grout.

STEP 6 Remove grout haze as you work, using a sponge and a bucket of water. Keep any traffic off of the finished surface for at least 24 hours of drying, and then use a sponge and water to remove the final remaining grout haze. Seal the grout after 72 hours in order to make the joints easier to clean.

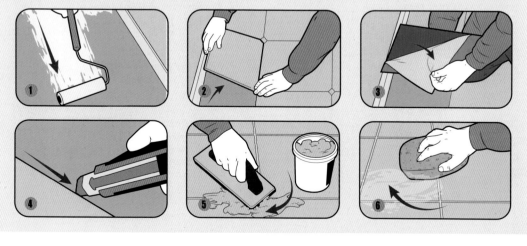

Decks are built with basic frame construction and are a popular DIY project. Take the time to thoughtfully design your deck for its intended purpose, area, and environment—and in accordance with local building codes. With proper planning, the project should go smoothly and you'll have a well-built deck that will last for many years.

290 CONSIDER YOUR DESIGN

Building methods for decks have changed over time, so you should be aware of that fact when you design one. Deck joists, which straddle the sides of a support post, are no longer approved by the International Building Code, and they should be supported by a load-carrying beam—or multiple beams.

The entire structure of the deck must be built sturdy enough to support everything above it, including people and furnishings. Therefore, decks that are supporting heavy items, such as hot tubs, will require additional reinforcement framing. Check with your local building official for specific construction guidelines, lumber size requirements (different wood species will have different strengths), and joist span limitations in your area.

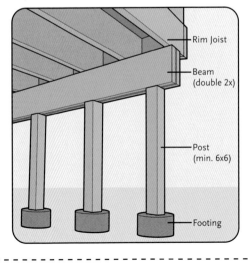

- Rim Joist
- Beam (double 2x)
- Post (min. 6x6)
- Footing

291 LEAD WITH A LEDGER BOARD

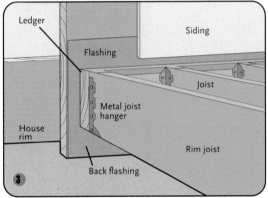

Ledger
Siding
Flashing
Joist
Metal joist hanger
House rim
Rim joist
Back flashing

Once you've done a thorough job of designing your deck, you're ready to begin building.

STEP 1 Construction usually starts with the ledger board, the piece that anchors the structure to the house. This will also establish your deck length and height (so account for the thickness of the building material). The ledger board, joists, and beam will support the weight of the deck, so use 2x8s or 2x10s, depending on the size of the deck you plan to build.

STEP 2 Make sure the ledger is level and fasten it with lag bolts or heavy-duty structural screws (-inch diameter with washers) that attach to your home's rim joist (some siding may need to be removed). Or, use expansion bolts if you are attaching it to a concrete foundation.

STEP 3 The ledger board needs to have continuous flashing installed according with your building code

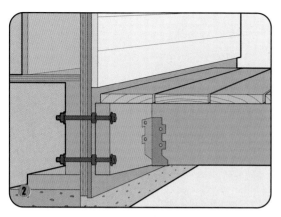

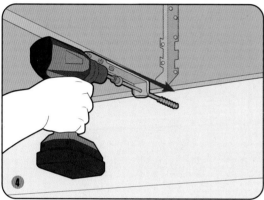

to prevent any water penetration into the house. The flashing should also lap up the house wall behind the exterior siding.

STEP 4 The International Residential Code requires a deck supported by an adjacent house to be built with a "positive attachment" to the house framing to help resist lateral loads. Check the local codes for requirements in your area. Simpson Strong-Tie offers a deck tension-tie for attaching a deck to a home that meets the latest code standards. The DTT1Z deck tension-tie fastens from outside the house, allowing the four required 750-pound lateral connectors to be fastened to the structural framing members within the house. This tie is screwed to either the narrow or wide face of a single 2x joist. Afterward, a long hex screw with an integral washer attaches the tension-tie to the supporting structure with a minimum of 3 inches of penetration.

292 **GET THE RIGHT LAYOUT**

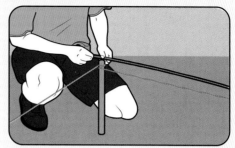

You can establish the layout of your deck by using string and wood stakes to determine where to locate the supporting concrete piers and support posts.

STEP 1 Drive stakes (or batter boards) at each corner, about two feet farther than the beam will be away from the house. Attach a string to each stake and attach the opposite ends to the ledger board. Make sure the strings are square to the ledger-board using the 3-4-5 method.

STEP 2 Drive two new stakes about 2 feet outside the first set of strings at the desired location for the beam (also called a girder). Attach a third string between the two new stakes and parallel to the ledger-board. At the point where the strings intersect, check for square by measuring diagonally from the intersection of the strings to the opposite corner of the ledger board, then check the other diagonal measurement; they should be the same. Move the stakes until the outline is completely square.

STEP 3 Use a plumb bob on the beam-layout string to mark the center points of the deck's support posts. Beams can overhang the posts a maximum of 1 foot. Spacing of your posts will be determined by local codes, joist size, beam size, and wood species. For example, if the deck's joist size is 2x6, and you use a doubled 2x6 beam, maximum post spacing is usually 6 feet (for woods such as Southern Pine and Hem-Fir). A deck with 2x8 joists and a beam made of two 2x10s will have maximum post spacing of 8 feet. Consult a lumber dealer or an engineer for design assistance; when in doubt, always over-build.

293 GET GOOD FOOTING

Deck posts should be supported by concrete pier footings. The footing hole depth will be determined by your location and frost line.

STEP 1 Check with local building codes to find out how deep you'll need to dig to prevent frost heave. Dig a hole to that depth, 14 to 24 inches in width.

STEP 2 Mix concrete and fill the footing hole. Tube-shaped cardboard footing forms can help keep the concrete in a cylindrical shape.

STEP 3 Insert an 8-inch J-bolt into the centers of each of your wet concrete footings, leaving enough threaded rod exposed to mount a metal pier bracket. Once the concrete dries, attach the bracket to the bolt with a washer and nut.

STEP 4 Use a support post size of at least 6x6 that's made of treated lumber and intended for ground contact. Place the post into the bracket, plumb and square it, then fasten in place with galvanized nails.

294 INSTALL YOUR FRAMING

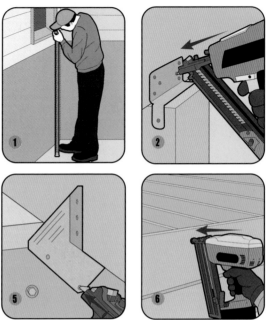

After your posts are set, you need to create the framing upon which you'll build the flooring of your deck.

STEP 1 Determine the anticipated surface height of your deck, then measure downward, subtracting the thickness of the decking and the height of the joists and beam. Transfer this measurement to the posts to determine where to cut them to accept the beam. A string level helps measure over longer distances. In some cases you should engineer a slight slope to the deck to pitch downward away from the house, especially if your decking material could collect water.

STEP 2 After the posts are cut, install the beam onto the support posts (and parallel to the ledger board) with metal post brackets to prevent uplift and lateral displacement. Beams can overhang the posts out to a maximum of 1 foot. All the hardware and fasteners should be hot-dip galvanized or stainless steel.

STEP 3 Deck beams that are made of 2x treated wood should be fastened together using staggered rows of 10d galvanized nails or #10 wood screws. If necessary to splice boards to form the beam, stagger the splices and locate the joints over the beams.

STEP 4 Install the side joists onto the ledger board using metal joist hangers. Ensure that the joists are

295 GET ON DECK

A deck's surface can be made from pressure-treated wood, PVC, wood-plastic composite, cedar, cypress, or an exotic hardwood such as ipe—there are even aluminum deck systems available. Each material has a different set of advantages: Some offer the genuine wood grain that you will only have with a natural product, while others may offer cool hidden-fastener systems a pre-finished appearance, and minimal maintenance requirements. Research your material options carefully, and explore the maintenance issues associated with each, as well as the cost of the product (which can vary greatly).

As you begin installing the decking, be sure the board is fastened perfectly straight, because all of the rest of the decking will run from this board. Keep the decking at least ½ inch from the house. Attach the boards using fasteners that are recommended by the manufacturer. Center joints over a joist or add 2x blocking so that you can attach both ends securely. Separate the deck boards approximately $\frac{1}{16}$ to $\frac{1}{8}$ inch to allow for expansion and contraction. As you are installing the deck boards, allow them to run long over the outer joists. When all of the boards are installed, snap a chalk line across the ends and trim all of the decking at once using a circular saw.

square to the ledger board and mount them to the beam with metal hardware. The joists can terminate at the beam or cantilever (overhang) by a couple of feet, according to span limitations.

STEP 5 Mark locations along the beam for the rest of the joists and install them using metal hardware to resist uplift and lateral movement. Joists are typically installed 16 inches on center (closer spacing may be required for some deck-board systems.)

STEP 6 If joist lengths vary, snap a chalk line over the ends and cut them to the same length. Fasten a rim joist over the ends and flush with the top edges using metal joist hangers. Double up on the rim joists to add strength and stability.

STEP 7 To help stabilize movement in a deck frame, you can place a long diagonal 2x4 brace across the underside of the joists. Alternatively, use perpendicular blocking between the joists, cut from the same size lumber as the deck joists; or, install diagonal 2x4 braces fastened onto the support posts and the adjacent framing members.

STEP 8 Construct handrail and stair systems before installing the deck boards. Handrail posts must be bolted to the deck's framing members according to building code.

296 ADD RAILINGS TO YOUR DECK

For decks more than 30 inches high, railings are a critical safety feature that are required by building codes. Various code requirements will dictate how to construct a handrail system; consult your local building inspector for any specific clarification.

Generally, the posts should be a minimum 4×4 size, and be solidly anchored to the deck joist and the rim joist of the structure. Use a pair of ½-inch through-bolts and a metal tension-tie for the upper bolt connection. Posts should be spaced no more than 6 feet apart. Rails can usually be built 36 to 42 inches high (check local codes for guidance).

Building a deck gives you ample opportunity to customize it with a personal touch, and the handrails are an opportune place to add to the décor. Designs and materials vary greatly. Posts made of treated 4×4 lumber are typically used for structural strength, and they can be stained, sealed and left exposed, or they can be sheathed in a PVC sleeve and integrated into a sleek vinyl railing system. Rails and balusters are often made of wood, and you can install metal balusters, steel cable, or even glass panels between the posts.

297 SELECT YOUR STAIR SYSTEM

Stairs, stringers, and guardrails must meet the IRC design and strength requirements for tread height and opening/spacing requirements. The steps should have a consistent tread depth with a 7¾-inch maximum riser height. (A deviation of ⅜ inch is allowed by code but should be avoided.)

If the stairs have open risers they should not let a 4-inch diameter sphere pass through them. Just as with the maximum spacing for balusters, this is intended to prevent small children from getting stuck or falling through.

Stair landings must be at least as wide as the stair and at least 3 feet deep. Usually made from block or concrete, the landing must provide a safe exit from the stair and may not have a slope more than ¼ inch per foot.

Laying out the staircase is the first step. The pitch of your stairs will largely be determined by the rise and run you need to traverse to reach the landing, factored with a comfortable tread and riser height that adheres to local codes.

Another factor in the pitch of your stairs might be the handrail system. Whereas you can custom-build your handrails to the slope of your preference, purchased systems usually only work in a limited range of predetermined angles (such as 30 to 35 degrees). These requirements need to be accounted for when designing the stair layout.

Stair layout can be very complicated. Measuring and designing the stringers can be such a challenge for DIYers; home centers usually offer precut stringers for sale. Metal connectors can be used to connect the stair stringers to the deck frame. Code typically requires that stairs be supported by stringers spaced no greater than 2 feet apart on center.

298 CONSIDER YOUR OPTIONS

If you don't want a handrail built from wood, you have plenty of other options. Deck railing systems are also available in metal, composite, and PVC. The systems vary in method of installation, so research your options carefully when selecting.

SLEEVE IT Some railing systems have a PVC sleeve to slip over a 4x4 treated post. The PVC protects he post from weather exposure and provides a sleek matching appearance to a vinyl baluster-and-rail system.

MAKE IT SOLID Other systems utilize a metal newel post inside a hollow PVC post sleeve, which is then filled with concrete.

LOOK THROUGH THE GLASS Glass balusters are available for a high-end look that optimizes visibility.

MAKE IT MODERN For a contemporary style with nighttime illumination, consider a stainless steel cable system with LED accent lights.

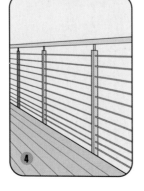

299 MAKE STAIRS SIMPLER

Another DIY-friendly alternative for stairway construction is to avoid using precut notched stringers and instead simply screw on L-shaped metal stair brackets to support the steps. The brackets eliminate the need to cut stair notches and reduce the measuring and marking as you fasten them to the full stringer boards.

STEP 1 Fasten the L-shaped stair brackets to the stringer boards.

STEP 2 Mount the stringers to both the deck and landing.

STEP 3 Install the treads over the tops of the stair brackets.

300 BUILD A FENCE

A fence can do a lot for a landscape: divide property lines, boost home equity, add to outdoor décor, and safely contain animals.

There are lots of options for materials and design. Fence building materials can vary, from metal and wood to vinyl and wood-plastic composites. For an easy-to-build fence, you might consider using pre-assembled panels to dramatically reduce building time.

If your yard is sloped, to keep the panel tops level you'll have to stagger the panel heights where they are fastened onto the posts. If your yard has a significant grade, these staggered panels will create gaps at the bottom of the fence.

An alternative is a privacy fence that's built to closely follow the grade of the yard. You can install the pickets along one side of the fence, or put in a shadowbox-style fence, which alternates the position of the pickets from one side of the stringer to the other.

Treated wood is often chosen for framing lumber. Posts can be made of 8-foot 4x4s, and the horizontal stringers (also called fence rails) can be made out of 8-foot 2x4s. The treated posts should be approved for ground contact.

For the fence boards (or pickets), use treated wood or a species such as cedar or redwood that has natural preservative oils to resist insects, decay, and chemical corrosion.

Set the posts with fast-setting concrete sold in ready-mix bags. Simply pour the mix straight out of the bag into the post hole. Once the post is buried, pour about a gallon of water per 50-pound bag over the dry mix, which then cures in about 30 minutes. Use roughly 1½ bags per post.

Fasten all connections with hot-dipped galvanized nails with ringed shanks for extra holding power. Be sure your fasteners are approved for exterior use in chemically treated lumber.

PRO TIP

TELL A STORY Prevent repetitive measurements with a story pole. Make one by marking each stringer height on a scrap piece of wood with masking tape, then place the pole alongside each post. Use the tape to determine each stringer location and mark it with pencil.

301 PLAN YOUR LAYOUT

Before building a fence, check with local officials regarding building codes and necessary permits. (Some neighborhoods might also have their own architectural guidelines or "covenants" that restrict design.) Double-check to be sure that the location of your proposed fence is not on a neighbor's property. Before digging, always dial 811 nationally to get any underground utility lines, cables, and pipes marked for free.

Within local code limitations, the height, décor, and trajectory of your fence will be up to you, and may be dictated by other obstacles in your yard, such as trees and sheds.

STEP 1 Mark your fence layout with stakes and twine.

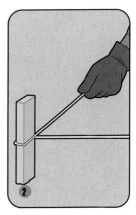

302 DIG DEEP

Generally, you should dig holes for fence posts deep enough to bury a third of the overall length of the posts (at least 2 feet deep). Go deep enough to set the post below the frost line to avoid frost heaving; dig an extra 4 to 6 inches deeper than the desired post depth for a gravel bed beneath that post for drainage.

Prepare for lots of digging. A traditional way is with a manual clamshell digger and trench shovel. Get some help to speed things up, and rent a two-man powered auger for digging.

STEP 2 Pull the line tightly between corner stakes, then stake it intermittently along the fence perimeter to keep the string tight and straight.

STEP 3 Walk the perimeter with a tape measure and spray-paint a large "X" to pinpoint the placement of each fence post. Posts are usually spaced 6 to 8 feet on center. The closer the fence posts, the stronger the fence. This measurement is also crucial for the sake of your materials, as dimensional lumber is sold in standard sizes. If your posts are accidentally spaced 8 feet, 1 inch apart, an 8-foot board will be too short. In that event, you would have to purchase a 10-foot board and cut off 1 foot, 11 inches to create a long enough stringer, which is a waste of material.

PRO TIP

GIVE THEM A SOAK While you're digging, soak the bases of your posts in water sealer. Place about 4 posts upright in a tall bucket all at once. Their mass displaces the water, which rises to the top of the bucket, thus soaking the bottoms of the posts. After soaking them for about an hour, rotate four new posts into the bucket to soak.

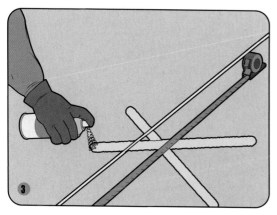

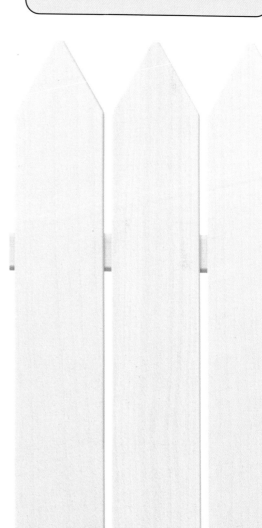

303 POST UP

Posts are the backbone of your fence, so install them right to ensure a strong construction.

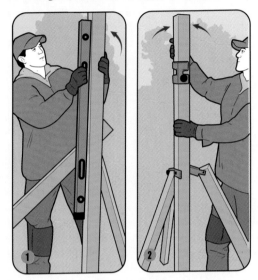

STEP 1 Begin by setting all the corner posts first. Have a helper hold the post upright while you use a hand level to make sure it is plumb on the gravel bed. A post level is also helpful, because it frees up your hands by strapping around the post while placing level vials on two adjacent sides.

STEP 2 Once the post is plumb left to right and back to front, then brace it in place. If you have a helper, they can hold it in position while you add concrete. Alternatively, nail scrap lengths of wood extending from the post to the ground to act as movable braces, with the nails serving as pivot points for adjustment. Plumb and square the post, adjust the braces to hold it steady, then add concrete. Use a sledge hammer to pound the posts into the ground once surrounded by concrete, then recheck for plumb, adjusting as needed once again. Leave the braces on while the concrete sets.

STEP 3 Once the corner posts are set, fasten a string between them to guide placement of the remaining posts. Keep the line on the outside face of the posts and secure it tightly. Set the rest of the posts, keeping their outside faces plumb and lined up exactly with the string.

STEP 4 Pour dry, fast-setting concrete mix into the post hole. Then just add water; no mixing is required. If you're using standard concrete that should be premixed, you can mix small batches with a wheelbarrow and shovel or hoe, following the manufacturer's instructions for the required amount of water. Allow the posts to set. Once the concrete is hardened, cover it with dirt and slope the earth away from the post to divert water.

304 STRING 'EM UP

With your posts properly set, your next objective will be to place the stringers.

STEP 1 For a standard 6-foot tall fence, position the bottom stringer 10 inches up from the ground and space the other two stringers evenly apart. You may need to alter placement depending on the height of your fence.

STEP 2 You have a variety of options for attaching your stringers, such as face-nailing, mortise and tenon joints, or toe-nailing. For a shadowbox fence, stringers are toe-nailed between posts by driving at least two nails into the side and one nail through the top of the stringer and solidly into the post.

STEP 3 If you're toe-nailing stringers that follow a slope, cut them at a miter to fit flush between the plumb posts. First, butt the square end of one uncut stringer against the penciled location on your left-hand post. Hold that end firmly against the post

while you position the other end of the stringer to overlap the right-hand post at the pencil marks. Mark the stringer, using the post as a pencil guide, and then remove the stringer and take it to the cutting table. Use an angle finder to transfer that angle to the left-hand end of the stringer. Before cutting the miters, recheck the post-to-post measurement to ensure you don't cut too short; remember to account for the ⅛-inch wide blade kerf of a circular saw.

STEP 4 Expect a lot of nailing. A framing nail gun (either air-powered or cordless) can really be a huge help. Use 3-inch hot-dipped ring-shank nails for all framing members.

STEP 5 With all stringers in place, cut the tops of the posts with a reciprocating saw so they're all the same height. Cut the posts in a manner that diverts water from standing atop the posts, which could contribute to rot. You can cut pyramid-like crowns, cover them with post caps, or just slice them off at an angle.

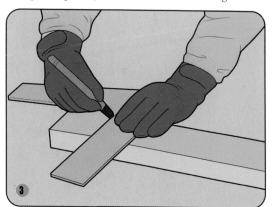

305 GO PICKETING

With posts and stringers done, it's time for the boards of your fence. Attach the pickets securely against the stringers. For a shadowbox installation, cut a spacing block slightly narrower than the width of the boards, so there will be a slight degree of overlap among the alternating pickets.

Place the first board along the corner post and use a 4-foot level to find plumb. Nail it home, using two nails per stringer location. Position the spacing block ❶ next to the first picket and then place the second picket against it. Drive in one nail at the top stringer. Use that nail as a pivot while you find plumb, then nail that picket home as well. Follow suit all the way down the stringer, spacing each picket with the block. If your fence boards vary somewhat in height, keep an eye on the tops so that they line up consistently, adjusting their placement against the ground if necessary.

For shadowbox installation ❷, once you reach the next post, return to the first post on the opposite side of the stringer. Center a picket across from each space provided by the spacing block to make the alternating picket style. Install the boards in the same manner—spacing, plumbing, and nailing.

If you prefer the picket tops to follow a straight line between posts, walk the fence and locate the high and low spots before installing. Tack pickets (preferably at the posts) to each of those high or low points. Start a nail in the top of those pickets, stringing line between them to guide picket alignment as you go.

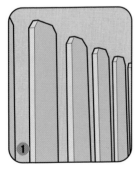
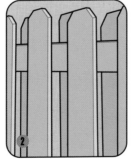

306 MAKE A BIG FINISH

Your fence should be protected with a good waterproof sealer. Although time constraints and inclement weather don't always allow it, it's much easier to pre-apply the finish to the fence components before construction. Also, pre-finishing the boards grants access to all sides of the pickets and stringers that might otherwise be inaccessible once built. Use a stain/sealer product offered by a reputable manufacturer to help protect against rotting, water damage, and UV rays.

307 GIVE YOUR FENCE A GATE

This fence shown has two gates: a single-door gate and a two-door gate for a pickup truck.

It's a good idea to purchase the beefiest hinge hardware available at the hardware store, because gate hinges are notorious for failure over time. Install according to the manufacturer's instructions. To construct the doors, fasten all pickets on the outside of the stringers to provide a solid plane to mount the gate hinges.

When constructing the gate doors, use ample bracing. For large doors, pass on the conventional Z-shaped bracing in favor of a double-Z. Build each door with three 2x4 cross braces perpendicular to the fencing, connected by two diagonal braces, with the fence boards nailed into each brace they cross.

Correctly constructing your support posts is also critical. You will get more stability from 6x6 posts rather than 4x4s. Anchor each post with a concrete footing. Bury the post in the ground to a third of its height. Add extra strength at the base of the two posts by installing a horizontal post flush between the two, or use a poured bridge of concrete, to keep both posts from pulling toward each other at the bottom due to the weight of the gate doors.

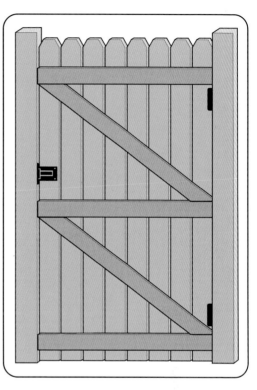

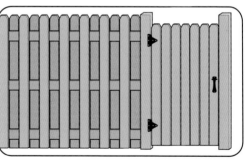

308 SHELVE IT

Built-in shelving requires opening up a wall and then constructing a basic shelf case inside the space.

Before removing any wall studs, be sure that the wall is not load-bearing. Exterior load-bearing walls aren't appropriate for built-in cases because removal of the wall eliminates insulation (and would require construction of a load-bearing header). If you want to locate shelves over a load-bearing wall, then build the case over the studs like a piece of furniture. For quick visual reference material as you work, try sketching your design on paper or diagram it on a computer.

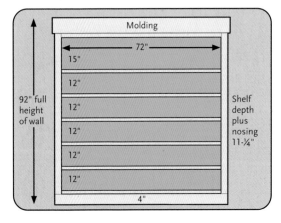

309 DEMOLISH A WALL

Before cutting into a wall, disconnect electrical power in case you accidentally run into a wire.

STEP 1 Outline the planned shelf on the wall using painter's tape, a T-square, and a pencil.

STEP 2 Seal off the work area with large vinyl sheeting for dust control.

STEP 3 Cut through the wallboard for access to the studs. Pry the wallboard off the studs with a flat bar.

STEP 4 Try to remove all the wallboard in large sections to minimize dust and debris.

STEP 5 Use a multi-tool with a flush-cut blade to cut through the nails holding the wallboard against all the studs on the opposite side of the wall. Then remove the wall studs from the area where you want to build.

310 CREATE A CASE

With your opening ready, it's time for the case.

STEP 1 Cut a couple of the old studs as trimmer studs, which will frame the new shelves. Make sure to install the studs perfectly plumb.

STEP 2 Install plywood backing over the exposed drywall. Attach it using a combination of Liquid Nails construction adhesive and some strategically placed drywall screws. (Don't screw through the drywall if it has a visible finished side.)

STEP 3 Use as few screws as you can to minimize wood-putty repairs. Clamp the plywood in place while the adhesive dries by tacking on temporary 2×4 cleats along the edges.

STEP 4 For the foundation, screw together 2×4 stud material in a rectangular box and strengthen it with blocking. This "toe-kick" box raises the

bottom shelf a few inches off the floor and makes room for decorative base molding at the bottom. Screw the box into the lower plywood panel.

STEP 5 These shelves are designed with 1¼-inch nosing (½ inch overhanging the ¾-inch shelves), so fasten a layer of ½-inch plywood over the box to raise the bottom shelf.

STEP 6 Install the side panels. Mount them into the trimmer studs with 3-inch self-countersinking screws. The sides must be perfectly plumb and square to the back. The sides can be made from ¾-inch solid wood or plywood.

STEP 7 Putty and sand all fastener holes. Stain or prime/paint the case before adding the shelves. Apply paint with a foam roller, which achieves thorough coverage without leaving brush marks or the stippling effect of a roller nap.

Shelves are often constructed of stain-grade ¾-inch plywood or solid wood. Nosing or edging can be added to the edge of plywood shelves to achieve the look of solid wood.

STEP 1 Rip the shelves to width and length using a table saw or a circular saw equipped with a ripping guide. If adding ¾-inch nosing, cut the shelves ¾ inch narrower than the sides of the case to leave room. Rip the ¾-inch solid wood nosing (1½ inches wide in this case), and cut it at length to match the shelves. You can attach the shelves to the back of the case with pocket holes, then each can be supported from beneath with a horizontal cleat. Screws driven into each end will provide extra support at the sides.

STEP 2 Decide if the pocket holes will go on the top or bottom of the shelves. For the top, you'll need wood plugs to hide the screws. If you choose the bottom, the shelves won't have as much holding power with the screw heads angled downward (but support cleats should solve the problem). Use a pocket-hole jig to guide a stepped drill bit, spacing the pocket holes 12 to 18 inches apart along the sides and back.

STEP 3 Finish-sand the shelves in the direction of the wood grain, progressing to finer paper to at least 220-grit. Dust with a tack cloth, then apply wood stain and polyurethane sealer.

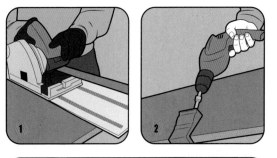

Now that you've built your shelves for your wall case, it's time to put them in their proper place.

STEP 1 Start at the bottom. The first shelf rests on the toe-kick box. Instead of using pocket screws, it's fastened through the face using countersunk trim-head screws. The tiny screw heads are easy to hide with wood filler.

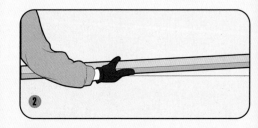

STEP 2 Locate the next shelf to conceal the joint between the plywood panels in the rear of the case. Once this critical shelf has been mounted, use it as a control point to install the remaining shelves at an equal distance apart from each other. (Note: The top shelf typically has some extra overhead space as room for storing any larger items.)

STEP 3 When installing, make sure the shelves are level in every direction. It helps to have an

assistant, or use clamps and cabinet jacks, to hold the shelves during installation.

STEP 4 Fasten the shelves tightly along their edges using pocket screws and a pocket driver bit. When locating the shelves, remember that if your shelf nosing is taller than the shelves, then the vertical midpoint of that completed shelf will not be the same as the center point of the plywood (nose-less) shelf. You'll need to account for this during the layout or your measurements will be off.

STEP 5 Once all shelves are mounted, install the nosing (stained and varnished to match). Make sure the upper edge of the nosing is flush with the shelf surface.

STEP 6 Fasten the nosing with wood glue and finish nails.

STEP 7 If you have installed the pocket screws from below the shelf, you can further support each shelf with a full-length horizontal support strip or "cleat" measuring roughly 1 x ³⁄₈ inch. Rip this strip from solid wood, then fasten it flush against the underside of the shelf with a combination of wood glue and pin nails.

313 ADD TRIM WORK

The trim package that encloses the shelves can be as simple or as elaborate as you want.

STEP 1 The case shown below has vertical face-frames ripped to 2 inches wide that cover up the edges of the side panels. These face-frames were nailed to the case sides as well as to the nosing of the shelves, with their outer edges flush with the sides. Face-frames can give visual weight to a case for a more substantial look.

STEP 2 The toe-kick box was wrapped with baseboard molding mitered at the outside corners. The new trim was matched the room's existing baseboard profile and intersected it with cope joints.

STEP 3 At the top, a "cap" panel of plywood hid the ceiling. The top of the case is then wrapped using a 1×6 that was mitered at the corners to serve as fascia for the case. Additional moldings are used to decorate the top and add shadow lines.

STEP 4 Pre-primed cove molding lines the sides of the case to conceal the joint against the wall for a finished appearance.

STEP 5 Once all trim was installed, fastener holes were puttied and all joints were all caulked as well. Repairs were sanded before a final coat of paint.

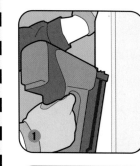

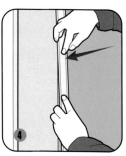

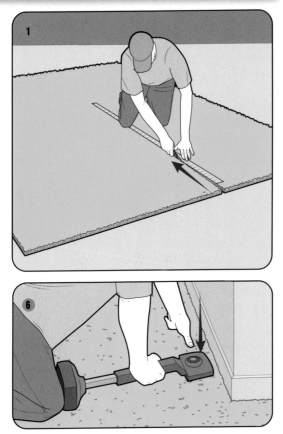

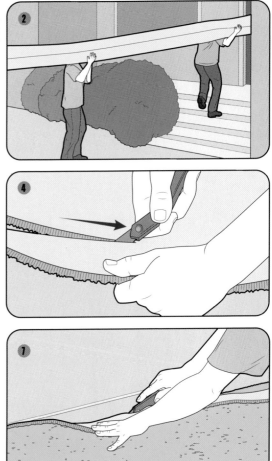

Do-it-yourself carpet installation is the best approach for small rooms that don't require a carpet stretcher. If there are no seams required, even better; carpet tools are available to rent, but rental costs will likely equal the cost of a professional installation job. The small-room scenario eliminates some of the pricier rental items and can sometimes be carpeted with little more than a knee-kicker, a carpet knife and carpet tucker (also called a broad knife).

STEP 1 Rough-cut the carpet to a workable size before hauling it into the room, to avoid lifting more than necessary and have less excess material obstructing the work area.

STEP 2 Recruit some help to lift the roll of carpet into the room—it'll be heavy.

STEP 3 Cut the wooden tack strips (which anchor the carpet) to fit around the perimeter of the room. Leave room between the tack strip and the wall equal to the thickness of the carpet. Nail these strips to the floor. Lay carpet padding over the entire floor, butting the seams and taping them together. Staple the pad every 12 inches, working toward the tack strips, securing the pad against the edge of the strips.

STEP 4 Use a carpet knife and straightedge to cut the carpet roughly 6 inches longer and wider than the room. (If the room is too large for a single piece of carpet, you'll need to join the seams using seam tape, a heat-bond iron, and a carpet-seam roller.)

STEP 5 Place the rug with the excess lapping up the walls. Relief cuts at corners will let the carpet lay flat.

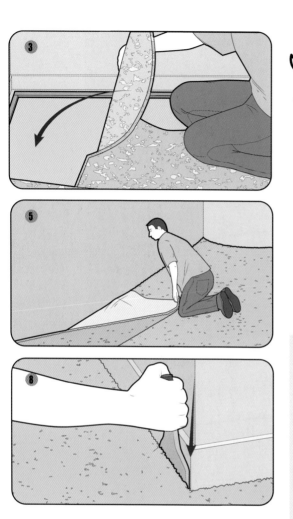

STEP 6 Once the first corner is anchored, go to the adjacent corner along the long wall and anchor both sides of that corner just as you did the first corner. For a larger room, you might need to work using a carpet stretcher to pull the carpet tightly from one end of the room over to the other corner. Once that second corner has been anchored, proceed down the wall between the two installed corners, knee-kicking the carpet in place and trimming as you go. Follow this procedure to anchor the short wall. Install the second long wall and finish with the final short wall.

STEP 7 Trim the carpet as you go, cutting away the excess along the wall with a carpet knife.

STEP 8 Use a broad knife to tuck in the edge beneath the wall or floor trim.

315 SEAM THE SECTIONS

If it is necessary to seam the carpet, plan the layout so the seams fall in low-traffic areas of the room. Butt together two straight seams and be sure the carpet lays flat and in line. Place a strip of hot-glue seaming tape centered beneath the edges. Slowly move the heated bonding iron under the carpet flaps and over the tape to melt the adhesive. As you move the iron down the seam, the flaps of carpet will fall back down onto the active adhesive. Use weights or a carpet-seam roller to firmly attach the carpet to the tape.

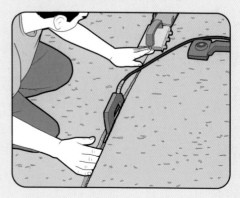

316 STRETCH YOUR CARPET

If you are using a carpet stretcher, start with the foot of the stretcher placed against the short wall of the starting corner. Make sure the carpet stretcher is placed against solid wall framing so that you don't inadvertently "stretch" the tool right through the wallboard of the house. Angle the stretcher about 15 degrees toward the opposite corner. A carpet stretcher is a modular device in which the installer adds lengths of tubes between the head and foot of the tool to traverse the distance across the room. Set the toothed head of the stretcher about 6 inches from the wall and push down on the handle to stretch out the carpet. Once stretched, used the knee kicker to anchor it in place.

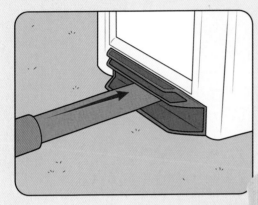 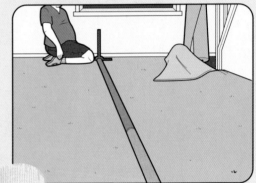

317 EDGE IT OUT

Where the carpet meets with the perimeter walls, the edges can be concealed by base molding and/or quarter round. Where carpet meets another flooring material, a transition molding such as a threshold, a carpet bar, or Z-bar binding strip may be installed for a more finished look. For low-pile carpets, some installers will simply fold the carpet under and staple it flatly. Other options include wooden thresholds, or you can hot-seam two carpet floors together if it meets another carpet of equal thickness.

318 GO MODULAR

An easy DIY approach to carpet installation is the use of modular floor tiles from companies such as Flor Inc. These 50-centimeter squares are available in a massive array of colors and styles. These can be used for wall-to-wall carpet or to accent certain areas of the floor. They're also portable. If you want to move the carpet to another room or another home, just pull up the squares and re-install. In case of stains or spills, just replace that single square rather than the entire rug.

STEP 1 Simply measure the dimensions of your floor to determine the quantity of tiles needed. Consider the use of various patterns, accent colors, and border tiles to develop a decorative style.

STEP 2 Lay the tiles on the floor with their seams butted together. In some cases it may help to snap a chalk line to keep the layout square with the walls.

STEP 3 Use the included adhesive discs to anchor the squares together. Peel away their backing and place each disc, adhesive-side up, at the intersection of four tiles to adhere to the four corners and hold them together. Do the same around the perimeter of the carpet.

STEP 4 For wall-to-wall applications, or other situations where the carpet tiles need to be cut, use a metal straight edge to guide a sharp carpet knife. Just score the flexible backing of the tile a few times to get a nice, clean cut.

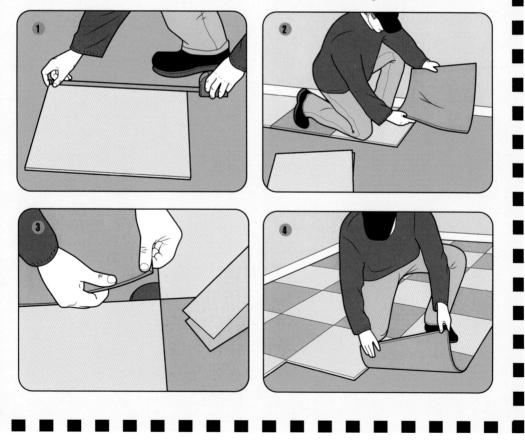

319 FIND LOST TREASURE

Sometimes, a hardwood floor is hiding under carpeting installed by the previous residents. Often, your first indication of this will be in a closet, where the carpeting stops. To check it out, use a pair of pliers to grab some carpet pile and pull it back. Pull back the pad to see what's underneath. You may find a floor that could be worth restoring.

STEP 1 To completely remove carpet to access the hardwoods, grab the pile with some pliers and pull upward until your utility knife won't reach to the hardwood floor underneath. Cut along the edges and fold it back, then roll up the carpet and pad into the center of the room for disposal.

STEP 2 Remove the tack strips and carpet-pad staples with a pry bar, hammer, scraper, and push broom.

STEP 3 If staples break off, sink them into the wood using a nail set.

320 FIX DAMAGED FLOORING

Normal wear and tear dulls a wood floor's finish. Furniture can scratch the surface; water damage can cause buckling, separation, and even rot in the flooring. Occasionally, homeowners may need to refinish the floor, replace some floorboards, or a combination of both. The biggest challenge when replacing flooring is to interlace the new section into the old. If the damaged area is very large, you may be better off replacing all of the flooring in the room rather than trying to patch it.

STEP 1 To remove a damaged section of the floor, cut across the boards just outside the damaged area. Set the blade depth to cut just through the flooring, not into the subfloor. Keep a good grip on the saw and wear eye protection as you cut across the flooring, because if the boards were blind-nailed through the tongue, you won't know when you'll hit a nail.

STEP 2 Pull out the cut boards without affecting the good part of the floor. Each cut board will need to be removed. Because they are locked in with tongue and groove, you will need to slide them toward the void left by the removed flooring. Start by drilling a pocket at 45 degrees with a ¾-inch spade bit.

STEP 3 Place the end of a pry bar or large punch in the pocket. Strike the bar to drive the floor board toward the void until you can tap the end with a hammer. Be careful not to damage the adjacent boards.

STEP 4 Remove all the boards in the affected area down to the subfloor and then thoroughly clean out all debris.

STEP 5 Install the new hardwood row by row with the first piece matching into the existing floor. Since you will be working with random length boards, be sure that end joints do not line up with joints on the adjacent row of boards. Make cuts only on the wall end of the last piece in each row.

STEP 6 Blind-nail the boards at an angle where the tongue meets the edge of the board. Finish nailers can also be used to nail through the face of the board in areas next to walls where the gun cannot be angled into the tongue. Identify any loose boards in the floor and nail those as well.

STEP 7 When all boards have been replaced or nailed, vacuum the entire floor using a powerful shop vac. Remove all dust and debris from nail holes, joints, and cracks.

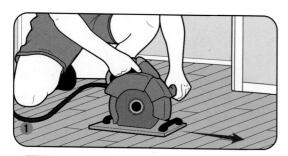

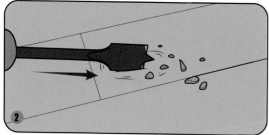

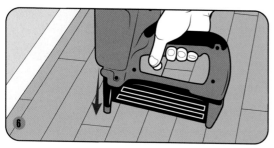

321 FINISH THE FLOOR

Once you've replaced the damaged flooring, it's time to finish, sand, and seal.

FILL UP You'll want to apply a quality latex putty over the entire floor surface. A drywall taping knife makes a good tool for applying latex putty. Apply enough pressure to force putty into the cracks and nail holes. Scrape off excess putty as you go.

SAND IT Before sanding, seal off any areas where you don't want dust to go using plastic sheeting and tape. Next, use a drum sander to sand the main part of the floor. Whether sanding off old floor finish or starting with new raw wood, you will need to start with a coarse-grit paper for the rough-sanding phase.

When you rent the drum sander, rent an edge sander as well. If your floor area has cabinets with toe kicks, make sure you get a sander with a low profile at the sanding disk so it will fit beneath them.

Make sure you know how to change the paper on both sanders. You will have to change paper as the grit wears off, as the grit clogs with old floor finish, or when you complete a pass with one grit number and need to graduate to a finer grit.

The rental outlet that supplies the sander will usually supply the paper as well. The supplier can make grit suggestions for your type of project. It's a good idea to take more paper than you might need and return what isn't used.

SEAL IT After the floors have been sanded and vacuumed, apply a penetrating sanding sealer. Use a sponge brush along the edges first. Next, just pour the sealer onto the floor to cover up the center and spread it with a T-bar applicator. Keep your movements smooth and coverage even, and don't overwork the product. Spread it in thin coats, leave it to dry, and then repeat the process according to the manufacturer's instructions.

INDEX

Numbers refer to the item number. Unnumbered items are indexed by the numbered item that they follow. So, "following 277" means that you can find this information in the box that appears after the text numbered 277.

A

B

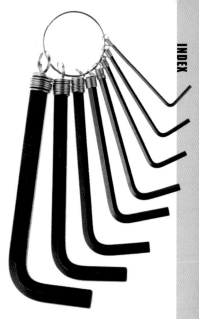

PHOTOGRAPHS

All photographs courtesy of Extreme How-To except as follows. *C. A. Technologies:* 169 (2); *CM:* 051; *Cen-Tech:* 049; *Craftsman:* 013; *Cuprinol:* 148; *Daptex:* 077, *Defy:* 151; *Dewalt:* 004; *Durham's:* 156; *Osmo:* 148; *Powerhorse:* 018; *Quickrete:* 159; *Roto-Rooter:* 092; *Sashco:* 160; *Shutterstock:* title page, all introduction images, contents, 001, 030, 031, 032, 036, 037, 039, 040, 045, 046, 048, 056, 063, 068, 078, 081, 083, 084, 088, 089, 091, 093, 098, 099, 106, 118, 127, 128, 132, 133, 134, 137, 151, 178, 192, 198, 225, 247, 254, 261, *Wagner:* 139, 169 (1 & 3); *West Marine:* 158

ILLUSTRATIONS

Conor Buckley: 09, 10, 14, 45, 178–180, 189, 202–204, 215, 224, 226, 229, 242, 303–307, 311 *Hayden Foell:* 76, 104, 113, 136, 145, 146, 193, 200, 201, 220, 243, 259, 298, 299 *Vic Kulihin:* 06, 15, 24, 27, 33, 107, 156, 176, 199, 211, 212, 216–218, 252, 263, 267–269, 270–272, 277, 313 *Liberum Donum:* 69, 73, 87, 109, 110, 129, 167 *Christine Meighan:* 25, 41, 47, 55, 56, 60, 65, 80, 81, 101, 119, 120, 123, 125, 140–142, 159, 173, 175, 186, 187, 190, 192, 194, 196, 198, 228, 231–234, 236, 240, 258, 260, 262, 275, 281, 284, 287, 288, 291, 294, 295, 309, 310, 312, 314, 315 *Robert L. Prince:* 35 *Lauren Towner:* 02–05, 08, 42, 44, 62, 64, 96, 100, 111, 116, 117, 157, 162, 195, 197, 207, 219, 221, 241, 261, 273, 274, 280, 290, 292, 293, 297, 301, 302, 316, 318, 319, 321

FROM THE PUBLISHER

ABOUT THE AUTHOR

Matt Weber has been editor-in-chief of *Extreme How-To* since 2003. He is an experienced home remodeler who has written hundreds of articles on home improvement and repairs. He lives just north of Birmingham, Alabama, with his wife, two young sons, a dog and a lizard. In his spare time, Weber plays bass guitar in the rock band Skeptic? and is also owner of Pint Bottle Press, where he authors/publishes works of fiction.

ABOUT THE MAGAZINE

Extreme How-To magazine is the enthusiast's guide to home improvement, providing hard-hitting information on tough, practical projects that build equity for the do-it-yourselfer. Seasoned handymen and savvy homeowners can follow the magazine's detailed, step-by-step instructions for a wide variety of indoor and outdoor projects, while generating their own ideas to put a personal stamp on their work. Get the latest information on tools and materials to get the job completed like a pro.

Extreme How-To not only offer tons of home-improvement content, but also supplements this information on the popular website, www.extremehowto.com, and with a digital version of the magazine. Browse through the pages with the click of a mouse, and interact with enhanced electronic features, such as video, audio, and links to articles offering further information on a particular topic.

Our mission is to pass along the latest and greatest home improvement knowledge, and any smart DIY'er will tell you that knowledge is the key to success.

FROM THE AUTHOR

I'd like to thank my dad Tom Weber—my DIY mentor—for teaching me the value of hard work and self-reliance, as well as a million other lessons that I use every day. I'd also like to thank *Extreme How-To* magazine's many talented contributing writers, including Monte Burch, Mark Clement, Rob Robillard, Clint C. Thomas and Larry Walton. Finally, I'd like to thank the publishers of *Extreme How-To,* Trent Boozer, Chad Gillikin and Jeremy Hollingsworth of Latitude 3 Media Group, LLC.

weldon**owen**

PRESIDENT, PUBLISHER Roger Shaw
ASSOCIATE PUBLISHER Mariah Bear
SVP, SALES & MARKETING Amy Kaneko
FINANCE DIRECTOR Philip Paulick
PROJECT EDITOR Ian Cannon
CREATIVE DIRECTOR Kelly Booth
ART DIRECTOR William Mack
DESIGNER Ian Price
ILLUSTRATION COORDINATOR Conor Buckley
IMAGING MANAGER Don Hill

Weldon Owen would like to thank Marisa Solís and Molly
Stewart for editorial assistance and Kevin Broccoli for the index.

Special thanks to Baron Weber for reviewing the electrical
projects for accuracy.

EXECUTIVE VICE PRESIDENT Chad Gillikin
PUBLISHER Jeremy Hollingsworth
EDITOR-IN-CHIEF Matt Weber

Extreme How-To
2300 Resource Drive, Suite B
Birmingham, Alabama 35242

ISBN 13: 978-1-68188-658-9
10 9 8 7 6 5 4 3 2
2024 2023 2022 2021 2020
Printed in China